*Women of
Blaxploitation*

Women of Blaxploitation

How the Black Action Film Heroine Changed American Popular Culture

Yvonne D. Sims

McFarland & Company, Inc., Publishers
Jefferson, North Carolina, and London

All photographs are from Photofest.

LIBRARY OF CONGRESS CATALOGUING-IN-PUBLICATION DATA

Sims, Yvonne D., 1969–
  Women of blaxploitation : how the black action film heroine changed American popular culture / Yvonne D. Sims.
      p.   cm.
  Includes bibliographical references and index.

  ISBN-13: 978-0-7864-2744-4
  ISBN-10: 0-7864-2744-2
  (softcover : 50# alkaline paper) ∞

  1. Blaxploitation films — United States — History and criticism. 2. African American women heroes in motion pictures.   I. Title.
  PN1995.9.N4S56   2006
  791.43′652208996073 — dc22   2006022231

British Library cataloguing data are available

©2006 Yvonne D. Sims. All rights reserved

No part of this book may be reproduced or transmitted in any form or by any means, electronic or mechanical, including photocopying or recording, or by any information storage and retrieval system, without permission in writing from the publisher.

Cover photograph: Pam Grier as Foxy Brown, 1974, ©MGM/Photofest

Manufactured in the United States of America

McFarland & Company, Inc., Publishers
  Box 611, Jefferson, North Carolina 28640
  www.mcfarlandpub.com

For my parents,
Clarence and Rosetta Goodwin Sims

Contents

Acknowledgments ix
Preface 1
Introduction 7

1. Reshaping African American Femininity: Mammy, Aunt Jemima, Sapphire and Action Heroine 25
2. Cultivating the Seed 51
3. Here Comes the Queen 71
4. Call Me Cleo 93
5. Love That Woman and Watch the Dynamite 111
6. The End of Blaxploitation 130
7. Aliens, Terminators and Outlaws: The Mainstreaming of the Action Heroine 147
8. Metamorphosis of the Black Action Heroine 169

Epilogue 191
Selected Filmography 193
Notes 201
Selected Bibliography 213
Index 217

Acknowledgments

Pardon the cliché, but this project really has been a labor of love. Under the best circumstances, writing can be laborious and made more difficult by outside demands that sometimes require so much energy that one wonders if there is enough left at the end of the day to come home and write. However, thanks to inner strength, a lot of drive and the aid of the individuals named here, I found the energy to write — not an easy task, but a necessary task to fulfill an objective, but more importantly, my dream. The actual process of writing is indeed a solitary one, but many people have played an integral role in shaping this book.

My parents, Clarence and Rosetta Goodwin Sims, have always been there for me; they know how important this project is and have seen me in various stages as I worked on this text. They have been so incredibly supportive of all my endeavors, and I am pleased that they are here to see this book come to fruition.

I have been extremely fortunate to have two individuals who lent their ears, eyes and shoulders. The first, Kristine Hartvigsen, provided extensive feedback on several chapters. During my too-many periods of self-doubt about the project, her reassurance was comforting. She has been there at every stage of the book and I am not sure if words can express the deep gratitude I have for Kristine. If there were a title that could describe her involvement in this project, I would call it *contributor* in the sense that she furnished so much feedback that saying I am grateful does not fully convey my appreciation. In academe, she would be considered a research assistant, but even that title is not quite apt for in addition to research, she has served as a coach, urging me on and, many times, reassuring me that this was doable. The second, Farida Cassimjee, provided so much highly useful commentary and also operated as a motivator, particularly during the final stages of the project when angst and pressure were building. I offer Kristine and Farida my gratitude, but somehow that simply doesn't seem enough so this project is as much for them as it is for me since we are all sisters of the cinema.

The Fairbanks Center for Motion Picture Study was extremely helpful in locating archival material. I would like to express my gratitude to the entire staff, but particularly Janet Lorenz for researching many insightful articles containing interviews with the actresses of blaxploitation. A film book is incomplete without stills and I want to thank Photofest for allowing me to use their stills to complete this project. Also, I wish to thank Frances Gateward, Bishetta Merritt, and Eric Pierson for their willingness to take time out of their very busy teaching and research schedules to discuss blaxploitation with me. Their comments were so helpful and they gave their time generously. Alma Deckert made a lot of excellent suggestions, but more important, she is responsible for helping me get this in book proposal in a workable format and was therefore very important to this project's foundation.

Donna Maurer has also played a crucial role at various stages in the writing process. Over the years, she has become a very good friend whose opinion I rely on very heavily. During the many incarnations of this project, Alicia Conroy, Alma H. Deckert, Tina Harris, and Doreen Piano have read portions of the text in the midst of working on their own research projects. Margaret Brocklan-Nease saw this book in early book proposal format and also read early drafts of chapters 1 and 4 of my dissertation, which underwent significant revisions and became the preface, chapter 1 and chapter 2 of this book. Even at that early stage, I was frustrated with a daunting writing project. Margaret spent many hours listening to me work out my ideas as well as commenting on pieces I gave her. Her advice has been invaluable. I would also like to thank Jennifer F. Wood, who has provided incredible moral support.

Alice A. Tait and Guy Meiss of Central Michigan University were very instrumental in my decision to take this book in another direction. An article that I wrote for their anthology was the basis for that decision to focus on the actresses themselves rather than to focus exclusively on their representations. Zia Hassan deserves recognition for providing funding towards the film stills. I wish to thank Eugene Wong and Mitali P. Wong for their feedback, copy editing and for helping me strengthen some areas of the book.

Acknowledgments

This book began as my dissertation and I wish to thank my former committee members Rachel Buff and Joe Austin of the University of Wisconsin-Milwaukee, Jeanne Ludlow of Bowling Green State University and Peter Shields of Eastern Washington University. I cannot express enough appreciation to everyone who has been involved in this project over the last two years. Rachel, Joe, Jeanne and Peter have seen the manuscript in dissertation format and this is the final product; I do hope they, and readers who are passionate about film, particularly the blaxploitation genre, will not be disappointed.

—Yvonne D. Sims
Summer 2006

Preface

Growing up, I saw few African American women role models on television and in film and never questioned their lack of presence. Like other African American girls, I played with white Barbie dolls and looked to white women in such television series as *Charlie's Angels, Police Woman,* and *The Bionic Woman,* as well as my mother, to shape my ideals of femininity. Then, after my father's transfer to Arkansas from South Dakota, I had my first encounter with blatant racism and its impact on femininity and cultural standards of beauty.

When I was 10, an argument between a white girl and me erupted in my new school. She told me that my mother had left me "in the frying pan too long." When I told my mother about this statement, she explained that "black is beautiful," and I should be proud of my skin color. However, I was too young to make the connection between skin color and beauty. In the meantime, I continued to play with my white dolls and idolize *Charlie's Angels* (1976–1982).

Even when black dolls became available and my mother bought them for me, I refused to play with them, preferring my white dolls. My mother wondered why I would not play with Christy, Barbie's African American friend, and I insisted that Barbie was prettier, and we had another discussion about beauty. Nonetheless, I continued to play with Barbie and ignored Christy. It must have been frustrating for my mother. Finally, when I started paying close attention to Christy, I realized that the only difference between her and Barbie was skin color, period; Christy had the same long straight hair and European features as Barbie. Then, I decided that she was pretty like Barbie.

Eventually, I noticed that all my black dolls had straight hair and did not require straightening to make it straight like my hair did. Getting my hair done was an uncomfortable ordeal; the process was quite tedious because my hair was very long and not naturally straight. My mother would wash it and let it dry overnight, and we would both cry for several hours as she straightened it with a hot comb the next day. After all this, she would put my hair in pigtails and tell me that I was a pretty girl. I was unaware that the hours of hot combing were only the beginning of a series of painful techniques in an effort to conform to standard, mainstream notions of beauty.

At the age of 12, I realized that I was not going to be beautiful like the women I saw on television or in film, or like my Barbie doll, and that these images could not provide me with the sense of identity I was searching for. Entering high school and still struggling to find my identity, it became clear to me that many girls who won acceptance from most of the other students looked like the Barbie I used to play with. They were tanned, had long, blond hair, blue eyes, and were the adulation of all races in school. The homecoming queen and her court were all white. The few African American girls who achieved the broadest degree of popularity appeared to fit one of two contrasting models. They either had long hair, light skin, and classic European features, or they were dark-skinned, wore a short hairstyle, and possessed features that were more "African."

Perhaps most disturbing to me was the small number of African American students in the high school who made fun of other African American students based on their "African" appearance. Several young African American males seemed to be the harshest critics and often made fun of other African American girls who did not fit the ideal standards of beauty. They teased one classmate on a regular basis because of the fullness of her lips, while black and white students alike held another classmate with light skin, long hair, and dainty features in adulation. I asked my mother why some black students made fun of other African American students. Her response was that these students did not understand the beauty of their African ancestry. I am not sure I fully understood my mother when I was in high school. It has only been through years of searching for my personal identity as an adult that I have come to comprehend her comment.

High school is a painful experience for many people; most hurtful for me was to be on the receiving end of taunts from people who shared my skin color. Perhaps I could have accepted my mother's explanation if the taunts had come from classmates who were not African American, but I could not accept my African American classmates teasing other African Americans about their features and skin tone. This hypocritical behavior led to critical self-examination, and I purchased skin lighteners and products to straighten my hair in an effort to conform to these mainstream perceptions of beauty. Clearly, the definition of beauty that I accepted was based purely on physical features. This definition has become so embedded in certain segments of the African American community that some women such as myself find it hard to function in a society that constantly judges us on the color of our skin, our weight, our other physical features, and our gender. My classmates and I had learned through toys, film, and television to define black femininity based on certain features such as skin tone, hair, and other physical characteristics. In some ways, I cannot hold them responsible for their behavior because I, too, participated in the myth by refusing to play with a black Barbie doll and by wanting to look exactly like certain African American celebrities, based solely on their physical appearances.

At the age of 10, I was not able to explain why I would not play with a black Barbie doll; at the age of 14, I could not explain the skin lighteners, straightening my hair, and my insistence on consulting cosmetic surgeons in an effort to change my physical characteristics. Looking back, the justifications were simple. I used skin lighteners to "even out" my complexion, chemical straighteners to have more hairstyle options, and consultations with cosmetic surgeons to boost my self-esteem. Earlier discussions about beauty with my mother did not resonate with me then, but have forced me to confront my own problems with African American beauty when I began working on this project. Old wounds surfaced as I struggled with whether I was going to do this project. In the end, I needed to examine what led me to make certain changes that, at first glance, seemed drastic, but in reality, were efforts to conform to white society's beauty expectations.[1]

As a graduate student at Bowling Green State University, I took a feminist film theory class in the spring of 1998. There, I became interested in analyzing the images of African American actresses. I wanted to learn more about the historic representations of African American actresses before critiquing contemporary images of African American women onscreen. I became keenly focused on how African American actresses evolved from servants and seductresses to gun-toting, stiletto-heeled heroines. I immersed myself in studying the blaxploitation movies of the early 1970s. Pam Grier and the revival of her dramatic career in Quentin Tarantino's *Jackie Brown* (1997) piqued my interest. Having seen a few of her earlier films, I became more interested not only in her career, but those of other African American actresses in blaxploitation movies. The 1970s marked a critical change in African American actresses' onscreen appearance and I became interested in how social, cultural and historical changes in the 1960s made this transformation possible.

When I was writing my dissertation in the spring of 2000, many of Pam Grier's films were not readily available on video; however, in later years all of her blaxploitation films came out on DVD and VHS. Interestingly enough, the movies of Grier and Tamara Dobson, another African American actress who starred in arguably one of the most definitive movies in the genre, outsell their male counterparts. Clearly, they are more familiar to segments of the movie audience who were not born at the height of both actresses' success and their mark has endured much longer than Fred Williamson and Jim Brown, two of the leading actors in blaxploitation movies.

In spite of her reconnection with audiences who remember *Coffy* and *Foxy Brown*, two of Grier's most successful movies, and her new impact on a younger generation, there are no full-length scholarly books on blaxploitation. There are excellent book chapters; film scholar Ed Guerrero's *Framing Blackness: The African American Image in Film* offers one of the most detailed, comprehensive discussions on the genre. But a scholarly book has not been written on a genre that has played an integral role in the shaping of African American films today, the emergence of an action heroine and the continued influence that only lasted five years in popular culture, most notably hip-hop culture.

While I wondered about discussing my own sense of beauty and identity when I was writing this book in dissertation form, I have since embraced the fact that any discussion of images of black women would be incomplete without an examination of my own experiences. Thus, I begin this book by keeping in mind that I am covering the experiences of Pam Grier, Tamara Dobson, Teresa Graves and Jeannie Bell *and* allowing old wounds to heal. Many women struggle with beauty-related identity issues because of the constant bombardment of images that tell them they must look a certain way if they want to be admired and even successful. While far too many women face these insecurities, for African American women the beauty struggle has been very difficult because so many negative images of African American womanhood were prevalent in film, advertisements, and literature for years. The results of seeing exaggerated, distorted and patently false images of African American femininity have been devastating, and attempting to dismantle images that have become ingrained in the very fabric of American culture is an arduous struggle. Nonetheless, as one of the most popular media outlets, film provides the opportunity to reshape and redefine African American womanhood. Grier, Dobson, Graves and Bell's blaxploitation movies provided alternative images of black femininity that signified empowerment and liberation for many African American women who were tired of viewing filmic images of black women as maids or seductresses.

I was too young to be fully aware of the responses that Pam Grier, Tamara Dobson, Teresa Graves and Jeannie Bell received from audiences, particularly Grier and Dobson, who enjoyed great success portraying women who protected their families at all costs, even if it meant adopting disguises that reinforced cultural myths of black women as loose. I was not surprised to read the reactions of film critics and many others in the African American community concerning Grier's depictions of black womanhood. Of the actresses starring in blaxploitation films, she received the harshest criticism for her willingness as part of her character to remove her clothing when necessary and engage in violent acts when necessary.

By 1970, as the black community made great political, social and cultural strides, blaxploitation movies portrayed caricatures and stereotypical images that many found disturbing and possibly a step backwards towards achieving progress in the film industry. Rightfully so, community leaders were concerned about the impact the genre would have on impressionable youths; however, they failed to recognize that voicing harsh disdain against the actresses who starred in blaxploitation films would also hurt the actresses rather than the film industry. In essence, by criticizing the most successful actresses in the genre, critics in the African American community may have inadvertently hurt Grier and Dobson's careers. Many of the actors and actresses in the genre had difficulty finding other roles after its demise in 1975 and were labeled as blaxploitation actors even though Grier in particular sought ways to move away from her status as "queen of blaxploitation."

I have always found the genre interesting on a number of levels. First, the political and social context in which blaxploitation emerged deserves a closer examination. The response by critics and audiences alike is also worth further scrutiny. Finally, many film books have focused on black actresses before 1970 with little attention paid to those who starred in blaxploitation movies.

I have also always been interested in the lives of the actresses who starred in many of the most popular, successful blaxploitation movies. While watching a Pam Grier movie years ago, I realized there were other images of black femininity that existed beyond that of Mammy of the Exotic Other.[2] I was too young to appreciate the contribution that Grier and Dobson in particular made to the face of the action heroine. Without a Foxy Brown or Cleopatra Jones, an Ellen Ripley[3] might not have become a popular icon and the prototype for the action heroine.

In spite of the failure on the part of critics and scholars alike to properly acknowledge the contributions of blaxploitation actresses to the genre of action heroine movies, the fact that there appears to be continued interest is a testament to the abilities of actresses such as Pam Grier, Tamara Dobson, Teresa Graves and Jeannie Bell. For her part, Grier *symbolizes* blaxploitation and despite her occasional efforts to distance herself from the acting period in her life, she will always be associated with the era. More recently, she has chosen to embrace the symbol and, with it, her groundbreaking role in creating a character that (while synonymous with Sigourney Weaver's Ellen Ripley) was nonetheless instrumental in changing the male-dominated action narrative in popular cinema. The genre itself has been so influential, particularly in the realm of popular music, that Grier has made an appearance in a music video with hip-hop musician Snoop Dog, and rapper Foxy Brown has adopted her moniker based on Grier's 1974 movie of the same name. In addition, over the years she has appeared in movies such as *Original Gangstas*[4] (1993), *Mars Attacks!*[5] (1998) and *Jackie Brown* (1997), due in large part to her status as the Queen of Blaxploitation. Film and cultural critic Nelson George notes:

> Pam Grier was a cult figure who was even embraced by many feminists for her ball-breaking action films. She remains one of the few women of any color in American film history who had vehicles developed for her that not only emphasized her physical beauty but also her ability to take retribution on men who challenged her.[6]

It is a legacy that, while underappreciated by many, deserves a place in the literature on action heroines in film. This book is dedicated to Pam Grier's Coffy and Foxy Brown as well as to Tamara Dobson, the late Teresa Graves and Jeannie Bell. The above actresses (particularly Grier and Dobson) redefined African American femininity in the 1970s, moving it beyond mammy and the exotic other to portraying a character that has cemented the status of the action heroine as a popular icon both in film and on television.

Introduction

> Films reflect not only the aspirations of individuals,
> but also those of society as a whole.[1]

Popular culture offers a fascinating glimpse of attitudes and perceptions about black masculinity and black femininity. Examining the role that popular culture plays in creating and sustaining derogatory images of African Americans in general is crucial to understanding how black femininity in all media outlets continues to be defined and reinforced by popular culture. It also offers an explanation of how highly problematic representations of black femininity continue to permeate and linger in American culture in spite of the advances made by African Americans since the 1960s. In her book *Aunt Jemima, Uncle Ben and Rastus: Blacks in Advertising, Yesterday, Today, and Tomorrow*, Marilyn Kern-Foxworth focuses on three dominant caricatures of African Americans in advertising with Aunt Jemima epitomizing black women and Uncle Ben and Uncle Rastus representing black men. Kern-Foxworth writes, "American popular culture has contained blatant stereotypical depictions of the black woman for a long time."[2]

Although her book focuses specifically on advertisements, Kern-Foxworth underscores the magnitude of distorted perceptions of black masculinity and black femininity that linger in other media outlets. The historic representations of African American women in advertising have been defined by the distinct image of Aunt Jemima and in film by the mammy, Exotic Other,[3] Sapphire and Aunt Jemima. As cultural artifacts, television, film and advertising have been a determining factor in shaping African American femininity. The roles that each outlet play in reinforcing and contributing to stereotypes are immense. The medium is not only the message; it shapes the image, and four of the most powerful media in the last half of the twentieth century — television, advertising, music videos and the press — have exerted the greatest impact on how black women not only are seen, but how they have come to view themselves. The message and the image haven't changed much during the black woman's history in America.[4] The perpetuation of the concept of black femininity in all media outlets, particularly film, is an ongoing discussion. But, the objective here is to reexamine a period in popular cinema where African American actresses for a brief time portrayed characters who were empowering and offered a repose from decades of mammy, the exotic other, Aunt Jemima and Sapphire images.

Many critics and film historians see blaxploitation movies as an embarrassing era for African Americans in general and actors in particular, but 1973 marked the first time that audiences saw African American women in non-servitude roles. Film scholar Cedric Robinson refers to blaxploitation movies starring black actresses such as Pam Grier and Tamara Dobson as the "Bad Black Woman"[5] motif. The label "Bad Black Woman" reinforces negative stereotypes of the actresses in blaxploitation and belittles the contributions of the actresses who starred in black action films that were more successful than their male contemporaries. However, I do agree that the genre itself did little to change the long-held images of African American women. In any case, to suggest that the blaxploitation genre had no redeeming values is reductive, particularly when one examines the political, social and cultural changes occurring within the African American community after the Civil Rights Movement. For two successful actresses involved in blaxploitation (which continues to draw new audiences today partly due to technological advances such as DVDs that allow consumers to purchase movies in box sets), this character has found a new audience. Pam Grier and Tamara Dobson brought a new character to the screen that was instrumental in reshaping gender roles, particularly those involving action-centered storylines, which have lasted for well over 30 years. It should be emphasized that blaxploitation greatly influenced the development of Sigourney Weaver's Ellen Ripley — a character that encouraged studios to begin making action-oriented movies with women in the lead.

As "Killer Dames,"[6] Grier, Dobson, Teresa Graves (who was a well-known comedienne before her television series) and Jeannie Bell had the opportunity to play empowered, independent heroines, despite the fact that many film critics and scholars found their work lacking in artistic and cultural aesthetics. Their roles were a significant departure from the historical representations of black actresses and, through the writers, producers, and directors of the films studied here, brought to the screen a new image of African American femininity. It was goodbye to the headscarves worn by Mammy and the wavy hair of the Exotic Other, and a refreshing and political greeting to the woman with a natural hairstyle modeled, according to Robinson, from civil rights heroines such as Angela Davis.

In her role as a gun-toting heroine who battles aliens in order to save humankind, Sigourney Weaver changed the landscape of the action narrative. Weaver's Ellen Ripley in *Alien* established her dominance as an action heroine who was tough as nails yet still feminine, and proved that actresses could star in and be as successful as their male counterparts in action-driven movies.[7] But her celebrated character was made possible by the action heroine in blaxploitation movies.[8] It was African American actresses who redefined the way women were depicted on the screen in the genre of movies commonly referred to as "blaxploitation."[9] Thus, the action heroine's emergence in popular cinema actually began in the early 1970s with two actresses who not only paved the way for Sigourney Weaver's Ellen Ripley, but also reshaped the way in which African American actresses had been presented onscreen.

Film scholars, reviewers and others have criticized blaxploitation movies for reinforcing negative stereotypes of African American men and women, but the matter cannot be so easily reduced to bad stereotypes pitted against good images of African Americans in films such as Martin Ritt's *Sounder* (1972) with Cicely Tyson and Paul Winfield. Not all African American actresses were afforded the opportunity to portray multi-dimensional characters and, as such, were confronted with blaxploitation movies as a way to gain entrance into the film industry. Historically, it has been very difficult for African Americans to gain the type of leverage needed to produce their own films within the studio system.

It is not widely acknowledged among scholars and critics of the genre, but many African American actors and directors fought to add elements to the characters and scripts in blaxploitation to make the movies more dimensional. Hugh Robertson, the director of *Melinda* (1972), stated, "I had to fight and fight for any human elements in the story."[10] In the original script for *Melinda*, the battle ended with the conversion of hopeless trash into stylish and diverting trash.[11] Robertson also noted, "They kept pushing for all sex and violence. I had to insist on the dinner scene between Melinda [Vonetta McGee] and Frankie [Calvin Lockhart] so we could see some kind of relationship between them, not just bring her into the story and suddenly have her dead the next morning."[12] The late African American actress

Rosalind Cash said, "I'm proud of what I did with Terry. When I go up to Harlem, the hard-working soul sisters come up to me and say, 'You were for real in that part; I know what that character was all about.'"[13] It is not unreasonable to assume that some African American women found admirable traits in Pam Grier and Tamara Dobson's heroines in spite of the problems of blaxploitation films in general.

Ironically, while critics pointed to the genre as reinforcing stereotypes of African American women, they did not seem to mind the contradictory aspects of films such as *Sounder*, which was viewed by many as a positive "black" film. Yet, Cicely Tyson's character is very much depicted as a mammy, right down to the attire that she wears in the film. While the clothing is in keeping with the movie's sharecropping theme, it is still a problematic representation, particularly since Tyson was one of the few black actresses to break the mold of what Hollywood deemed as beautiful. Scholars disagree as to whether Tyson's character was truly different or simply represented an updated version of the mammy character. Edward Mapp suggests that Rebecca (Tyson's character in the film) wears a bandanna and an oversized faded feedsack dress throughout much of the drama.[14] Rather then start her own vegetable garden or put up preserves in her spare moments on Sundays, Rebecca joins her family in sports and singing, two pastimes stereotyped as being very popular among Negroes.[15] Yet, another critic views Rebecca as multi-dimensional and complex, calling her "a forceful human, not a groovy sex-object."[16]

Consequently, black actors have suffered and for many years have had to take roles deemed racist, presenting the African American community with little complexity. By the 1970s, much had changed in Hollywood, but much had remained the same. Sidney Poitier was the first black actor to win a Best Actor award for his film *Lilies of the Field* (1963) and, during the 1960s, audiences began to see a diverse, eclectic mix of African American actors on television and in film. Still, the diversification did not necessarily translate to better roles for actors in the early 1970s. Thus, in that sense, the film industry lagged in its treatment of black actors.

The emergence of blaxploitation allowed unknown actresses such as Pam Grier, Tamara Dobson, Jeannie Bell and the established Teresa Graves an opportunity to create an alternative image of African American femininity that greatly differed from the stock roles assigned to black actresses. As a comedienne who appeared on many USO tours and a regular performer in other venues, Graves was not new to the television landscape.

Thanks to the increasing visibility of prominent women in the civil rights movement with natural hairstyles that reflected pride in their African heritage and made a statement against the idea that African American women had to look a certain way to be considered beautiful, particularly by media outlets such as film, television and advertising, an alternative image appeared. The Afro symbolized by Angela Davis, but worn by many women, did not conform to the ideals of black femininity which was not defined by African Americans themselves. Cicely Tyson received a great deal of exposure, in large part because of her acting talent but, equally important, she could not easily be categorized and fit the "new" African American actress onscreen in the 1960s. Thus, her casting in roles beyond historic images of black women represented significant strides in the 1960s for African American actresses.

In order to understand the significance of this, one need only examine the roles of African American actresses prior to the 1960s. Hattie McDaniel immortalized Mammy in *Gone with the Wind* (1939), for which she became the first and only African American actress for many years to win an Oscar in the Supporting Actress category. Upon her acceptance of her Oscar, McDaniel expressed hope that doors would open for African American actresses, yet that did not happen. Instead, McDaniel and other actresses such as Louise Beavers and Ethel Waters found themselves in servitude roles that forced them to play derogatory characters. In sharp contrast, actresses such as Nina Mae McKinney, who is widely credited by film scholars as the first Exotic Other onscreen, Lena Horne and Dorothy Dandridge were typecast as seductresses who led men astray in many films.

These stereotypes centered on physical characteristics rather than talent.[17] Since McDaniel, Beavers and Waters were darker complexioned in comparison to McKinney, Horne and Dandridge, studios forced them to play roles in which they nurtured white families, had no families of their own and focused all of their attentions on appeasing their employers. Studios thought McKinney, Horne and Dandridge were too pretty to portray maids and were better suited to play seductresses. For actresses such as Josephine Baker, whose physical characteristics did not fit either category, the film industry had little to offer.[18] Of the African American actresses working in Hollywood prior to the 1960s, Hattie McDaniel arguably encountered the most resistance from studios and audiences alike: They were unable to see her as any character other than Mammy, and she came to epitomize Mammy in her public life.

In her article "But things is changin' nowadays an' Mammy's gettin' bored: Hattie McDaniel and the Culture of Dissemblance," Victoria Sturtevant notes, "McDaniel's white employers and much of her public were not fully cognizant that she was acting the part — that she was an actress, not a

Mammy who worked in Hollywood."[19] Sturtevant traces the industry's (and audiences') unwillingness to see McDaniel as any other character beyond Mammy to what historian Darlene Clark Hine calls the culture of dissemblance, a survival mechanism used by black women during slavery to defend themselves against the constant threat of sexual harassment and rape. Clark Hine uses the culture of dissemblance theory to discuss African American women in slavery; however, Sturtevant argues that her usage is quite applicable to African American actresses such as Hattie McDaniel as the name of her article suggests. The black actress as domestic further illuminates the extent to which the culture of dissemblance allowed black women to adopt not a second personality but a role, an act which was divorced, consciously and completely, from their private identity. Yet, many African American actresses were unable to separate their onscreen personas from their private, real selves because they were typecast in a particular role. Equally important, the film industry would not *allow* them to do so. When McDaniel made her way to the podium to accept her Best Supporting Actress Oscar, famous gossip columnist Louella Parsons wrote, "[T]ears came to Mammy's eyes."[20] In *Bright Boulevards, Bold Dreams: The Story of Black Hollywood*, Donald Bogle provides illuminating insight as to how so many African American actors and actresses during the early years of the film industry negotiated their onscreen personas of jesters and domestics as a livelihood only to return to a fashionable home of their own once they left the studio. Having to go back and forth between two worlds illustrates the fine line black actors and actresses often walked to pursue a career that sometimes put them at odds with the African American community, but also allowed them the opportunity to pursue a career in film. Hattie McDaniel was consistently criticized by Walter White,[21] president of the Beverly Hills chapter for the NAACP in the 1940s, for accepting mammy roles. Why she was singled out while many other African American actors portrayed similar roles, I do not know. However, an argument can be made that McDaniel's high visibility (particularly after winning a Best Supporting Actress award for Mammy) may have placed her in a position where White felt that, instead of accepting the same role over and over again, she should use her status to reposition herself in the film industry. To convince studio executives to cast her in other types of roles would have been impossible given the political nature of the film industry and the racist structure of the studio system. Also, reshaping black femininity onscreen was a heavy burden to place on one African American actress with no voice. McDaniel was literally confined to playing mammy throughout her acting career as was the case with Lena Horne and Dorothy Dandridge as tragic mulattos. Even in the year 2006, one wonders how much of a voice African American actresses possess. Voice translates into power and, while the opportunities have grown for black actors, black actresses still face enormous obstacles, particularly as they see their roles diminishing in favor of other actresses of color.

Thus, we see the limitations and struggles imposed on Pam Grier's predecessors and why blaxploitation movies, in spite of their flaws, offered a venue that allowed African American actresses to begin to redefine their image even though studios still controlled the types of characters they portrayed. Particularly for Pam Grier and Tamara Dobson, once their respective studios saw the popularity and success of their onscreen characters, the actresses were allowed some control over their images. For Grier, her early work in low-budget films led to cross-over success in mainstream films. This is demonstrated in the input Grier had in her follow-up to *Coffy* (1973), *Foxy Brown* (1974), where she insisted that the character be allowed to wear more glamorous attire. She notes:

> I wanted to show in films what we are doing when everyone says things are getting better.... I showed this in the pictures and it was just so ugly and people saw it and said Wow! That's really the way it is. And all of a sudden there was a kind of violent reaction to it. It kind of sparked people. They kind of woke up because they saw it 20-feet tall, our lifestyles up there on that screen.[22]

Perhaps in working for Warner Brothers instead of AIP, Dobson could ensure that she did not need to perform nude scenes. After the success of their respective movies, both actresses were able to get producers to *listen* to their input.

Much to the chagrin of critics of the genre, blaxploitation was crucial in redefining African American femininity in film and on television. Esther Rolle's portrayal of the matriarch on the television series *Good Times* showed that for black actresses, when given the opportunity to portray women and not a category, success was possible in an industry that relies heavily on one's physical attractiveness rather then talent in many cases. For years, African American actresses were limited to roles that called for their physical characteristics. The 1960s changed this, in part because for the first time, race relations in America were displayed on television and not just the newspapers. That forced many Americans to examine the status quo of African Americans in the South and other parts of the country. For every film or television role that defied labeling, many familiar stereotypes of African American women still existed onscreen. That is to say, mammy, the exotic other, Aunt Jemima and Sapphire co-existed with all too much regularity alongside images that challenged the dominant way[23] of thinking about black women. Yet, a few independent filmmakers and producers managed to portray African Americans in a variety of roles that were not very diverse and functioned very similarly to the films created by Hollywood, but still depicted African Americans in different societal functions.

Early African American Production Companies

By 1910, William Foster, an African American entrepreneur, began producing a series of comic films which had all-black casts.[24] In describing William Foster, Mark Reid writes, "[H]e was the first African American to establish a film production company and has been described as a clever hustler from Chicago who had been a press agent for the Bert Williams and George Walker revues and Bob Cole and Billy Johnson's comedy musical *A Trip to Coontown* (1898)."[25] Foster focused on comedy shorts. Another African American production company, Lincoln, was created in 1916. Established by a group of black Los Angeles citizens, its "productions, like those of the Foster Photoplay Company, deliberately used a black slant because brothers Noble and George Johnson, the primary founders of Lincoln, agreed with Foster in that blacks should make movies with black performers for black audiences ... that there was a market waiting for such films and that the black entrepreneur would profit financially."[26] Lincoln produced films demonstrating the concept of American individualism and were serious narratives with plots constructed around a black, rural hero's realization of some admirable ambition.[27] The company produced "mostly family-oriented pictures."[28]

Another African American entrepreneur emerged, his films differing greatly from those of William Foster and the Lincoln Motion Picture Company. Of the three production companies, Oscar Micheaux's was the most revolutionary in the sense that his storylines focused on all aspects, from violence to love. Critics and scholars have debated the aesthetics of Micheaux films; however, like Foster and the Johnsons, he offered an avenue for black movie audiences who simply had no movies of their own. Whereas Lincoln Motion Picture productions were serious melodramas that espoused conventional middle-class puritanical ethics, Micheaux productions attracted audiences by dramatizing subjects that Lincoln films avoided.[29] His films introduced audiences to black-oriented themes like interracial intimacy, lynching, passing, urban graft, wife beating, rape, and prostitution.[30]

I believe that, in many ways, Micheaux was the predecessor for blaxploitation movies. This is verified by Reid, who states, "[I]nstead of emphasizing the long-suffering virtues of black Americans, Micheaux felt his audiences would accept violence, lowlifes, interracial love scenes and steamy love scenes."[31] While these themes displeased some in the black community, Micheaux's action films, like other cultural productions of the Harlem Renaissance, were imaginative reflections of a proud, aggressive, New Negro whose new morality condoned retaliatory action against white racist aggressions.[32] Micheaux's place within the Harlem Renaissance is exemplified in his choice of dramatic themes.[33] His portrayal of black urban life, which included gangsters, sexually liberated women, and self-assertive blacks, reflected a community of cosmopolitan blacks.[34] He pioneered the development of the black action film genre.[35]

In sum, Micheaux's films attracted an audience that found blaxploitation movies appealing some fifty years later, when the genre became popular among urban audiences in the early 1970s. One has to wonder if studio executives in the industry had seen or heard of Oscar Micheaux, particularly when blaxploitation movies that centered on action heroes and heroines became popular. Foster, Lincoln and Micheaux were the first independent black filmmaking production companies in the United States, but could not compete with the major studios both in terms of financial backing and in keeping talent. They folded when the Great Depression hit in 1929.

The Civil Rights Movement and Its Impact on the Film Industry

Clearly, the Civil Rights Movement had a major impact on mainstream Hollywood and consequently, for the first time, television and film began to show an array of African American beauty that did not fit in the mammy, exotic other, Aunt Jemima or Sapphire categories. Consider again the fact that Cicely Tyson's natural hairstyle signaled a cultural phenomenon that was sweeping the African American community which, as part of the Black Nationalism movement, produced "Black is beautiful" as a mantra that many embraced as they sought ways to proudly display a social consciousness and political, perhaps even spiritual connection, to Africa.

By the late 1960s, black is beautiful was in full force, in part because of the visibility of prominent African American women activists who dared to defy conventions by adopting hairstyles that forced many African American women to consider the ways in which they had tried so hard to conform to beauty ideals based on European standards. With the increasing number of actresses who could not be easily categorized (Nichelle Nichols, Gail Fisher, Diahann Carroll and others), for the first time audiences could see that the range of diverse beauty among African American women was not defined by mammy, the exotic other, Aunt Jemima, or Sapphire roles.

Consequently, in the early 1970s when Grier and Dobson emerged onscreen, audiences saw two things. First, their beauty represented the standards of the time rather then Hollywood's notion of black femininity. Second, the bold heroines that Grier and Dobson portrayed took a backseat to no one; there had not been such characters played by African American women before. Most significantly, studios built characters and storylines with African American actresses such as Grier and Dobson in mind.

By the time Weaver's Ripley appeared, action heroines had been around for several years: They appeared with regularity on television and, most importantly, made their first mainstream appearance with a bell-bottom-wearing, gun-toting heroine named Coffy played by Pam Grier.

Grier, Dobson, Graves and Bell,[36] with the help of the writers, producers and directors of the films considered in this book, gave black audiences another character to consider. Although the action heroine was unwittingly conceived by studios whose sole objective was to make money, she was brought to life by Grier and Dobson in particular. They are not given due recognition for their contributions to the action heroine character because of the character's origins. Exploitative films (also known as movies) that cater to a particular audience, and are usually based on a trend of the moment, are hardly respected by many, given their tendency to capitalize on trends and phenomena in American culture. The objective of directors, studios, and writers who produce such movies is to make money while offering a cursory glance that does not accurately portray societal concerns, but is meant strictly for entertainment value.

Randall Clark is correct that the criteria used to judge mainstream films should not apply to exploitation films. In *At a Theater or Drive-In Near You: The History, Culture, and Politics of the American Exploitation Films*, he notes that studios who produce exploitation films are willing to take risks that the mainstream will not. In the process, studios such as American International Pictures break ground as they produce movies featuring characters who have not previously appeared onscreen or have been toned down so that the significance of the character is almost non-existent. Clark notes, "[I]t is, in fact, typical of the differences between mainstream and exploitation films that even when Hollywood studios were producing blaxploitation films, they avoided films about powerful African American women. That was left to the exploitation film producers."[37]

Exploitation film producers created an African American female character who was well-equipped to handle herself in any given situation, and, as we've seen, became the early prototype for the action heroine. The significance of her role in American popular cinema was not felt in mainstream Hollywood productions until after Pam Grier's character created a stir. It is important to note that the action heroine had appeared for quite some time in martial arts movies made in Hong Kong and Taiwan. Thus, while audiences who watched martial arts movies were already familiar with the character, audiences in the United States did not get a full glimpse of the action heroine until she appeared in blaxploitation movies.

Hollywood has always produced films with strong heroines, but the action genre had been dominated by white male actors until blaxploitation movies were released. Given the historic representations of African American women in cinema, a black actress starring in a genre dominated by actors was unheard of until the early 1970s. Regardless of how cultural and film critics may have felt about Grier's protagonist, it is clear that she gave the action heroine a persona that would later be used as a model by the studios and by the actress who became synonymous with action heroines — Sigourney Weaver.

In sum, audiences saw the metamorphosis of the action heroine from low-budget blaxploitation movies to full-scale mainstream studio productions. In the process, the studios erased the action heroines' racial construction, thus dismissing the African American actresses who help bring Ripley to life onscreen. African American actresses in this genre not only paved the way for other action heroines, but also redefined the ways in which women in general were represented in film by portraying a new character who held her own among men *and* women. Moreover, African American actresses proved through blaxploitation movies that when given the opportunity, they could carry action-oriented storylines in a genre dominated by men.

The films *Coffy* (1973), *Foxy Brown* (1974), *Friday Foster* (1975) and *Sheba Baby* (1975) ensured Pam Grier's status as "Queen of Blaxploitation" but also earned her public scorn from many African American leaders who were concerned about derogatory onscreen representations of African Americans. Grier and the other actresses in the genre took exception to the labeling of blaxploitation as exploitative, stating, "[A]ll across the country, a lot of women were Foxy Brown and Coffy. They were independent, fighting to save their families, not accepting rape or being victimized."[38] Her heroines' strengths were based on characteristics she saw in the African American women in her own family.

Grier, Dobson, Graves and Bell became the mediators between studios and the audiences for this new character. Their portrayal of the action heroine represented the antithesis of the Mammy (as seen in Hattie McDaniel's character in *Gone with the Wind* (1939) and Dorothy Dandridge's dangerous seductress *Carmen Jones* (1954). Presenting an African American woman who epitomized the struggles and gains of African American women in the 1960s and early 1970s altered the onscreen perspective of African American femininity. To accept these groundbreaking roles, audiences had to reinvent the narrative by disregarding weak story lines and obvious caricatures. Grier, Dobson, Graves and Bell achieved this objective by taking a character created by the studio, producers and directors, and giving her an image that connected with young, urban African American audiences (especially women).

The Chapters

In Chapter 1, "Reshaping African American Femininity: Mammy, Aunt Jemima, Sapphire and Action Heroine," emphasis is placed on film as a media outlet that shapes perceptions about African Americans. I discuss Grier, Dobson, Graves and Bell's contributions to the action heroine genre and end the chapter with conclusions about action heroes, the action genre and the origins of the action heroine.

Chapter 2, "Cultivating the Seed," opens by looking at the social, political and cultural framework of the 1960s that was integral to the rise of blaxploitation movies in the early 1970s. It is generally acknowledged that the racial turmoil of the 1960s directly impacted the film industry. In the midst of a myriad of changes in American culture, the film industry finally began to take note of a segment of the moviegoing audience they had ignored for years — African Americans. Sidney Poitier made great strides as a black actor and became the first black actor to win an Oscar; however, young urban African American audiences were restless and wanted a change. They craved a hero of their own. This market wanted heroes that they could identify with more readily and Jim Brown appeared to fill that niche. Thus, the black action hero emerged in the form of a former star collegiate and professional football player. Mainstream studios were slow to respond to this market. However, one studio, American International Pictures (AIP), with its history of capitalizing on trends in American culture, quickly rushed to fill the void by producing many of the blaxploitation films.

AIP's niche was discovering trends in American culture and basing their films on popular political and social phenomena. Thus, it was no surprise when Melvin Van Peeble's *Sweet SweetBack's Baadasssss Song* (1971) and Gordon Parks' *Shaft* (1971) became box office bonanzas that AIP found a way to capitalize on this "new" market and audience by creating the majority of blaxploitation movies — particularly those that were focused on action.

Chapter 3, "Here Comes the Queen," interweaves an analysis of Grier's films with the actress's perspective on her heroines. In her first film, *Coffy*, it is clear that producers relied on African American women activists such as Angela Davis in shaping Grier's onscreen persona. However, the action heroine began as a groundbreaking heroine but became more exploitative with the succession of films. By 1975, Grier's action heroine had softened from a no-nonsense woman to a less-empowered woman in *Friday Foster*. Although earlier traits of her action heroine were present in her final AIP film, *Sheba Baby* (1976), interest waned, and Grier found herself stigmatized and unable to find mainstream roles. Nonetheless, she remains the most visible and successful actress from the genre.

Chapter 4, "Call Me Cleo," examines Tamara Dobson's role in *Cleopatra Jones* (1973) and the sequel, *Cleopatra Jones and the Casino of Gold* (1975). The chapter considers her perspective on playing a new type of heroine, with a careful analysis of the characteristics that make Cleo an action heroine. *Cleopatra Jones* was also highly successful, establishing Dobson's onscreen presence as a prototypical action heroine. Released a month after Grier's *Coffy*, *Cleopatra Jones* presented an upscale version of the action heroine in blaxploitation movies. Although Dobson's action heroine differs occupationally from Grier's, her character's objective is similar — to eradicate crime in her community. Despite the box office success of *Cleopatra Jones*, when *Cleopatra Jones and the Casino of Gold* was released, the audience base had dissipated, along with interest in the character. The sequel became an unwitting caricature, with Dobson adopting outlandish costumes and mannerisms to portray Cleopatra Jones. Dobson appeared in a few more films before ultimately disappearing from Hollywood and returning to modeling in the late 1970s.

Chapter 5, "Love That Woman and Watch the Dynamite," discusses the impact of the action heroine on the small screen as well as a lesser-known action heroine in another blaxploitation film, *T.N.T. Jackson*. In contrast to Grier and Dobson, Graves followed a different path, having already established a television presence. She traveled extensively entertaining troops during Vietnam. Other African American actresses had television shows before Graves, but her show became the staple for other action heroines on television. Beverly Garland portrayed a female cop in a short-lived television series titled *Decoy* (1955) that lasted a few episodes before television abandoned the idea of a woman detective. *Get Christie Love!* marked the return of the character and the series is responsible for the wave of shows starring female detectives that began to appear in 1975. Moreover, as a mass medium, television reached a broader audience, thus offering increased visibility for this new character. Television audiences had seen women appearing in action-oriented roles before, but always alongside a male counterpart. Diana Rigg's Emma Peel in the 1960s British series *The Avengers*, her earlier counterpart Dr. Catherine "Cathy" Gale portrayed by Honor Blackman, and Linda Thorson's Tara King who replaced Rigg in the 1968-69 season are examples. Christie Love offered quite a contrast to Waters' *Beulah* (1954) and Carroll's *Julia* (1967–68). Philip Green calls Graves' character "the most unexploitative use of a black hero or heroine at the time."[39]

Critics did not think much of the series, and Graves' increasing aversion to portraying a character that was at odds with her personal religious faith did not help. But *Get Christie Love!* was groundbreaking if for no other reason than a Best Actress Golden Globe nomination for Graves. After *Get Christie Love!*, women as private eyes and detectives appeared regularly in TV series and enjoyed tremendous success thanks to copying the formula of Graves' series. Additionally, although the Golden Globe is a prestigious award now, there was a time when it wasn't and the fact that Graves won one can be seen as a very positive feat.

Of the African American action heroines, Jeannie Bell was not as well known as Graves, Grier and Dobson, and her heroine was probably the weakest in terms of plot and character development. Nonetheless, she is important because she took martial arts a step further than Dobson's heroine by using it as the primary mode of defense in *T.N.T. Jackson*. Indeed, her action heroine infused the martial arts with blaxploitation, bringing the two sub-genres together, which in itself was significant: Producers were able to appease audiences who enjoyed both martial-arts and black action movies. Philip Green noted that "in every way imaginable Bell is a more imposing and credible action hero — except, apparently, for the color of her skin."[40] Indeed, it appears that if Pam Grier and Tamara Dobson's heroines had not been categorized as blaxploitation heroines, they might have gained recognition as the first mainstream action heroines in popular cinema. Such an argument is strong in Dobson's case, particularly since *Cleopatra Jones* was produced by Warner Brothers, a bigger studio that could have marketed the film beyond the blaxploitation audience.

Chapter 6, "The End of Blaxploitation," explores the demise of the genre. By 1975, African Americans had grown weary of blaxploitation movies. The films had become too formulaic, and the lack of character development hurt, too. When studios such as AIP and Warner Brothers discovered that African Americans wanted to see a diverse range of movies and that they no longer had to make films specifically geared towards this market, they stopped production on them and moved on to the next trend.

Chapter 7, "Aliens, Terminators and Outlaws: The Mainstreaming of the Action Heroine," discusses the mainstreaming of the action heroine in popular cinema. In the early 1970s, the action heroine was an empowered, liberated African American woman with a social and political message. By the late 1970s and onward, the action heroine represented a woman who was out to save mankind from destructive forces, whether manmade or extraterrestrial. The transition began with Weaver in the *Aliens* tetralogy and continued with Linda Hamilton in *Terminator II* (1991). I should note here that Hamilton appeared as an "action heroine in training" in the first *Terminator* (1984) movie. Susan Sarandon and Geena Davis's *Thelma & Louise* (1991) took the action heroine in another direction. Feminist film scholars continue to debate the merits of the Weaver, Hamilton, Sarandon, and Davis heroines as groundbreaking, but their characters have become ingrained in contemporary cinema as presenting women in new roles. The action heroine differs from portrayals of women as the femme fatale and the ambitious, career-climbing professional of films in earlier cinema history.

Although interest in blaxploitation films may have waned, the action heroine persevered as a result of the trailblazing genre in the 1970s. Despite the willingness or unwillingness of some feminist film critics to embrace the action heroine, she is here to stay, and studios continue to make big-budget movies in the genre because of the responses from audiences. In fact, many of the action heroines have out-produced their male counterparts at the box-office with better storylines and stronger characters. Several actresses have carried the action heroine into the new millennium, and film scholarship continues to play an integral role in the ongoing discussion of this character. The chapter concludes that linking the action heroine's past to her present and her future is important in demonstrating her emergence.

Chapter 8, "Metamorphosis of the Black Action Heroine," discusses the factors that led to a resurgence of interest in blaxploitation movies with Quentin Tarantino's rediscovery of Pam Grier in *Jackie Brown*. The chapter also explores whether audiences are as excited about an African American action heroine as they were initially by Pam Grier's *Coffy* and Tamara Dobson's *Cleopatra Jones*. The social, political and cultural times have changed significantly since Grier and Dobson's heroines. Halle Berry offered the best hope as the African American actress who could reinvent the action heroine storyline, again addressing issues of race and class. At one point, there was discussion that her character Jinx from the James Bond movie *Die Another Day* (2002) would receive her own movie. However, since Berry's weak performance for *Catwoman* there have been no further discussions on producing a movie based on Jinx. Moreover, four years have elapsed since the last Bond flick, so an interest in a spin-off character has tapered off. Still, Halle Berry enjoys the distinction of being the *first* James Bond actress to carry her own movie and producers are still remaking Foxy Brown with her as the star. It remains to be seen whether Berry or another African American actress can add further discussions about the action heroine, particularly in regards to race.

Mediocre reviews and lackluster performance at the box-office may mean another long period before an African American actress is given the opportunity to carry an action-oriented role in film. Vivica A. Fox portrayed a strongwilled FBI agent on the television series *1-800-MISSING*. Seeing such a character in film would be nice.

Additionally, it remains to be seen whether or not the sub-genre of action heroines remains a viable commodity in Hollywood. Like so many trends in the film industry, it appears that while the action heroine genre has been highly successful, it is beginning to lose its appeal as actresses in general move towards other roles that continue to redefine the gender narrative. Without a strong character similar to Sigourney Weaver's Ellen Ripley, there may be little interest in producing more action heroine movies.

Despite concerns that the genre itself may be diminishing, with good scripts and strong characters, there is hope that a new black action heroine will emerge and capture the attention of critics and audiences alike. While Berry's *Catwoman* was unable to return the action heroine to her racial roots, the possibility remains strong that her remake of Pam Grier's *Foxy Brown* may attract new audiences to blaxploitation while returning the action heroine to her position in popular cinema and with it a willingness to offer African American actresses more opportunities to portray such a heroine.

It is important to acknowledge the contributions of African American actresses to the action heroine genre and its subsequent trail blazing for *all* action heroines in decades to come. The question remains whether Grier, Dobson, Graves and Bell brought to life a new heroine that was revolutionary or whether their characters replaced the mammy, the exotic other, Aunt

Jemima and Sapphire with alternate sexual stereotypes of African American women. I have refrained from answering this question by allowing the reader to draw his or her own conclusion about these actresses and their contributions to blaxploitation presented in this book. Part of the objective here is to begin a long-overdue dialogue on what Peter Shields has called a misunderstood historical moment in film among scholars, critics and fans.

1

Reshaping African American Femininity: Mammy, Aunt Jemima, Sapphire and Action Heroine

As a cultural artifact, film has the power to shape, reinforce, and change cultural perceptions about ethnicities, gender, class, and sexuality. Lawrence Reddick writes, "[T]he movie, radio, newspaper, and library are the most important agencies for the communication of information and ideas in the American society."[1] Although this statement was made in 1944, its message still resonates loudly today as scholars, cultural critics, film critics and movie audiences grapple with lingering images of certain ethnic groups that have become ingrained and absorbed in American popular culture.

As one of the most powerful communicative transmitters, films have played an integral role in influencing the development, shaping, creating and changing cultural myths about ethnic groups and gender roles in American culture. James R. Nesteby notes, "[T]he African American images captured on film present a valid historical document reflecting predominant attitudes, conscious or unconscious, in American culture during the era in which the film is produced."[2]

For African Americans, film has largely reinforced derogatory caricatures with which African American actors, producers and directors still struggle today. While alternative representations of black life can be found in independent cinema, particularly in those films by some African American directors, mainstream studios continue to produce films that present African American men and women in one-dimensional roles. It has been a difficult task for African American actors and actresses to move beyond their onscreen representations. Acknowledging the challenges faced by African American actors, I would like to draw attention to the plight of African American actresses in the film industry since that is the focus here.

As actresses and voices of racial and gender-driven experiences, Grier, Dobson, and Graves became the mediators between studios and the audiences for this new character. Their portrayal of the action heroine represented the antithesis of the mammy as seen in Hattie McDaniel's character in *Gone with the Wind* (1939) and Dorothy Dandridge's dangerous seductress *Carmen Jones* (1954). Presenting a woman that epitomized the struggles and gains of African American women in the 1960s and early 1970s altered the onscreen perspective of African American femininity. Character portrayals by Pam Grier, Tamara Dobson, Teresa Graves and Jeannie Bell offered a significant departure from the historical representations of African American women and, through the writers, producers and directors of the genre, brought to the screen a new image of African American femininity.

During the blaxploitation period, the action heroine was an every woman. However, mainstream studios appropriated her from blaxploitation movies and, beginning with Sigourney Weaver's Ellen Ripley in *Alien* (1979), the image of the action heroine underwent a radical transformation. She changed from an African American woman who worked, within or outside of law enforcement, to protect her family and community from crime, to a white woman whose task was to save the world from alien forces. Weaver's role as an armed heroine changed the landscape of femininity in Hollywood films. *Alien* established her dominance as an action heroine who was hardy yet still feminine and desirable, proving that actresses could fill a starring role and become as successful, if not more so, than their male counterparts.

Over the years, audiences have seen the metamorphosis of the action heroine from low-budget blaxploitation films to full-scale mainstream studio productions. In the process, the studios erased the action heroines' racial construction, thus dismissing the African American actresses who brought her to life onscreen. Pam Grier, Tamara Dobson, Teresa Graves and Jeannie Bell not only paved the way for other action heroines but *redefined* the ways in which women in general were represented in film by portraying a new character that could hold her own among men and women equally.

Unfortunately, studio executives stripped away this trailblazing heroine's racial essence. It is the goal of this book to explore this transformative process and understand the rarely reported origins of the action heroine in popular cinema.

Theory and Context

There are various methodological approaches to studying and analyzing film. Laura Mulvey's "Visual Pleasures and Narrative Cinema" appeared in the Autumn edition of *Screen* (1975) and is considered a highly influential article in film theory. In summary, her article suggests through psychoanalysis that the camera is masculine and facilitates erotic pleasure for male audiences, while female audiences remain passive and serve as the objects to pacify men's viewing preferences. Mulvey's essay sparked spirited debate about the extent to which gender affects a person's perspective when viewing a film. Her essay lacks an account of how race *and* class impact spectators, thus her argument is limited when applied to the experiences and images of African American actresses as well as the spectatorship of African American audiences. While still very relevant to film studies, many scholars of film are using other theoretical apparatuses to advance their argument.

When critiquing film, scholars use many theoretical apparatuses such as Psychoanalysis, Marxism, Cultural Studies, and Audience Reception analysis, to name just a few examples. Much of my research in film is centered on placing blaxploitation in a historical, cultural, political and social context while examining the perspectives of the actresses both onscreen and off. Discussing the representations of African Americans, and separating the historical, cultural and political demarcations from the industry, is not possible because so many of the stereotypes are rooted in American societal and cultural attitudes.

I have chosen to look at how Grier, Dobson, Graves and Bell's offscreen life experiences may have served as markers for their onscreen heroines. It becomes clearer in the ensuing chapters that, at least for Grier, Dobson and Graves, their off-screen experiences and lives as African American women played an integral role in their onscreen characters — particularly for Graves, whose faith had a direct impact on her character's development in the television series *Get Christie Love!* As Grier and Dobson became more successful, they too were able to take an active role in how their heroines were characterized. This was not the case for Bell and, after her starring role in *T.N.T. Jackson*, her fledging acting career dissipated coinciding with the demise of blaxploitation movies in general.

Rather then relying on one method of analysis, I employ an interdisciplinary lens to analyze African American actresses' contributions to the action heroine in popular cinema. There is not one specific theory that addresses the issues that I am concerned with in this book. Instead, I have chosen an interdisciplinary methodology that brings together the sociological aspects of black women from an economic, social, political and cultural background along with an analysis of black actresses in film. African American women's onscreen personae are linked to their status as black women in American culture. A close examination of cinematic history will reveal that typecasts of black actresses are based on long-held cultural attitudes associated with African American femininity. Dismantling ingrained perceptions, particularly when they are so one-sided and have been held for generations at a time, is a large undertaking. However, one way to begin is by drawing from a body of theoretical work that addresses African American women in society and as spectators in film. Through this analysis, it becomes clear that their filmic representations extend beyond the film industry and into society itself.

When examining literature on the representations of African American women, it is useful to look at cultural and film critic bell hooks, whose article "Oppositional Spectators" in her book *Black Looks* examines how African American women can adopt an oppositional gaze when viewing images that are painful to watch. She writes that African American women can interrogate these constructed personas onscreen only by adopting such a gaze and notes that as spectators, "most black women I talked with were adamant that they never went to movies expecting to see compelling representations of black femaleness. They were all acutely aware of cinematic racism — its violent erasure of black womanhood."[3] For hooks, the oppositional gaze is practiced by black female spectators exercising their "power in looking through the contestation confrontation" of dominant images.[4] Understanding blaxploitation within its social, political and cultural context allows viewers to confront the painful distortions of stereotypical images while seeing glimpses of empowerment from the heroines' perspectives. That is to say, the films of Grier and Dobson in particular may have provided some African American women with the ability to identify with the traits of an empowered woman who is trying to take care of her family and working while dismissing and ignoring the negative aspects of a character created by a producer who could not relate to the burdens endured by black women in a culture where gender and race often become determining factors in their status of some individuals.

In Chapter 3, there is discussion of how Grier herself notes the impact of her characters on some African American women. Leaving aside the label of blaxploitation for a moment and focusing specifically on those traits that were appealing to some African American women, particularly younger African American women, it is easy to understand the appeal of Grier's heroines. In keeping with hooks' oppositional gaze, some black women could identify with Grier's heroines by discarding the negative aspects of Hollywood's notion of black femininity while keeping those attributes that were positive. To "adopt an oppositional stance" means to interrogate the images that one sees in film by "creating alternative texts that are not solely reactions."[5] Understanding that blaxploitation movies in general presented many negative images of black femininity, African American women could still engage and enjoy the films of Grier and Dobson and even identify with certain traits of these heroines by adopting an oppositional stance — taking the positive traits of the heroines and reclaiming them, while discarding the negative attributes associated with these heroines.

hooks, Patricia Hill Collins, Jacqueline Bobo, and K. Sue Jewell also provide the analysis for this book. Viewing African American women's experiences through a sociological and cultural lens offers a full critique of Grier, Dobson, Graves, and Bell's lives as African American women attempting to make a living in an industry that allowed them limited entry and no creative freedom. Ironically, the film industry offers one of the few media outlets where African American women can change the cultural myths. Yet, the industry is also a media tool that has reinforced a system that simultaneously involves minorities and marginalizes them. Still, the film industry is a dominant outlet that can help dismantle lingering cultural myths about African American women when they are allowed to tell their own stories and when they are in positions of authority in the studio system. In their interviews, it becomes clear that Grier, Dobson, and Graves exhibited more control over their onscreen images.

As a sociologist and the author of *Black Feminist Thought*, Patricia Hill Collins examines the underlying sociological effects of race, gender, and class on African American women. She has suggested "portraying African American women as stereotypical Mammies, Matriarchs, Welfare Recipients, and Hot Mommas helps justify U.S. black women's oppression."[6] These images of African American women have become ingrained in all media outlets but particularly in film, where African American actresses have been forced to portray the very roles that Collins labels as stereotypical since their appearance in film. K. Sue Jewell also notes that the media have defined "African American womanhood in four categories: Mammy, Aunt Jemima, Sapphire, and Jezebel/the bad black girl."[7]

Before the 1960s, African American actresses dominated these categories and were rarely seen in complex, multi-faceted roles. Blaxploitation films changed that by showing tough, no-nonsense women who were capable of holding their own among men and using justifiable violence to achieve their ultimate objective. Grier, Dobson, Graves, and Bell's action heroines greatly differed from the mammy, jezebel, Aunt Jemima, and Sapphire characters previously played by African American actresses.

Collins writes that a core theme of black feminist thought is challenging these controlling images."[8] Extending her analysis to blaxploitation films, Grier, Dobson, Graves, and Bell's experiences as African American women allowed them to shape the direction of their characters despite the fact that their characters were written by European American writers. The heroines may have turned out differently in the hands of an African American woman writer. But, there was (and continues to be) a lack of visible black women screenwriters. Since few African American women participated in the decision-making process during the blaxploitation explosion, actresses had to take matters into their own hands. This is particularly true of Grier and Graves, who were established enough to force directors — and, in Graves' case, a television production company — to make changes in their characters' personality make-up.

Using Bobo's work on African American women's responses to Steven Spielberg's *The Color Purple* (they were able to find value in the film despite its white director and, at times, controversial images of black men and women), I suggest that some African American women could relate to Grier and Dobson because of the strength their characters exhibited in tough situations. Grier's heroines would be particularly appealing to this audience because they seemed more believable than Dobson's glamorized Cleopatra Jones, who has been compared by film critic Mary E. Mebane[9] as well as other film critics to a female James Bond.

Finally, I am also a textual critic who analyzes film as a text and tries to find an ideological framework which is also part of the larger theoretical foundation that I am writing about. Notable film scholar Robert Stam states that the historical roots of textual analysis touch on many fields including "biblical exegesis, nineteenth-century hermeneutics and philology, and the French pedagogical method of close reading."[10] Other scholars, such as Douglas Kellner, adhere to a different interpretation of textual analysis, as "concerned with showing how the cultural meanings encoded into a text's various 'languages' convey ideological effects."[11] In order to illustrate an empowering image of onscreen black femininity, I employed both a textual and ideological analysis along with an oppositional gaze and ultimately linking the social, political and cultural status of black women in American culture with their position in the film industry.

To my knowledge, little statistical data exist from 1972 to 1975 on how African American women responded to these heroines. Therefore, my conclusions are based on archival interviews with the actresses at the height of their popularity. I aim to give voice to the actresses behind the persona of this new character and, through their stories, offer an analysis of their portrayals by providing a first-hand glimpse into their feelings about this new heroine and what she represented for black women.

Through primary and secondary archival interview material, I trace the crucial roles these actresses played in presenting a heroine that redefined the action genre for actresses in general and African American actresses specifically. In the process, I reinforce and pay homage to the contributions these actresses made in giving the action heroine an image.

Mammy, the Exotic Other,[12] Aunt Jemima and Sapphire

In order to understand the significance of the new African American heroines onscreen in the 1970s, a history of African American actresses in cinema would be helpful. There were two stock roles for African American actresses before the 1960s. The mammy and exotic other were introduced in early cinema. There has been a lot of speculation in history concerning whether an actual mammy ever existed.

Jessie Parkhurst states, "[T]he 'African American Mammy' tradition in the Southern household became a plantation tradition, bloomed when the plantation was in its glory and so took hold of the imagination of the people of the South that the 'African American Mammy' eventually entered the homes of the middle class and the poorer farmer."[13] Mammy became an imaginary figure created by White Southern families longing to become part of the Southern aristocratic class.[14] During slavery, there were African American women who performed household tasks that might conceivably make people think they were mammies when, in reality, their work consisted of laborious domestic duties.

Mammy's onscreen characteristics were based on her appearances in minstrel shows. She was a dark-skinned woman with African features who wore shapeless dresses. Her physical characteristics contrasted sharply with the Exotic Other. This distortion made her in Cheryl Thurber's words "an asexual figure who invited an ambiguous resolution of sexual tensions."[15] A Rubenesque figure has been defined as aesthetically appealing during different periods in history and in certain cultures. However, mammy's shape was overly exaggerated, marking her physically unattractive by Victorian standards of beauty. Her personality was aggressive in nature when dealing with other servants, but very docile in the company of her white employers. On the one hand, she is presented as masculine in her abilities to perform strenuous physical labor, and yet very nurturing when taking care of her employer's children.

Another image of African American femininity that emerged was the Exotic Other. Originally introduced onscreen in the 1920s, she appeared regularly in the 1940s as a seductress. In contrast to mammy's characteristics, the Exotic Other was light-skinned, with long straight hair and a thin nose, features considered "classic" in nature. She was destined to remain on the fringes of both the black and white communities. Her one-percent of African American blood kept her from becoming part of the Caucasian community, and the African American community rejected her as well. Thus, the tragic mulatto became an outsider and was given the "tragic" label because of her inability to reconcile her dual heritage. The style of dress was different between mammy, the tragic mulatto, Aunt Jemima and Sapphire. While mammy wore shift dresses, Jezebel wore nice skirts or tightly fitted evening gowns that showed off her curvaceous figure.[16] Aunt Jemima's attire was similar to mammy and Sapphire did not have specific clothing.

Despite concrete evidence that suggests the mammy did not exist as a real woman, her image remains distinctive. The most recognizable actress to bring her to life was Hattie McDaniel. This begs the question of how the image came to appear onscreen and as part of the answer, one must look at how African American women were viewed in American culture during and after slavery. In the eyes of many, African American women did not represent the ideal Victorian image of womanhood, and mammy was created according to Jewell as "the antithesis of the American conception of womanhood."[17] Her counterpart, the tragic mulatto, was also created to counter images of Victorian womanhood and, more importantly, to juxtapose African American women against each other.

At the heart of the juxtaposition lies physical characteristics such as skin tone, facial features, and hair texture that were integral in determining the types of roles available to African American actresses. These factors limited their ability to create multi-faceted characters until the 1960s. Kathy Russell, Midge Wilson, and Ronald Hall state, "[F]or women, skin color was a critical factor in casting: light-skinned African American actresses were given sympathetic roles; women who were dark were cast as Mammies."[18] Directors created a system in which African American actresses competed for tiny roles and, more importantly, with each other. African American actresses who could not be easily categorized, such as Josephine Baker, found little work in show business during the 1930s because their complexion was not considered light or dark enough for a role as a domestic or a seductress. Subsequently, she left America and became a sensation and icon in France for many years. Ironically, while producers could not find a place for Baker in the American film industry, she found an energetic reception from French audiences precisely because she did not fit a predetermined mold that American producers used to cast African American actresses.

Mammy, Jezebel, Aunt Jemima and Sapphire's images are crucial to understanding the rise of alternative black heroines in blaxploitation movies. The problem, as Edward Mapp suggests, is that the African American actress has always been "defined by others rather than herself. When she is not a figment of white male fantasy, she is a product of white female thinking."[19] During the period of film shorts before WWI and before African American actresses appeared onscreen, white actresses portrayed black women characters in blackface — a common practice in the early years of film, most notably in D. W. Griffith's *Birth of a Nation* (1914). Although hailed by film critics as a cinematic masterpiece, the film presented highly disturbing images of African Americans and was instrumental in how the industry presented future images of African Americans. These two roles defined African American femininity onscreen from the 1920s to the 1960s. Onscreen, mammy, the tragic mulatto, Aunt Jemima and Sapphire functioned as a way of affirming Victorian womanhood by reassuring audiences that African American women were not a threat to the European ideals of femininity. Talented actresses such as Nina Mae McKinney, Fredi Washington, Butterfly McQueen, and, in later years, Lena Horne and Dorothy Dandridge never were able to fulfill their true acting potential because of the unwillingness of studios to see them in other roles beyond mammy and the tragic mulatto. In the careers of McKinney, Washington, Horne and Dandridge, they regularly portrayed a variant of the Exotic Other. Sociologist David Pilgrim asserts:

The portrayal of Black women as lascivious by nature is an enduring stereotype. The descriptive words associated with this stereotype are singular in their focus: seductive, alluring, worldly, beguiling, tempting, and lewd.[20]

Historically, white women, in film, were portrayed as models of self-respect, self-control, and modesty — even sexual purity, but black women were often portrayed as innately promiscuous, even predatory. This depiction of black women is signified by the name Jezebel.[21] The film industry used these stereotypes to reinforce and not challenge the preconceived notions of largely white audiences of black femininity.

McDaniel became the first African American to win an Oscar for Best Supporting Actress in *Gone with the Wind* (1939). Along with Louise Beavers, she portrayed a mammy until her death in the early 1950s. Yet, even with that role, McDaniel and Beavers did what other African American actresses would come to utilize in later years and that meant injecting their own sense of what the character could be despite the limitations of playing Mammy. George Alexander notes that "though they both often played maids, they brought a fierce energy to the screen that earned them an enduring place in the film world."[22] Film scholar Donald Bogle notes, "[T]hey were a presence on screen, and each became a presence within the film community itself, and each became known to general audiences."[23] With McDaniel especially, her size, deep voice, and attitude were all key in shaping her commanding screen presence. Bogle asserts, "[W]hen she worked opposite women like Vivien Leigh in *Gone with the Wind* and Jean Harlow in *Saratoga* and *China Seas*, she would look at these women directly in the eyes. She had such a full sense of self and no real feelings of being inferior."[24]

Similar to the typecasting McDaniel and Beavers endured, Horne and Dandridge also faced obstacles moving beyond the Jezebel role to characters with depth. Neither was successful in breaking through the typecast. Horne was ultimately blacklisted for her vocal opinions on racism and for her interracial marriage. After a Best Actress nomination for *Carmen Jones* (1954), Dandridge was under-utilized and suffered both professional and personal tragedies.

Hattie McDaniel and Louise Beavers

During the 1930s, African American actresses made their mark by appearing in numerous mammy roles. Hattie McDaniel and Louise Beavers became associated with the mammy image and ultimately were typecast in this role. Hollywood had found a new place for the Negro — in the kitchens, laundry rooms, and pantries.[25] Two distinct images of the mammy icon appeared in film. The first image was that of the strong-willed, vocally assertive African American woman who openly voiced displeasure with her employer's judgment. The second image was a more typically sedate domestic who did not engage her employer in conversation and willingly performed her duties in the employer's household. Aunt Jemima falls into this category. Hattie McDaniel fit the bill as the outspoken mammy while Louise Beavers portrayed the latter image. In fact, McDaniel won an Academy Award for her portrayal of the loyal, faithful servant in *Gone with the Wind*, but this did not lead to a surplus of roles for her. As a robust, dark-skinned woman, she possessed the physical characteristics of mammy and used these stereotypical traits to "display her remarkable talent and affinity for pure broad comedy."[26] The role of mammy solidified McDaniel's career in Hollywood as a servitude actress. *Gone with the Wind* picked up where *Birth of a Nation* left off in the depictions of African Americans in general, and African American women in particular. The film's glorification of Southern aristocracy and docile African American servants became a box-office hit and continues to appear regularly on cable television. With limited screen time, McDaniel brought mammy to life by portraying her as a boisterous, sharp-tongued woman. The role did not allow McDaniel to explore her full acting ability but, utilizing her comedic talents, she made a strong impression in a role with little depth. Not surprisingly, critics adored McDaniel's portrayal of mammy. She took the limited role of mammy and, using her creativity and talents as an actress, left an enduring image onscreen and in Hollywood for other African American actresses in later years. After McDaniel won the Oscar, Hollywood (prone to replicating successes) was now convinced that audiences could "walk a million miles for one of Mammy's smiles"[27]: They wrapped bandanas around the head of each working black actress faster than you can say "Ah's a comin'."[28]

Louise Beavers was another African American actress who appeared in many mammy roles during the 1930s. I would categorize Beavers' mammy as more of an Aunt Jemima role since her depiction of the character was more pleasant and cheerful than assertive. Beavers predates McDaniel as one of the first mammies, but the latter's visibility made her more recognizable in this role. Beavers received critical acclaim for her portrayal as Aunt Delilah in the film *Imitation of Life*. Based on Fannie Hurst's bestselling novel, the 1934 version starred Beavers and Claudette Colbert (as Miss Bea) in the title roles. Beavers' Aunt Delilah perfects a family recipe, and Miss Bea decides to market it. As a result, both women become rich, but instead of leaving, Aunt Delilah opts to remain. The two women become business partners while raising two stubborn daughters. Fredi Washington, a light-skinned African American actress, played Beavers' daughter Peola, who is unhappy with her position in a racist society. She longs to have the advantages of Jessie, her white playmate. Peola becomes resentful and ashamed because of her mother's dark skin.

On the surface, *Imitation of Life* illustrates the struggles of two women of different colors and their relationships with their daughters, and as friends. Yet, the film is also one of the first to explore the issue of skin color in the African American community. *Imitation of Life* explores a side of the African American community not openly discussed, much less put onscreen: intraracial discrimination. The film was a precursor to films that explored miscegenation in mainstream Hollywood productions during the 1940s. For the most part, *Imitation of Life* ignored differences between African American women and white women and the status that each woman occupied in a patriarchal hierarchy. The film was a critical and box-office hit, but unfortunately for Louise Beavers this did not translate into more acting roles. Audiences were not ready to see African American women in any other role and studios in particular did not want to create roles for black actresses beyond one of servitude. Beavers was *the* mammy until McDaniel usurped the image in *Gone with the Wind*. Beavers arrived in producer David O. Selznick's office for her interview dressed in her best furs while Hattie McDaniel arrived in his office wearing a head scarf, apron, and Civil War–era housedress borrowed from the studio costuming department.[29]

McDaniel and Beavers are to be commended for invoking their own individuality given the restrictive nature of the film industry. Yet, they were subjected to a lot of criticism from African American leaders. McDaniel and Walter White feuded for years concerning her roles.

During the 1930s, employment opportunities (beyond domestic work) for African American women were sparse. If they were lucky, a job as a teacher was one way to escape poverty. However, many African American families did not have the money to send their daughters to college. Region also played an important role in determining job prospects for African American women. For example, opportunities for domestic servants were plentiful in the South. However, the Northern region relied heavily on industrial work. Consequently, African American women competed against African American men and white men for factory work in the North. They were often excluded in the North not only because of their race, but also because of their gender. For those African American women who wanted to act, finding acting opportunities was extremely difficult. They were ever mindful that the duties they performed in film were the duties many African American women around the country executed on a daily basis. Although actresses such as McDaniel imbued her characters with a rebellious spirit, mammy has always been relegated to "her place" in the kitchen or pantry.[30] A mammy should never be confused with a nanny, which is a dignified, good-paying position for whites. As mother surrogate, scapegoat, and unpaid servant, the screen mammy was an enigmatic perversion.[31] She was always there to assist her employer at the expense of her own family and life. Audiences and studios alike viewed Hattie McDaniel as mammy and she earned a good living playing that one role. But when the word mammy is uttered, one cannot help but think of McDaniel the actress and not McDaniel the person.

Lena Horne and Hazel Scott as the Tragic Mulatto

In the 1930s, African American actresses were relegated to servitude roles, but this changed during the 1940s. During the 1940s, African American actresses such as Hazel Scott and Lena Horne became associated with the image of a sex object, the tragic mulatto and entertainer melded into one. Roles for African American actresses as entertainers became commonplace as a number of black musicals were made during the decade. Nina Mae McKinney served as the model for the Exotic Other's appearance onscreen. Originally from South Carolina, she caught the attention of King Vidor who cast her in *Hallelujah* (1929). Audiences were transfixed by McKinney's seductive and sassy moves,[32] which Horne and Dandridge adopted later in their roles.

Although she is not well known today, Hazel Scott was extremely popular in Hollywood during the early to mid–1940s. Portraying mainly entertainer roles, Scott's closest rival was Lena Horne, who eventually surpassed her in status. Unlike other African American actresses, Scott had an established reputation as a pianist before coming to Hollywood. She refused servitude roles and often played herself in films,[33] a luxury that few African American actresses had.

As Scott's career began to fade, Lena Horne's star began to rise. She starred in a range of black musicals during the 1940s. Horne was established as an entertainer before coming to Hollywood, having appeared as a very successful nightclub performer in New York. Recognized for her beautiful complexion, she received publicity in mainstream magazines such as *Time* and *Life*, which was unusual for an African American actress at the time. As a matter of fact, audiences did not believe she was African American. Like Hattie McDaniel and Louise Beavers in the 1930s, Horne was typecast as the *tragic mulatto*.

She became an object on display and remarked, "[T]hey didn't make me into a maid, but they didn't make me anything else either. I became a butterfly pinned to a column singing away in Movieland."[34] Along with the president of the Beverly Hills NAACP chapter Walter White, Horne worried that she would be typecast as a Jezebel. She stated:

> [M]y and White's concern was that in the period while I was waiting for *Cabin in the Sky* they would force me to play roles as a maid or maybe even some jungle type. Now these were the roles, as I have said, that most Negroes were forced to play in the movies at that time. It was not that I felt I was too good or too proud to play them. But Walter felt and I agreed with him, that since I had no history in the movies and therefore had not been typecast ... it would be essential for me to try to establish a different kind of image for Negro women.[35]

Horne recognized the dilemma faced by many African American actresses. Audiences were not ready to see them in roles other than those conjured up in fiction about African American women. Moreover, once they arrived in Hollywood, African American actresses faced pressure from the African American community for taking roles that demeaned African American women. Intent on *not* being typecast, Horne included a statement in her contract clause that she would not play a "jungle type,"[36] which upset studio executives. It was not just this stipulation that ultimately led to her decline in the film industry. An interracial marriage and outspokenness about racism ultimately put Horne on the infamous blacklist, and in the 1950s she lost the pivotal role of Carmen Jones to Dorothy Dandridge. The 1940s remain her most productive years as an African American actress in Hollywood. She returned to the screen in the 1960s playing a tragic mulatto who was the mistress of a white gunfighter.

Dorothy Dandridge and the 1950s

In the hands of Horne and Hazel Scott, the tragic mulatto remained demurred. However, her depiction changed in the 1950s largely because of Dorothy Dandridge's portrayal in the 1954 film version of Bizet's opera

Carmen. Similar to Lena Horne, Dandridge received a great deal of attention because of her golden complexion, straight hair and "European" features. *Life* magazine put her on the front cover, marking the first time an African American celebrity achieved this distinction. She was a show business veteran, having appeared at the famous Cotton Club in Harlem before making her film debut as an extra in *A Day at the Races* (1937). Much like her predecessors Nina Mae McKinney and Lena Horne, Dandridge's physical characteristics fit Hollywood's image of the Jezebel. In the same way that Hattie McDaniel's face became synonymous with mammy, Dandridge's Carmen Jones cemented the image of this stock character.

One of the most successful black musicals in film history, *Carmen Jones* featured a stellar cast of African American performers (Harry Belafonte, Pearl Bailey, Brock Peters, and Diahann Carroll). Dandridge's Carmen Jones manipulated men around her. The camera played on this appeal with lingering shots of Dandridge's figure, from the scene where she stands on a table in a black off-the-shoulder-top form-fitting skirt and black heels, to the scene where she is dressed in a short satin robe while Belafonte's character blows her toenail polish dry.

Class may have been the determining factor in how the Jezebel was portrayed onscreen and often put African American actresses at odds with each other (at least on screen, and sometimes off-screen). An excellent example of this can be found in Lena Horne's portrayal of the Jezebel in *Cabin in the Sky*, in which she attempts to entice Eddie Rochester's character, Joseph "Little Joe" Jackson, away from his wife Petunia, portrayed by Ethel Waters. In contrast, Dorothy Dandridge's character Carmen had an animalistic quality; she not only seduced men, causing them to kill for her, but she did not mind engaging in her own fights with other women. In sum, Horne's jezebel was more coy then Dandridge's, and this may have been the direct result of Horne's own middle-class upbringing which was diametrically opposite of Dandridge's tumultuous early years. Hazel Scott also had middle-class roots, and she was well established as an accomplished pianist before becoming an actress; producers may have taken greater care to present the image of the jezebel as portrayed by her and Horne as less cunning or outright brazen as Dandridge's Carmen. Horne played (in Bogle's words) a "dignified" seductress while Dandridge's character was bold. Dandridge's performance in *Carmen Jones* was impressive enough to earn her an Academy Award nomination for Best Actress, marking the first time an African American actress had achieved such an honor. She did not achieve this level of success in subsequent films and was stuck with this character.

In an effort to satisfy audiences and to reinforce the cultural myths about African American womanhood, the film industry demanded that African American actresses remain in stock roles that would not upset audiences. In the 1930s, Hattie McDaniel and Louise Beavers fulfilled this role in their depictions of mammy. In 1959, Dandridge earned another Best Actress nomination for her portrayal as Bess, the tragic mulatto, in *Porgy and Bess*. Ironically, African American women received praise from critics only when they played these stock roles. It seems that these stereotypical roles (particularly mammy) brought familiarity to those who longed to relive the South's "glory days." For white audiences who harbored such longings, the appeal of these characters was undeniable and allowed them to remain firmly entrenched in their nostalgia of the Old South.

In many ways, the dilemma of portraying a character that did not fit in the black community or the white community affected Dandridge's personal life. The pressures of being an African American actress in a white male–dominated industry, along with failed interracial relationships and poor business advice from her second husband, may have contributed to her early death at the age of 42. Her death symbolized the oppression and heavy burdens many African American actresses encountered in Hollywood.

With little opportunity to expand their acting range, they remained typecast. The dilemma was clear for African American actresses: Either they would play roles that demeaned and reinforced cultural myths about African American women, or they would have to give up acting. Sad to say, the critics only took notice of African American actresses when they appeared as mammy, the tragic mulatto, Aunt Jemima or Sapphire. Thus, actresses such as Dandridge, Horne, McDaniel, and Beavers could only hope to take their role and turn it into a brilliant performance. A stunning tribute to their talented acting abilities, many African American actresses were able to do just that.

If one were to judge African American actresses' onscreen images from the 1930s to 1950s, a distorted view of black femininity emerges. Hattie McDaniel, Louise Beavers, Lena Horne, and Dorothy Dandridge may have represented some African American women; however, their films had audiences believe that they in fact represented *all* African American women.

Breaking the stereotypes of mammy and the exotic other has been extremely difficult for black actresses who for years have fought to shed their identity with these images. Hattie McDaniel's portrayal of Mammy and Dorothy Dandridge's role as Carmen Jones cemented the image of African American femininity onscreen and made it hard for African American women outside of Hollywood to disassociate themselves from these images.

African American women in film have taken roles that devalued their very essence as African American women and managed to make the most of their limited presence onscreen.

There are two more stereotypes that manifested itself onscreen in the form of Aunt Jemima and Sapphire. Aunt Jemima evolved from the mammy image and is very similar in terms of appearance. The primary distinction between mammy and Aunt Jemima is that Aunt Jemima's tasks of domesticity are usually limited to those of a cook. Aunt Jemima's physical characteristics were very similar to mammy's.

Sapphire was known for being verbally combative. The similarity between mammy, Aunt Jemima and Sapphire is related more to their emotional make-up than to any other qualities that they possess. The Sapphire image of African American womanhood, unlike other images that symbolize African American women, necessitates the presence of an African American male. Specific physical characteristics are not part of Sapphire's make-up. While she rarely appeared in film on the scale of mammy and the exotic other, her image was first ingrained on television by Ernestine Wade's character on the TV series *Amos 'n' Andy*. On that show, Sapphire was always engaged in verbal disputes with her onscreen husband "Kingfish" (portrayed by Tim Moore).

It is not ironic that the character on this television show which ran in the early 1950s (and originated on radio) was named Sapphire. The producers must have known that such a stereotype existed—if not from seeing in film, then in avenues such as popular advertising of the day (African Americans often appeared in derogatory ads), on postcards, as memorabilia and so forth. On the show, "Kingfish" was always getting into some kind of trouble and Wade's Sapphire responded with a verbal tongue-lashing that included pointing her finger at her husband's antics with one hand on her hip.

Based on the cultural pervasiveness of mammy, the exotic other, Aunt Jemima and Sapphire symbols, it is easy to see that audiences would think these two prevailing images literally define African American femininity. Of course, this is simply not true. The beauty of African American femininity lies in the wide spectrum of color hues and cannot be defined solely by light skin versus dark skin. In fact, more true to form were the images of African American women's strength and endurance in the face of a structure that kept them at the bottom of the social and economic ladder based on race, gender, and class. The heroism of African American women as social activists was absent from the screen. To show them in any other role required dismantling cultural myths associated with African American women as asexual or promiscuous. The film industry was not interested in creating multi-dimensional roles for African American actresses. More importantly, the power structure of the film industry left black actresses at such a disadvantage that they had little choice concerning roles.

In the 1960s, audiences began to see an array of black femininity though mammy and the tragic mulatto remained. The 1960s offered an alternative image of African American femininity with actresses such as Cicely Tyson, who wore an Afro in the television series *Eastside/Westside* (1963); according to Bogle, "her Afro became her badge of honor long before the Afro gained wide acceptance within the black community. She brought in a new aesthetic, because she knew who she was and had so much pride in herself that she made the audience rethink its definitions of beauty. And that's power."[37] Tyson's physical characteristics represented a rethinking of African American femininity that audiences began to see reflected in television with Nichelle Nichols (Lieutenant Uhura on *Star Trek*) and Gail Fisher (Peggy Fair in the *Mannix* series). A diverse group of black actresses made it easier in some ways to cast Pam Grier and Tamara Dobson's roles in the early 1970s.

The caricatures of the past remained, but they were sharply contrasted with images of African American women in occupations ranging from Nichols on *Star Trek*, a revolutionary television series known for its groundbreaking depictions of minorities and women, to a widowed nurse and mother balancing duties at the hospital and home, played by Diahann Carroll on *Julia*.

In sum, the mammy, exotic other, Aunt Jemima and Sapphire were integral in defining African American femininity onscreen. They represented dehumanizing cartooning of a perceived range of African American femininity that continued to reinforce negative depictions of African American women in film. The social damage wrought by their iconic images seeped behind the screen as well as being projected on it. McDaniel, Beavers, Horne, and Dandridge, who made these images real for audiences, suffered long-lasting strife emotionally, professionally and, in some cases, physically as they struggled to utilize and perhaps transform the only avenues available to them in Hollywood before the 1960s. The characters lacked depth and were stereotypical, but laid the foundation for changing images of black women in film during the 1960s. There are certain traits present in each character that contributed to the personality make-up of the action heroine in blaxploitation movies. For example, McDaniel's mammy was aggressive and that can be found in Pam Grier, Tamara Dobson, Teresa Graves and Jeannie Bell's heroines. Grier's heroines in particular were cunning—

an attribute of Jezebel. The mothering instinct present in Aunt Jemima was clearly part of the personality characteristics of Grier and Dobson's heroines, particularly when their loved ones and community were at risk. Finally, Sapphire's verbal sparring was present in blaxploitation action heroines. Grier and Dobson in particular often made the male characters around them look inept.

Action Hero

In order to understand the early origins of the action heroine in popular cinema, it is necessary to examine the genre of action movies. As Jason Meyer suggests,

> Action movies are an undeniable presence in popular culture and have been arguably one of the most successful genres in the history of film. They have a genealogy that ties their heroes and anti-heroes with everything from comic books to Greek myth. They present agents of power and change, characters who have the ability to affect their environments, characters ripe for audience identification.[38]

Blaxploitation films, particularly those that focused on action-oriented storylines, provided audiences who craved alternative heroes with an outlet in which they could, for the first time, identify with a protagonist who looked like them. As a genre, action movies were confined to white males, excluding African American men as well as women — of any race. In the old boys club school of action movies, women tended to play the role of rescuee, or often just decoration.[39]

In the 1980s, the standard action hero was Sylvester Stallone's John Rambo, a misunderstood loner. Arnold Schwarzenegger's Terminator became the symbol of the action hero in the early 1990s. During both decades, others emerged, such as Bruce Willis and Mel Gibson, but the emphasis on the action hero, particularly his physical characteristics, was that of a white, muscular male — often a loner who was charged with the task of making things right in a chaotic world. Much attention in film scholarship has been focused on action movies, but little has been focused on action movies in the blaxploitation era, particularly those centered on African American heroines.

Action movies trade in classifiable character types, but women have been especially confined to extremely narrow types.[40] However, this was not the case with Pam Grier and Tamara Dobson. Surprisingly, given the historic treatment of African American actresses, they were allowed to move more freely and, in many ways, redefine the way African American femininity had been portrayed onscreen. The move away from mammy, the exotic other, Aunt Jemima and Sapphire to a tough, liberated heroine, quite adept at handling herself in different settings, could only occur in blaxploitation movies, as mainstream studios were not ready for such a heroine and, frankly, had not created a woman character along these lines. Strong heroines have always existed in cinema's history, but the action genre has been male-dominated.

As noted in the introduction of this book, exploitation films do not shy away from introducing topics or characters that mainstream films would not consider. They are able to do this primarily because the budgetary risks are lower. Also, as previously noted, studios that make exploitation movies are often exploiting trends in popular culture; therein lies greater flexibility and freedom to create characters that would seem revolutionary in mainstream popular cinema. The black action heroine was a character that mainstream studios would have deemed risky to build a movie around. Until the emergence and success of Pam Grier's characters for American International Pictures, African American action heroines were non-existent in mainstream popular cinema.

Actors such as Clint Eastwood and Charles Bronson symbolized the action hero in the early 1970s as a disenchanted, cynical loner who worked within the system, as was the case with Eastwood's Dirty Harry Calhoun, or outside of it, as Bronson's protagonist in *Death Wish* (1974), to exact retribution or a reckoning. By the 1980s, the action hero had moved from loner, as portrayed by Bronson, and a "renegade" police officer, as portrayed by Eastwood, to a veteran forced to take matters into his own hands when the government failed him, as portrayed by Sylvester Stallone in *Rambo: First Blood* (1982). Stallone's hero was so popular that the character became a political symbol when then–President Ronald Reagan invoked his name in speeches. Mainstream action heroes in the 1970s and 1980s reflected the attitudes, mood, and social climate of the country, and film historians have often noted that heroes depicted by Eastwood, Bronson, Stallone, and Schwarzenegger symbolized the shift of the political landscape to a more conservative era. Yvonne Tasker notes that "the success of these films and stars could be read in terms of a backlash against the feminism of the 1970s, as indicative of a new conservatism in both national and sexual politics."[41]

In the 1990s, the action hero underwent another transformation as a cyborg warrior out to save the world from destruction. In the interim, an interesting phenomenon was occurring with the action heroine who began to build as large a following in mainstream popular cinema as her male counterparts. In the words of Bishetta Mishett, the "female action heroes seem to take on all the characteristics of their male counterparts which means that they are outside the mainstream, are outspoken, irreverent, and they use legal and barely legal methods to accomplish their goals."[42] She adds, "Many times the males have a female friend or best male friend. However, generally, the women are more sexual and may begin an attachment to a male in the film."[43] All of these characteristics fit the action heroines in blaxploitation movies as well as the action heroines in later mainstream movies. In reference to Grier's heroines, Mishett says,

> I consider Grier one of the women of the blaxploitation period who could be characterized as a "female jock." There were women who used their physical characteristics and brawn to rid the community of drugs. I believe that these images were two-sided — negative in that the women were often used as sex objects or shown nude and positive because they had determination and purpose and were dedicated to remove drugs from the African American community. Their methods included using their bodies in this crusade.[44]

The contradictory facets of the black action heroine in blaxploitation movies was that she was required to disrobe while simultaneously serving as the liberator of the evils confronting her family and community. Grier had to find a way to negotiate and defend herself against criticism for nudity while arguing that her heroines were actually empowering for black women. It was not easy to maneuver and, given the history of African American women performers and black women in general in America, sometimes it was difficult to justify what seemed in some cases to be gratuitous nudity and violence in her movies. However, it is important to keep in mind the real differences between studios such as American International Pictures and a studio such as Warner Brothers, which produced Tamara Dobson's *Cleopatra Jones* (1973).

AIP employed tactics that might not appeal to mainstream studios. Thus, the blaxploitation action heroine had more latitude then her mainstream counterpart, particularly when examining the transformation of her character from "street and sassy" to her reemergence as a scientist exploring life forms on other planets. The street and sassy action heroine is directly tied to her creation by a studio known for its marketing sensationalistic strategies, designed to target the urban market. But AIP was formed by two creative, business-minded individuals, Jim Nicholson and Samuel Arkoff, who were not interested in directly competing with major studios, but rather seeking to offer audiences alternative movies that would be difficult to sell to (say) Columbia or Warner Brothers. Nicholson and Arkoff decided not to use glossy promotions for their films, relying on the shock factor. As their strategy pertains to blaxploitation films, particularly those starring Pam Grier, they used sex appeal to show a street, sassy and curvaceous action heroine using her body and brains to exact revenge. Giving Grier's character street smarts would appeal to those audiences in the urban market who were attracted to characters such as Richard Roundtree's John Shaft. Adding the physical attractive factor would appeal to teenage and young males and the spunk might appeal to young women who admired Grier's action heroines because they showed strength in the face of adversity and represented a can-do attitude towards the world while taking care of their families and community. The studio had latitude in creating the character, but Grier and Dobson (particularly the former) added a layer to what often turned out to be one-dimensional role. As is the case with a prototype, it takes time to develop a character and audiences did not see such a development until Sigourney Weaver made her entry with Ellen Ripley.

The contrast between the black action heroine in blaxploitation movies and mainstream, popular cinema is startling. In many ways, race and class are a factor along with the fact that studios with larger budgets sometimes produce characters with more depth. What the action heroine lacked in blaxploitation was a depth found in *Alien* (1979) and what she lacked in her mainstream form was interesting, believable to a certain extent, everyday women. Whereas the focus was communal, as portrayed by Weaver, the character was a loner, a renegade in cases, when she directly challenged the system, and a warrior who was forced to take matters into her own hands when her superiors proved inept or were destroyed. It became her task to save humankind from the ravages of an alien force. Interestingly enough, Weaver's action heroine initially was there to support her male superiors who were charged with the task of completing the mission. However, they were killed, and it became Ripley's purpose to ensure the safety of the crew by battling the alien, particularly after the loss of a male character that she was very fond of.

Unlike the action hero, there were not alternative ways of looking at the action heroine. Weaver's character entered mainstream popular cinema at a time when strong women protagonists appeared to be fading as the women's movement lost momentum.[45] Ellen Ripley represented "a shining symbol of feminine fortitude"[46] and Weaver's portrayal of the character "exuded a confidence on the screen"[47] that was hard to ignore and became popular across the gender spectrum. It is little wonder then that Ripley became the "gold standard"[48] for action heroines. Ximena Gallardo notes, "Ripley was the first female protagonist of either science fiction or horror who actually saves herself and kills the monster on her own."[49] Ripley epitomized the action heroine until the early 1990s, when audiences were introduced to action heroines as outlaws, female versions of *Bonnie and Clyde*, portrayed by Susan Sarandon and Geena Davis in *Thelma and Louise* (1991), along with other action heroine images such as Geena Davis' pirate character in *Cutthroat Island* (1995) and Jamie Lee Curtis' police woman in *Blue Steel* (1991), to name a few.

Arguably, whether these latter characters fit into the action heroine model depends on how the term action heroine and action heroine genre are defined. It may be useful here to briefly establish definitions for the action movie, action hero, action heroine and action heroine movies. Meyer notes: "[M]otivation is a central problem in all Action Movies ... the heroes commit acts of criminal brutality, and they must somehow be justified."[50] The heroes' context and character must provide both motivation and pathway for the violence. In defining the action genre, he adds, "[T]he Action Movie needs more justification for its action, some plausible (at least from the suspension of disbelief standpoint), understandable reason. Usually the Action Movie looks for a reason which the audience can in some way approve."[51] This definition is sufficient for movies focused on male protagonists. It becomes a little more complicated when heroines are presented with the opportunity to rescue their family, community and possibly the world. Not surprisingly, action heroines are constructed in a manner that reinforces their traditional roles as nurturers. This is certainly true of blaxploitation heroines, particularly Grier's characters. To borrow Bogle's term "woman as nurturer," protector of her family and community was a trait that carried over to mainstream popular action heroine films. Action heroines are not merely films that have women protagonists in an action-oriented storyline. Contrary to many film scholars' assertions that Pam Grier and Tamara Dobson were the female counterparts to Richard Roundtree and Fred Williamson, blaxploitation heroines were more developed then many of their male alter egos. Though the storylines may have required violence and enough action to satisfy an audience, Grier managed to bring a depth to her heroines (especially in *Coffy* and *Foxy Brown*) that was lacking in many blaxploitation action movies centered on heroes. Weaver's Ellen Ripley is more complicated than Schwarzenegger and Willis heroes. Storyline plays an integral role, yes, but what the actor or actress brings to the character also adds dimension to some heroines. What makes some action heroines compelling, then, is how the actress chooses to portray the role, storyline, and other factors that are not necessarily tangible. Her appearance first in exploitation movies versus mainstream cinema is in itself interesting.

Mainstream popular cinema lagged in presenting the alter ego of the action heroine, for exploitation films had long explored the character as an outlaw. In fact, Grier's heroine, particularly in *Coffy*, can be seen as an outlaw for her refusal to allow the judicial system to bring those who have harmed her loved ones to justice. In her later action films, producers attempted to soften Grier's action heroine and show her on the right side of the law but still pursuing justice, always on the edge of the system.

Although Weaver's heroine continued to dominate public minds as the action heroine, Sarandon and Davis' portrayals of suburban women turned outlaws caught the attention of film critics, scholars, and audiences alike. Some critics hailed Sarandon and Davis' heroines as empowering women despite their outlaw status. Ironically, when Grier was battling villains, she received criticism for reinforcing in the minds of some critics the black woman as vengeful and one who enjoyed violence. Grier's characters received a great deal of negative responses for her heroines' seeming lack of remorse in exacting retribution. Ironically, when some 28 years after *Coffy* was released, a film starring two actresses as what could arguably be described as female versions of Bonnie and Clyde received acclaim for its "liberation" of women and their retribution was deemed justified. In addition, Linda Hamilton received a great deal of press centered on her physique in *Terminator II* (1991), more so than as an action heroine in *The Terminator* (1984).

In the first film, Hamilton's Sarah Connor was supported by a male protagonist and only became the focal point when her boyfriend was killed by Arnold Schwarzenegger's Terminator.[52] True to action heroine form, action heroines in mainstream popular cinema and in blaxploitation movies did not instigate action; there was always a provocation, typically one that involved their families or community, at least in blaxploitation movies, that spurred them to react.

There are many differences between the action heroine of blaxploitation and her later prototype in mainstream popular films. The most obvious differences involve race and class. Grier and Bell's heroines were not portrayed like Dobson and Graves' heroines, who, as part of their professional duties, were sent to eradicate crime. Part of the blame for this characterization lies with AIP, which wanted a female counterpart to Richard Roundtree's Shaft but who lacked his cool demeanor and focused more on exacting revenge, thus making them "angry black women." This is applicable to Grier's heroines, particularly *Coffy* and *Foxy Brown*, and Jeannie Bell's *T.N.T. Jackson*. In contrast, mainstream studios such as Warner Brothers created a character that was so unbelievable in *Cleopatra Jones* that audiences may have found themselves unable to relate to her on any level. Yet

Grier and Dobson made their heroines appealing because this was the first time audiences had seen African American woman who onscreen had full autonomy — something that the actresses themselves lacked in their portrayals of these heroines in some cases.

In blaxploitation movies, the action heroine — with the exception of Tamara Dobson's character — was an every woman, either seeking retribution or closing down criminal organizations. They were not glamorous Secret Service agents working for the government in a Bondian sense. In mainstream popular cinema, action heroine movies often turn to a time-honored subject and motivator — motherhood.[53] While Grier, Dobson, Graves, and Bell's heroines were not mothers, they took care of siblings, extended families, and, in Dobson's case, the community where Cleopatra Jones grew up. This is a trait shared by Weaver and Hamilton's action heroines.

Despite their ability to hold their own among their male counterparts and having better developed characters with a stronger plot, they were unable to escape the male fantasy label. Grier and Dobson's heroines were labeled as "macho supergoddesses"[54] by some film scholars, which is reductive. There is no question that studios, particularly AIP, played up Grier's physical attributes as a way to draw audiences to her films. Given the nature of AIP's role as a studio that produced exploitative films, such a market strategy would not have been unheard of. However, she was more than a macho goddess and more than a response to her male counterparts in blaxploitation movies. These heroines, particularly Grier and Dobson, were the early prototypes for Weaver, Hamilton, and other action heroines who emerged after 1974 on television and in popular film.

For a brief period in the 1970s, in low-budget films specifically geared towards an African American audience, a new heroine emerged that was subsequently co-opted by mainstream studios. The action heroine is a mainstay in popular cinema today, and it is no longer revolutionary to see a woman carrying an action-oriented storyline. However, since the end of blaxploitation films, African American action heroines have been all but invisible in popular cinema.

Halle Berry's *Catwoman* (2004) had the potential to bring the second African American action heroine to mainstream audiences, but it was a box-office failure despite her strong performance as an action heroine in the James Bond movie *Die Another Day* (2003). There are many reasons why Berry's action heroine failed to capture audiences across racial lines. The fact that a major studio was willing to write a story around an African American action heroine had not occurred since Warner Brothers' *Cleopatra Jones* in 1973. The early accomplishments of Weaver, Hamilton, Sarandon, and Davis and, in the millennium, Drew Barrymore, Lucy Liu, and Cameron Diaz in big-screen versions of *Charlie's Angels* (2001 and 2003), along with Angelina Jolie's Lara Croft in the *Tomb Raider* movies (2001 and 2003), are indicators that action heroines enjoy a great deal of success at the box-office.

What is missing in the ongoing dialogue on whether action heroines are empowering roles for women in film is the lack of acknowledgment by scholars and critics about the contributions of the genre as the first mainstream introduction of the action heroine. She has always been present, particularly in exploitation films, but she gained greater appeal among a diverse audience when Grier burst into her first starring movie, *Coffy*, followed by Tamara Dobson in *Cleopatra Jones*, Teresa Graves in TV's *Get Christie Love!* and Jeannie Bell's *T.N.T. Jackson*. When production of these movies ended, the racialized construction of the action heroine was erased. Upon her reemergence in mainstream popular culture, the action heroine's racial origins no longer existed.

2

Cultivating the Seed

The 1950s marked the beginning of changes to come for the film industry in the 1960s. Evidence of a different type of hero for this younger audience could be found in the wide appeal of James Dean's *Rebel Without a Cause* (1955), in which Dean portrayed an angst-ridden teenager who disliked his father for what he saw as a weakness in his character (the father was not being able to stand up for himself, to his wife and for his son). The entire movie centers on teenagers who have problems with authority figures; this leads to tragedy. Dean's character is a teenager with pent-up anger who reacts to problems with his parents by getting into trouble.

Dean's parents and the parents of the other teenagers are portrayed as a generation that simply does not understand their children and who appear to be unable to cope with the angst displayed by the teenagers. Additionally, an interesting sub-plot involves a teen who does not fit with the clique because of a white father (who refuses to acknowledge him) and a black mother (who is unprepared to teach him how to live in a world where he does not fit because of his mulatto origins). Dean subsequently bonds with an outsider because he does not fit either.

This type of character would have been difficult to bring to the screen in the 1940s because of the social, cultural and political climate. First, the film industry's primary objective during the 1940s was arguably to produce films that lifted the spirits of audiences amidst World War II. In addition, melodramas featuring actresses with a strong screen persona such as Bette Davis and Joan Crawford were popular with audiences. Also, studio executives were interested in making films that were for the most part wholesome, perhaps musical in nature, with heroes and heroines that audiences could readily identify with. The youth market had not been targeted because the industry itself was relatively financially stable. Financially, the studios did not begin to lose a significant amount of money until the 1950s and they still held a firm grasp on the audience despite the presence of television. Although films that focused on teenagers were made before *Rebel Without a Cause*, few focused on the angst of the youth and the restless spirit among some. Movies such as *Reefer Madness* (1936) that explored the exploits of teenagers who used marijuana were mainly propaganda films; they were not meant to examine drug usage, but to show the effects of such usage. Instead, studios concentrated on movies such as Mickey Rooney's *Andy Hardy* series that portrayed a lad who has a dilemma, but a resolution is reached by the end of the film so audiences leave the theater feeling happy. Dean's "antihero" was the first to challenge a series such as Rooney's; by the 1950s, political and social changes were occurring at such a rate that the film industry was forced to take notice. With the rise of the Beatnik generation and studios that focused on sensationalistic themes such as American International Pictures, a character such as Dean's rebel was suddenly in vogue. Thus, the film demographics dictated that studios change their conception of films and bring in audiences that wanted films which focused on their concerns.

Younger audiences did not connect to the films that their parents had enjoyed for years; consequently, the industry faced enormous challenges as it attempted to satisfy the needs of a growing market while retaining its traditional audience. It became crucial to not only appeal to Baby Boomers. Equally important was a segment of the film audience that had been overlooked since the inception of cinema—African Americans.

Given the bleak financial status of some studios, the industry could no longer afford to alienate this market. The demographics of the moviegoing audience actually began to change before the 1950s. Hollywood's once unified audience had declined and become fragmented. With the rise of television, younger, better-educated, and liberal filmgoers, and with the addition of foreign films, Hollywood profits were at stake.[1] With the advent of television, movie attendance declined steadily to an ebb of 17.5 million Americans a week in 1971 after a peak of 80 million in 1946.[2] Production and salaries dropped off over the years and unemployment rose.[3]

Ideally, the film industry would have recognized the importance of including African Americans and produced films with them in mind, but as Ed Guerrero noted "Hollywood is a system entirely motivated by short-term profit. Because of this, the industry is conservative and changes only when forced to do so by the combined pressures of multiple influences, no matter how just or important any single condition may be."[4] Quite simply, if the industry had been in better shape financially, then it would have continued to operate at the status quo and to ignore African Americans. During its heyday during the thirties and forties, the high-living moguls virtually ignored black people, both as artists and consumers.[5] And yet, in perhaps one of the greatest ironies of our time, it was black people who brought life back into a dying industry.[6]

It should be noted that organizations such as the NAACP had vehemently protested the representations of African Americans in film, to no avail. When D.W. Griffith's *The Birth of Nation* (1915) made its debut, many African Americans in several cities picketed the film for its racist portrayals. Ironically, it is considered by many reviewers and historians as a cinematic masterpiece despite its gross distortions of African Americans and that it became the point of reference film for those depictions.

By the 1960s, the film industry was poised to make major changes in how it viewed and depicted African Americans. This was partly economic as many studios, now facing financial crises, began to acknowledge that African Americans represented a large percentage of movie-goers, particularly in cities. Television brought the images of racism home to many Americans and also took a percentage of viewers away from movie theaters. Finally there was a changing of the guard, so to speak, as younger executives took control of studios and were more attuned to the rapidly changing face of America.

The new filmmakers and studio heads actively sought to make political statements using film as a means to protest and to force audiences to develop a social conscience. In the words of Michael Ryan and Douglas Kellner, these Hollywood films "articulated critiques of American values and institutions. They transcoded a growing sense of alienation from the dominant myths and ideals of U.S. society."[7] All of this led to structural changes in the film industry and it was during this era that the foundation was laid for the creation of a genre specifically geared towards urban African Americans in the early 1970s.

Most obvious to observers of film history of the late 1960s scene is that blaxploitation movies were made possible by the rising political and social consciousness of black people which translated into a large black audience thirsting to see their full humanity depicted on the commercial cinema screen.[8] According to film scholar Daniel Leab, "the growing Negro audience"[9] could no longer remain marginalized, as it accounted for a large percentage of box office revenues. According to a 1967 estimate, although blacks represented only about 15 percent of the American population, they accounted for roughly 30 percent of the movie-going audience in the nation's cities, where the biggest movie theaters were located.[10] As the civil rights movement progressed, so did the surge in African American identity politics in which the African Americans comprised of black leaders, entertainers and intellectuals openly challenged Hollywood's persistent degradation of African Americans in film.[11]

A once thriving film industry entered the 1960s at one of the lowest financial points since the inception of filmmaking. One challenge facing Hollywood was the need to find a new audience in the midst of the great social changes taking place. The Baby Boom generation, often referred to as such because of the large number of children born after World War II, came of age in the early 1960s. Many Baby Boomers no longer responded to the saccharine romance movies of the 1950s, or the clear line between good and evil depicted in many Westerns and gangster films. In short, a younger audience did not connect to the films that their parents enjoyed in the 1930s, 1940s and 1950s. Consequently, the industry faced enormous challenges as it attempted to satisfy the needs of a changing demography while retaining their audience base. It became crucial to appeal not only to Baby Boomers but, equally important, an African American audience that Hollywood had ignored for many years. Indeed, the 1960s, particularly the latter portion of that decade, was a period of fractions within the African American community. It was the growing split within the African American community between generations and class status that also provided the foundation for the emergence of a new genre in the early 1970s. The link between political, social and cultural movements in the film industry and American culture is inextricable at times. For often the film industry mirrors society and such was the case in the 1960s.

Film scholar Mark A. Reid has suggested that "Afro-Americans' rising impatience with white intransigence and black second-class citizenship produced two major results in the late 1960s: racial violence and black cultural nationalism."[12] By 1967, and as a logical result of the frustrated attempts to gain first-class citizenship for blacks, many black grass root organizations became more aggressive in their tactics.[13] This frustration split the black community as many younger African Americans were no longer drawn to the appeal of Martin Luther King's Gandhi-inspired approach to the civil rights movement. They were drawn to Malcolm X's approach, and subsequently became involved in Black Nationalism that would later show up in certain elements in blaxploitation movies (particularly the theme of "Whitey as the bad man"). It was also this group that studios, especially American

International Pictures (which produced the bulk of blaxploitation movies), catered to in the early 1970s. Between 1969 and 1971, 74 percent of American movie-goers were under 30, according to a survey cited in the October 13, 1971, *Variety*. However, the idea of catering to the youth market began in the early 1960s and AIP was one of the first studios to recognize the potential of making movies for younger audiences in general. The black youth, of course, represented an even more specific group of youths to which producers needed to direct their work[14] and it was this group that ultimately derived the greatest satisfaction from seeing a proliferation of action-oriented storylines with black male and female protagonists.

Some of the movies that began to appear reflected a change in attitudes by "the younger generation." Films such as *Bonnie and Clyde* (1967) starring Warren Beatty and Faye Dunaway and Peter Fonda and Dennis Hopper's *Easy Rider* (1969) were particularly appealing to audiences seeking onscreen changes.

Studio executives such as Jack Warner of Warner Brothers and Darryl Zanuck of 20th Century–Fox left the industry in 1967 and 1971, respectively. As younger executives came of age, so did the promising filmmakers who would go on to change the cinematic landscape in the 1970s. Francis Ford Coppola, William Friedkin, Steven Spielberg and countless other talented filmmakers had a new approach to creating films. The demographics of the film industry were changing and, with that, so did the focus of films in general. Part of the reason for the changes can be found in the advent of television. By the mid–1960s, Hollywood had become increasingly dependent on television leases of their films as a secondary market, with the average film going for $150,000 to be shown twice over a three-year period.[15] By 1968, the stakes in the leasing game had risen considerably, with Hollywood getting up to $800,000 per lease; with rates so high and a glut of already leased films jamming the system, television networks suddenly stopped buying.[16] The film industry had a major financial crisis with "majors losing between $15 and $145 million and Columbia and Fox tottering on the edge of bankruptcy."[17] Finding a new genre or genres of films and actors that appealed to different segments of the population seemed like one salient solution to reinvigorate the industry.

Although the industry's interest in the African American market was motivated by profit, it was clear that, even without concerns about box-office grosses, film (like society) had to restructure the way it presented and dealt with issues facing African Americans. Television allowed many Americans to see how racially charged the country was and to see that the gross economic, social and political disparities that African Americans experienced could no longer remain unsettled. Broadcast images of marchers and protesters attacked by police dogs, pummeled with water from fire hoses, beaten and spit upon by crowds underscored escalating racial tensions in America. The riots that erupted in the inner cities during the 1960s were the result of a country deeply divided along racial and socio-economic lines. It was a defining point for all Americans.

For many blacks, the American dream was overshadowed by the reality of high unemployment in urban areas. Many sought refuge in better-paying jobs in the North, in contrast to the agriculturally based, low-wage work available in the South. The riots signaled an effort by many blacks to underscore the economic and social disparities they faced in the inner cities. Several urban riots occurred in Afro-American communities between the Watts (Los Angeles) Riot on August 9, 1965, and riots in other cities in spring 1968.[18] Images of black inner-city life seemed to define the Afro-American community.[19] Much like now, many people form their opinions about African Americans from television. The news coverage contributed to many believing African Americans were violent people. Television disrupted the ease of many Americans as they watched defining moments in America's social and cultural history of the 1960s peak. The idealism of the 1950s was being replaced by the harsher realities of the 1960s. Unemployment and poverty were significantly higher among African Americans, and the tension that lurked beneath the surface for so long erupted. Television captured these images, shattering the comfort zone of many in suburbia.

The 1960s

Films of the 1960s that focused on race were not as blatant in their attempts to get to the underlying roots of racial divisiveness but instead chose to focus on racial healing by suggesting that the American Dream was open to all Americans. *A Raisin in the Sun* (1962) is an excellent example. Adapted from Lorraine Hansberry's play, the film examined a working-class African American family that comes into some insurance money and tries to decide what to do with it. The film starred Sidney Poitier as Walter Lee Younger, Ruby Dee as his wife, a rising young African American actress named Diana Sands as his sister, and veteran actress Claudia McNeil as the family matriarch.

The film offered a sensitive portrayal of the tensions facing many African American working-class families trying to survive. It focused on three crucial aspects of the American Dream: owning a home, getting a college education, and being self-employed. Owning a home meant establishing roots and an identity, which was difficult for those living in closed quarters like the inner city. Obtaining a college degree provided opportunity to leave the ghetto, as did owning a business.

Through the Sands and Poitier characters, the film successfully explored the frustrations of inner-city living and the longing to escape the ghetto in search of a better life. It suggested that "the American Dream was open to blacks if white attitudes shifted and blacks pursued their ambitions relentlessly."[20] Many African Americans had limited access to primarily middle-class benefits such as home ownership, college choice, and the GI Bill during this period.

In 1963, the National Association for the Advancement of Colored People (NAACP) threatened to take legal and economic action against the film industry, which had relegated African American actresses and actors to one-dimensional, subservient roles. But African American actors and actresses soon began to appear regularly in roles outside this confine.

New studio executives were acutely aware of the racial tensions and began to make a conscious effort to change images by tackling subjects once considered taboo, such as interracial marriage. Despite its simplistic depictions of racial inequality, the industry demonstrated a willingness to examine and try to comprehend the state of race relations. Film scholar Daniel Leab has suggested that "the faith that social change could be effected through personal understanding and affection between blacks and whites was further explored in Stanley Kramer's *Guess Who's Coming to Dinner* (1967)."[21]

This film addressed the issue of interracial marriage on a surface level between a black man (Poitier) and a white woman (Katharine Houghton). Spencer Tracy and Katharine Hepburn played Matt and Christina Drayton, the wealthy white parents of Houghton's character; the parents' real concern about the marriage centered on the social pressures an interracial union would face. In the same year, the Supreme Court ended state bans on interracial marriage stemming from the case of *Loving vs. the State of Virginia* (1967). Yet, younger African Americans still longed for heroes that they could relate to.

A New Black Aesthetic

African American cultural critics and authors such as James Baldwin and independent filmmaker William Foster applied pressure to studios to produce films based on novels by black writers and directed by African Americans. *The Learning Tree* (1969) is one example of a film showcasing African Americans in a variety of settings. Directed by Gordon Parks, Sr., a famous *Life* magazine photographer, and based on his life story as a young African American man growing up in segregated Kansas, the film was very successful and groundbreaking because Parks "employed a black crew at all levels of production."[22] Parks later solidified his name as a director in Hollywood by directing *Shaft* (1971), one of the most successful and influential films in the genre.

The division along class lines escalated throughout the civil rights movement and contributed to rioting. But it became more apparent when examining the criticism of blaxploitation movies that the most vocal critics were bothered by what they saw as stereotypical representations of African Americans. Many blaxploitation movies by and large reinforced painful caricatures of African Americans during a crucial period when blacks reaped the benefits of the social and political progress made during the 1960s. Yet, for many, the genre (particularly those movies that focused on black action storylines) represented a positive change in the form of a new hero or heroine. Audiences who responded favorably to the genre were young and urban, and they related to Jim Brown rather than Sidney Poitier, who represented the bourgeois to this particular audience. Consequently, it is not surprising that similar class chasms would find their way into the controversy surrounding blaxploitation films.

While middle-class African American audiences may have found Poitier's characters appealing, some thought them out of vogue and not reflective of the turmoil occurring in the political and social landscape of the 1960s. He portrayed "positive," one-dimensional role characters who were always non-threatening and accommodating to others, which explains why there was not as much of an uproar by audiences over *Guess Who's Coming to Dinner*. Poitier was not only criticized by some audiences in the African American community, but African American reviewers also began to critique and analyze his onscreen image. James Baldwin's analysis was perceptive and, in some ways, could also be applicable to blaxploitation movies.

In response to Larry Neal's scathing remarks about Poitier, Baldwin wrote an essay for *Look* in which he examines Poitier's career in its entirety at that point. Baldwin recognized the demeaning nature of the roles Poitier had played, as well as his lack of relevance in the changing times.[23] He "rightfully insists that Poitier's roles and identity as an artist must be considered within the context of American race relations, racial injustice, and the entertainment industry's ideology of racial subordination, that is to say, Neal's 'tar baby.'"[24] The same could be said of blaxploitation films that were created to fill a void for urban audiences. The void existed because prior to the 1960s, the film industry was not interested in producing films with African American audiences in mind. There were exceptions to this with the reoccurring theme of miscegenation from time to time, but the film industry did not make a concerted effort to market films for an African American audience. This changed in the 1960s as the political, social and cultural terrain underwent a transformation that can only be described as tumultuous but necessary in order for African Americans to achieve equal status in this country.

In the late 1960s, some younger African Americans "channeled their anger by focusing on developing black studies programs in higher education and putting into practice Black art, discussions of black aesthetics and the development of collectives that continued black creative traditions."[25] As a result of this energy, a new black aesthetic formed, creating a wave of African American creativity in the arts. The emphasis of finding a black art which reflected black culture could be found as far back as 1937 when Richard Wright wrote in "his seminal essay Blueprint for Negro Writing ... in a folklore molded out of rigorous and inhuman conditions of life ... the Negro achieved his most indigenous and complete expression."[26] In other words, it has always been during a tumultuous time and the will to endure that African Americans have been inspired to create poetry, art and music that has had a lasting effect on American culture. The Harlem Renaissance is an excellent example of creative endeavors by black artists, writers, poets and musicians that remain influential long after the Renaissance ended. However, blacks of the sixties saw theirs as a new movement.[27] Black Arts critic and poet Larry Neal wrote that the movement was an ideology which stressed the importance of creating art directed at problems within Black America.[28] Earlier, black independent filmmaker William Foster had recognized that there was a black audience which was interested in black-oriented art.[29] But, "the first wave of independent black filmmakers including Foster" and Oscar Micheaux were not concerned with addressing the issues confronting the African American community. In contrast, the new black aesthetic movement which was born out of "the ashes of riot-torn ghettos"[30] wanted to create a criterion that examined "the artistic value"[31] of black art, poetry, literature and film. The demand for a black criterion became more important with the emergence of blaxploitation movies. The criticism and insistence on establishing such a criterion was underscored when younger African Americans en masse went to the theaters to see so-called black-oriented movies, better known as blaxploitation. If one remained within the parameters of film production, as many film historians do, the occurrence of blaxploitation would seem to constitute a paradox, except for the facts that Poitier's stardom and the subsequent appearance of blaxploitation coincided with the most militant phase of black liberationism.[32] Thousands of young blacks, in colleges and high schools, had determined that integrationism, the ideology which had dominated the Civil Rights movement in the post–Second World War era, was a liberal conceit, premised on the belief that a kind of Christian forbearance would transform the hegemony of white racism.[33] Their faith exhausted by the spectacles of bombings, beatings, insults, murders, and judicial and police injustices, many blacks turned to the more muscular postures of Black Power, Marxism, or separationist programs.[34] These events, coupled with the attraction of younger African Americans to Black Nationalism, played an integral role in the rise of urban movies produced specifically for urban audiences.

Sidney Poitier: A New Urban Hero?

In spite of unfavorable criticism, Poitier was the leading box-office draw. This was significant particularly during a time when blacks were not obtaining roles beyond the Tom, Buck, Mammy, Exotic Other, Aunt Jemima and Sapphire. At the height of his career in 1968, his fee per film had risen from $300,000 to $700,000 in a few years.[35] In the early 1970s, Poitier directed his own films, thereby maintaining complete control over his image. Once he gained control over the types of movies he wanted to produce, Poitier did seek ways to explore characters that differed from what some saw as his unassuming characters of the 1960s.

But, in the late 1960s, the urban market simply was not interested in onscreen heroes like Poitier because they viewed many of his characters as too accommodating. Part of the dissatisfaction with Poitier is centered on a generational gap. By 1967, Poitier had been in the film industry for at least ten years, playing in many instances variations of the same character — always dignified and never the hint of aggression that would turn off white audiences. *In the Heat of the Night* (1967), also starring Rod Steiger, marked a turning point in Poitier's career, but younger African Americans looked to Jim Brown and Woody Strode, who had appeared previously in other films, as the models for their heroes. Urban African Americans were not interested in Martin Luther King's peaceful integration message and favored

Malcolm X's by-any-means-necessary mantra, and this was demonstrated in increasing demands for onscreen heroes like Brown, Strode and, later, Fred Williamson. Historian Robert Fogelson has noted, "[T]he violence of the 1960s riots can only be understood as a manifestation of the grievances of the black ghettos."[36]

The 1960s were tumultuous on many different levels, as the split between younger African Americans and older African Americans in the civil rights movement took on significant proportions and the roles of African American women within the movement became better delineated. African American women in growing numbers were gaining the spotlight, taking on more significant roles in the civil rights movement. For the first time, black women were highly visible and received as much attention as their male counterparts.

This change was not accepted by many of those previously enjoying the limelight. For the first time, African American women in the movement met with open hostility and male chauvinism. The Black Panther Party furthered the chasm when its leaders openly chastised women for daring to take leadership roles in the civil rights movement.

In the late 1960s, however, after years of urban riots and rebellions, shifting demographics accelerated as racial boundaries eroded with the development of more suburbs, and whites abandoned the city centers, and their movie houses, to inner-city blacks.[37] Further contributing to the power of the black box office, suburban middle-class blacks would come to theaters in the city centers for a night out, thus making urban areas like Chicago's Loop and Atlanta's downtown predominantly black entertainment centers.[38] The demographics of urban cities were changing and, with it, the face of urban movie theaters.

To create alternative heroes was a daunting task for an industry which was to blame for constructing and presenting negative onscreen images of African Americans. However, it was possible with new executives, many of whom came from privileged backgrounds. They understood the film industry had to change to reflect all aspects of America. These studio heads were more attuned to the political heartbeat of this country because of their youth and made a conscious effort to change the film industry's image, taking chances on subjects that had not been considered before. Equally important, they attempted to deal with the complexities of America's racial problems without offering heavy-handed social messages.

It would be untrue to say that the industry never attempted to produce films that focused on race. The "racial" films that Hollywood produced prior to the 1960s were conciliatory and often made to give audiences a surface level treatment of racism. Filmmakers who grappled with the racial construct always found a way to have a neatly wrapped ending that would not offend white audiences.

For example, in 1949, a film about miscegenation, *Pinky*, starring Jeanne Crain, appeared on the screen and was problematic on many levels. First, the main character was not portrayed by an African American actress. The character was a dramatic role, and studios confined African American actresses to whatever stereotype they felt like. Also, the film's theme was superficial in the sense that the ultimate message of the movie is that Crain's Pinky knows her place is in the African American community and should be content to stay there. It is an interesting film because, in the beginning, Pinky is presented as a sophisticated, liberated African American woman who has a wonderful career as a nurse and is going to marry a Caucasian doctor. However, her world is shattered by a visit to the South to care for her ailing grandmother; she is not accepted by either the African American or European American community. *Pinky* was not the only film to attempt to address racial issues. The 1959 remake of *Imitation of Life* (directed by Douglas Sirk) appeared in addition to Stanley Kramer's *The Defiant Ones*, starring Sidney Poitier and Tony Curtis. Kramer would revisit racial themes in *Guess Who's Coming to Dinner* (1967).

While mainstream studios maintained a status quo for the most part by distributing films that did not challenge ideological thinking, another studio targeted a different audience based on trends in American culture. Jim Nicholson and Samuel Arkoff founded American Releasing Corporation in 1954, changing it to American International Pictures (AIP) in 1957, with the objective of appealing to a different audience.

Nicholson and Arkoff succeeded largely because they hired directors who worked within the structure of a strict budget and were either unknown or no longer part of the Hollywood A-List. These directors worked with actors who were no longer marketable or were just beginning their careers. They used current popular trends to make cheap movies that, while perhaps lacking in artistic quality, were profitable as double-features at drive-ins, which appealed to much of the youth market. AIP earned its reputation by shamelessly copying and mass-marketing trends or whatever social problem received great publicity in American culture. Through all of the company's incarnations it continually functioned under a standard set of rules outlined by Jim Nicholson[39]:

OBSERVE trends and emerging taste.
KNOW as much as possible about your audience.
ANTICIPATE how you will sell your chosen subject.

PRODUCE with prudence, avoiding expense for what won't show on the screen.
SELL with showmanship in advertising and publicity.
USE imagination.
HAVE good luck: Even if you do everything else, you'll still need it.[40]

The young and unsophisticated audience ignored by the major studios was the life blood of AIP. The relationship with drive-in audiences and AIP was integral to their success as Nicholson and Arkoff appealed to audiences that did not necessarily want to see the melodramas, musicals or romance comedies produced by major studios such as Warner Brothers, Columbia and MGM. Moreover, and what cannot be underscored enough, is that as a studio not reliant on established actors and actresses, AIP had more creative freedom and opportunities to make movies built around themes that executives at other studios would not touch and could create characters that might never appear in a Katharine Hepburn, James Stewart or Cary Grant film.

Careful examination of the films of the 1950s, particularly those made by AIP, shows that anxieties and fears about Communism and nuclear weaponry were manifested onscreen in such features as *Invasion of the Body Snatchers* (1956), *Day the World Ended* (1956), and *It Conquered the World* (1956). Many of AIP's films reflected attitudes about Communism and youth culture that began to escalate during the 1950s. AIP continued to emphasize youth disillusionment, particularly within the counter-culture movement, via films such as *Hell's Angels on Wheels* (1966), *The Wild Angels* (1966), and *The Trip* (1967). Arkoff stated, "When it came to the youth market — and to combinations — we led the pack."[41] The studio focused on this market "producing and exhibiting monster films, adolescent rebellion films, teen party films and horror films."[42] Typically, in the early years, according to Arkoff, the creation of a film began with a title (Nicholson's contribution), which inspired an ad campaign which then eventually produced a shooting script.[43]

James Dean became an overnight icon in *Rebel Without a Cause* (1955). With the appearance of Marlon Brando's *The Wild One*, a new wave of movies that focused on teenage rebellion in one form or another appeared, mainly in exploitation films as mainstream studios tried to stir clear of tackling social issues such as juvenile delinquency and motorcycle gangs. Yet, movies such as *The Wild One* were pivotal in creating a generational chasm between older audiences who enjoyed the light musicals and dramas of the 1940s and younger movie-goers carving out their own identity by rejecting films that appealed to their parents.

The emergence of rock 'n' roll deepened the divide between teenagers and their parents. Singers such as Elvis Presley created a stir with gyrating performances, unheard of in the new television medium. Musicians such as Chuck Berry, Little Richard, Fats Domino, Buddy Holly and the Crickets, and so many others changed the musical landscape, and the film industry saw an opportunity to make films centered on parental dissatisfaction with rock 'n' roll.

For a time, AIP focused on rock 'n' roll in such films as *Shake, Rattle and Rock* (1956) starring Fats Domino. While AIP was the not the first studio to capitalize on this popular phenomenon, it made many movies that dealt with the generation gap, particularly in the form of drag racing features that portrayed youths rebelling against their parents and society in general. Nicholson and Arkoff's first film was a highly successful drag racing feature called *The Fast and the Furious* (1954). *Hot Rod Girl* (1956), *Dragstrip Girl* (1957), and many more in this genre soon followed. AIP was alert to popular trends and produced films that focused on them.

In contrast, mainstream studios would not touch subjects that might offend some audiences sensibilities. If they produced a film about teenage romance, it was along the lines of *Gidget* (1957) starring Sandra Dee, who with her blond hair and blue eyes looked the part of the all–American girl. The movie made many parents feel more at ease because of its portrayal of a carefree teenager who was more concerned about romance, enjoying the beach, and having clean fun than rebelling against her parents. Arkoff noted that the reason mainstream studios had trouble courting teenagers was because they had adult actors playing adolescents, and "the last thing teenagers wanted was a lecture during an evening of entertainment,"[44] which they inevitably received in Mickey Rooney's *Andy Hardy* series. There is irony here because, not only did mainstream studios use actors twice the age of the teenagers they portrayed, but in the few movies of the time that featured African American women characters, they were portrayed by white women. Is it any wonder that teen audiences and African Americans — two markets the film industry badly needed to persevere financially — had difficulty relating to certain types of characters? AIP was ahead of mainstream studios in recognizing the untapped market and developing movies with this market in mind. An excellent example of AIP's innovative approach was a series of successful Beach Party movies aimed at teenagers (and audiences in their twenties) in the early 1960s, starring former Mouseketeer Annette Funicello and Frankie Avalon. The studio made a series of films focusing on young teenage love in a beach setting while also producing a number of horror flicks based on Edgar Allan Poe's works. Roger Corman directed many Poe-oriented movies for AIP and usually cast Vincent Price in the lead role. The films were successful and also drew in a market that had grown up with actors such as Peter Lorre and Boris Karloff in earlier years. AIP was successful because they did not spend a lot of money on actors' salaries, sets, and costumes. One key to their success lay in the genius of Nicholson and Arkoff in marketing their movies by using sensational headlines to stir curiosity. The ability to produce movies for a certain segment of the audience that mainstream studios chose to ignore would work well in the early 1970s with blaxploitation.

By the mid–1960s, AIP turned towards the counterculture movement, which had picked up momentum, and produced a number of films that focused on hippies, drugs, and resistance to the establishment. In spite of their budget limitations and tendency to sensationalize trends, many AIP films represented a social and political commentary about American culture. As previously mentioned, during the height of fear and anxiety concerning Communism and nuclear weaponry, AIP made a number of horror films leveraging "Red Scare" paranoia. Don Siegel's *Invasion of the Body Snatchers* (1956), made by Allied Artists, involves alien pods landing and inhabiting human bodies in an ultimate effort to take over Earth. I concur with many film critics who have suggested that the pods symbolized Communism and its effects on the populace if it were allowed to run rampant. It could also symbolize growing concerns about the civil rights movement and the fears that some may have felt about the changing of the status quo, particularly for African Americans.

Senator Joseph McCarthy fueled the anti–Communism fervor with the House on Un-American Activities Committee as a way to root out those who participated in organizations he deemed suspicious. Many actors, producers, writers, and directors were blacklisted for "subversive" activities (according to the Committee) against America. African American actors such as Paul Robeson and Lena Horne were blacklisted because of their active involvement in civil rights during the 1950s. Robeson, a gifted thespian and former college athlete, was very vocal about the social and political displacement of African Americans. Aligning himself with the Communist Party, he came under intense scrutiny in the early 1950s for advocating that blacks needed to "incorporate a socialist perspective, and also needed to be at the forefront in promoting peaceful co-existence with the Soviet bloc."[45] Well aware of the attention Robeson received as a speaker both within the African American community and beyond, the House on Un-American Activities sought to suppress Robeson's powerful voice. A cultural and social critic who had carved a niche as a respected authority on racial inequality, Robeson posed a threat to those who did not want social change for blacks.

McCarthy showed a reckless disregard for basic civil rights, and his venomous attacks were often groundless and rooted solely in an individual's political affiliation. Unable to find roles in Hollywood because of her outspokenness and losing the leading role in *Carmen Jones* (1954) to Dorothy Dandridge, Horne retreated to her singing career.

The entertainment industry faced intense scrutiny from McCarthy. Yet during World War II, Hollywood was among the strongest supporters of the war effort. Many actors eagerly participated in a variety of war-related promotional and morale-building activities. Many toured Europe, meeting with American GIs to show their commitment to the war.

Despite the film industry's efforts to support the U.S. troops, the perception of an ultra-liberal entertainment industry made it an easy target for those who did not approve of the lifestyle of many actors. Unlike some writers, recognizable actors could not work anonymously and had no place to turn when they were blacklisted. Consequently, many top studios stayed away from films that might cause discomfort or depart from the status quo.

AIP for the most part escaped the scourge because of its status as a Hollywood outsider. In the 1950s, the studio's biggest challenge came from segments of the general public upset about the teenage rebellion themes permeating its films. Towards the end of the decade, the studio faced difficulties unrelated to the political landscape. Horror films centered on nuclear disasters or focused on teen angst no longer sold tickets. AIP was not immune to problems facing mainstream studios and, in spite of the success of its beach movies, needed a new formula to keep audiences interested. By moving to Italy to reduce movie production costs and borrowing the concept of British studio Hammer, which focused largely on Dracula and Frankenstein horror movies, Nicholson and Arkoff maintained their success for a time.

By 1967, many young African Americans had become disillusioned with Hollywood's version of the black hero portrayed by Sidney Poitier. Once AIP saw the success of Mario Van Peebles *Sweet Sweetback's Baadasssss Song* (1970) and Gordon Parks' *Shaft* (1971), they began producing their own version of this black hero with many movies starring Fred Williamson, who had a little more acting talent then Jim Brown. Black movie-goers demanded onscreen heroes who, while not representing the charged political climate of the 1960s (especially during the middle to late years of the decade), at least had persona that differed greatly from the gentlemanly characters that Poitier portrayed in his films. When studios saw audiences respond to Jim

Brown as the alternative African American hero, they sought ways to expand the black audience base. As an actor, film critic Pauline Kael wrote, Brown is "handsome and stiff— the essence of straight"[46] in reference to one of his first action movies, *The Split*, but that he "looks like an Indian and he acts like a wooden one; he's totally unconvincing."[47] Brown did not appeal to younger black audiences because of his acting ability or lack thereof. Instead, his popularity stemmed from his gridiron days in college and then as a professional football player and that, in appearance and mannerisms, he was the polar opposite of Sidney Poitier. Moreover, there was a thirst for action-driven movies among many younger audiences in general, and to have an African American actor starring in a genre traditionally dominated by Caucasian actors was progress for the action genre. His popularity as a former professional football player more then anything else explains part of Brown's appeal. Kael writes "[E]ach time he comes on the screen the kids in the theatre yell as if he had just scored a touchdown and an actor who has the public on his side like this is almost sure to loosen up.... Brown is the equivalent of the old Arrow-collar-ad idols, and he may be the new Robert Taylor or Gregory Peck."[48] Before starring in movies built around him, Brown portrayed a stereotypical character who became the sacrificial lamb for the sake of the main characters. *Dark of the Sun* (1968) was one such movie in which Brown dies after saving the lives of Rod Taylor and actress Yvette Mimieux.

Nonetheless, his appeal lay within a segment of the black community that was youthful, militant, and more vocal in their dissatisfaction with the status quo of African Americans. It was the same appeal that made Williamson a major black action star in blaxploitation movies. The demand for a different type of African American hero onscreen was greatly influenced by the rise of Black Nationalism and the Black Panther Party. Black audiences in urban areas had adopted a different tactic for articulating social change and an identity for African Americans as "violence peaked between 1967 and 1968 with 384 uprisings in 298 cities."[49] Conditioned by this building sense of insurrection and cultural separation (as well as by an overall sense of rebellion in emergent collectivities of Chicanos, Hippies, women, antiwar groups, and the rest), blacks and black intellectuals in particular were becoming increasingly dissatisfied with the demeaning portrayals of African American life that Hollywood was still putting on the screen.[50]

Blaxploitation movies originated when the film industry capitalized on the success of *Sweet Sweetback's Baadasssss Song* in 1971. Directed by Melvin Van Peebles and extremely successful (particularly among young, urban audiences), the film is widely credited with the emergence of blaxploitation — although many of the films that tried to duplicate Van Peebles' story failed to capture the politics of *Sweetback*. With the success of Van Peebles and Gordon Parks' *Shaft* (1971), AIP released a number of films specifically geared towards this long-ignored audience.

Although demands for African American images to fit the mood and attitudes of the community were answered primarily by black male actors, African American actresses were shown in an array of roles during the 1960s. Actresses such as Cicely Tyson, Nichelle Nichols, Diahann Carroll and many other African American women made inroads in the industry, but it was not until the early 1970s that black actresses began to find recognition and leading roles in Hollywood. Moreover, the images of mammy, the jezebel, Aunt Jemima and Sapphire were still frequently shown in film and on television in spite of the political strides made by African American women. So damaging was the representations of African Americans in *The Birth of the Nation* that the film industry has consistently used these stereotypes for many years to suit the needs of studios.

Soon after the influx of blaxploitation movies, audiences began to see what one film scholar, Donald Bogle, labeled the "black woman super woman"[51] and another film scholar, Cedric Robinson, called the "Bad Black Woman."[52] The heroines in blaxploitation movies were attractive and glamorous, and not afraid to confront violence with violence. These macho goddesses answered a multitude of needs and were a hybrid of stereotypes, part Buck, part Mammy, part Mulatto.[53]

The emergence of Pam Grier playing the title role in *Coffy* in 1973 ushered in a wave of films featuring African American actresses in action-driven storylines. Grier achieved superstar status for her roles as a practical, liberated black woman taking on drug dealers in her neighborhood. As a nurse seeking revenge on the drug dealers who left her sister in a catatonic state, Grier's Coffy showed no fear of taking on the villains. The poster advertising *Coffy* and featuring Grier with an Afro, curve-hugging bell-bottom pants, and a gun made her an icon, the leading action heroine and the queen of the genre.

AIP released *Coffy* in May 1973, and Warner Brothers released *Cleopatra Jones*, starring model Tamara Dobson, in June of that year. Dobson's character was a fashion model who worked as a government secret agent. Her mission was to discover and rid her neighborhood of drug dealers. Both films were highly successful, and the next year, AIP made a *Coffy* sequel with Grier, titled *Foxy Brown* (1973). It marked the first time African American actresses appeared in leading action-oriented roles made particularly for them.

The genre offered new opportunities to fill roles that represented liberation and empowerment. However, many critics suggested that Grier and Dobson, as well as other African American actresses, contributed to the stereotyping of black women in general.

In a 1973 edition of *Black Creation*, a group of 400 black actresses, actors, writers, producers and others working in Hollywood, under the name of the Black Artists Alliance, published an open letter to the Rev. Jesse Jackson. In its letter, the group expressed

> common outrage at the gross and deliberate distortion of Black life in motion pictures, television, radio, and commercials. "We will no longer tolerate the cheap movies about us. Cheap in terms of the range of human emotions expressed, and cheap in their one-dimensional investigations of human problems. We will no longer tolerate visual images of Black people that are paraded across the screen as little more than reincarnations of racist stereotypes which demean our women and make ludicrous caricatures of our men." The group implored Rev. Jackson to help them change the inaccurate depictions of Black people and invited public support for their cause.[54]

Ironically, Jackson, Griffin and others saved their harshest criticism for the actors and actresses themselves rather then arranging formal discussions with studios such as American International Pictures — the studio most responsible for producing the proliferation of blaxploitation movies. Samuel Z. Arkoff stated in his autobiography *Flying by the Seat of My Pants* that at one point the studio received threats about blaxploitation movies. The studio was never able to find out who set a car bomb in their parking lot. Ultimately, when the genre was no longer profitable, AIP and other studios discarded blaxploitation movies and moved on to the next trend.

The scathing remarks directed towards blaxploitation movies will be discussed in detail in Chapter 6. However, criticism that the genre forced African American actors and actresses to take a back seat as it pertains to salary is valid. For example, Richard Roundtree was not an experienced actor and worked as a model before *Shaft*. The film and soundtrack grossed millions, but Roundtree only made $13,500. While he is perhaps an extreme example of starring in a successful movie and not earning a salary anywhere near the millions actors make today, some stars such as Pam Grier and Fred Williamson were able to command a good salary and live relatively comfortably making blaxploitation movies. The genre offered an early means by which African American actresses in particular could take on obstacles, both in society and within the film industry, and only actresses such as Grier and Dobson had the authority to do that. Even then, their power was limited and Grier in fact started her own production company with her earnings.

Though critizized for reinforcing negative stereotypes of black womanhood, blaxploitation movies offered African American actresses such as Grier, Dobson, Graves and Bell the opportunity to challenge prevailing images of African American women as mammies, Jezebels, Aunt Jemima or Sapphire in favor of self-assured heroines who took charge and possessed the ability to remain level-headed in potentially volatile situations. Their trailblazing performances traded on negative stereotypes as a means towards female empowerment of a more global scope in the decades to come.

As the Civil Rights Movement shifted in the mid– to late 1960s, the economic reality that many studios were losing money forced the film industry to change. By recognizing and listening to African American audiences, particularly those who were not interested in Sidney Poitier, they were able to make political gains with some segments of the community and by creating heroes portrayed by popular athletes such as Jim Brown, who starred in many blaxploitation action movies in the early 1970s.

3

Here Comes the Queen

> Long before Thelma & Louise struck their first celluloid body blows in defense of womankind, Pam Grier was singlehandedly keeping the neighborhood safe from junkies, pushers, and The Man himself with karate chops, jujitsu kicks, or any other instrument of destruction within her reach.[1]

The year is 1997. The industry is reveling in the buzz generated by a former queen of "B" action flicks who is making her first appearance in decades on several late-night talk shows. For African American actresses, any positive recognition of their art is historic, given the industry's racism and sexism. The actress in question basked in the resurgence of a career that spanned 27 years and earned her the title "Queen of Blaxploitation." In this moment, Pam Grier finally enjoyed the success that had eluded her in the early 1970s. Some film critics quickly labeled Quentin Tarantino's *Jackie Brown* as an older Foxy Brown. But, *Jackie Brown* cannot be regarded in the same fashion as Grier's earlier characters, who truly stood on their own. Still, the movie created a new generation of Grier fans and sparked renewed interest in a genre where studios remained more interested in profits than in creating multi-dimensional roles for African American actresses.

Her succession ensured Grier's status as the *actress* of the genre. However, the films also earned public scorn from many African American leaders, including Junius Griffin (1970s-era president of the Beverly Hills chapter of the National Association for the Advancement of Colored People), Jesse

Jackson and Roy Innis, whose main concerns centered on derogatory onscreen representations of African Americans. The genre received its appellation of "blaxploitation" from Griffin, who argued that these films exploited African Americans and offered no redeeming aesthetic or cultural value. The emergence of the action heroine in mainstream popular cinema began with Pam Grier, who became *the* icon for blaxploitation movies. With a strong screen presence, Grier's stardom began in *Coffy* (1973). Prior to *Coffy*, Grier had minor roles in movies such as *Beyond the Valley of the Dolls* (1971) and starring roles in *The Big Doll House* (1971), *The Arena* (1971), *Black Mama/ White Mama* (1972), and *The Big Bird Cage* (1972). It became evident very quickly that Grier's screen presence overshadowed the one-dimensional roles that focused on her physical attributes and the weak storylines in AIP productions. According to famed exploitation movie director Roger Corman, "[T]he audience responded more to Pam than to any of the other actresses."[2] For African American actresses working in blaxploitation movies, a crucial element in their success lay in the ability to transform weak characterizations and storylines into strong characters. Grier was highly successful at creating an empowering screen persona.

After the success of Melvin Van Peebles' *Sweet Sweetback's Baadasssss Song* (1971) and Gordon Parks' *Shaft* (1971), AIP released a series of films oriented towards the young, black urban movie market, much to the dismay of African American cultural critics and community leaders who expressed dismay at what they saw as derogatory, stereotypical roles in these movies. Critics felt that African American actresses and actors were reinforcing cultural myths of black men and women as bucks, mammies, Jezebels, pimps and hustlers. The civil rights movement restored positive visual images of African Americans by highlighting leaders influential in instituting social and political change in the 1960s.

Junius Griffin, Jesse Jackson and many others feared that negative images perpetuated in these movies would dismantle the progress made by the civil rights movement. African American women activists such as Angela Davis, Fannie Lou Hamer, Barbara Jordan and Shirley Chisholm orchestrated the push to show African American women in multi-faceted roles. Griffin and Jackson demonstrated their position through boycotts and open disdain towards actresses and actors who gained recognition in blaxploitation movies, sometimes calling for boycotts. Through his organization, People United to Save Humanity (PUSH), Jackson put media organizations on notice that the African American community would "challenge the nation's major corporations on their responsibilities to blacks."[3]

By the end of 1972, organizations such as PUSH, the Coalition of Blax-

"I want answers or else": Sheba (Pam Grier) confronts someone who knows why her father was killed.

ploitation (which counted among its membership leaders from the NAACP), the Congress of Racial Equality and the Southern Christian Leadership Conference,[4] as well as cultural critics such as Lerone Bennett, a senior editor for *Ebony*, and Dr. Alvin Poussaint, a prominent African American psychiatrist, openly criticized the studios and the industry. Still, they reserved their harshest criticism for black actresses and actors who appeared in these movies.

Because of her rising stardom, Pam Grier became a frequent target of scorn for taking roles that critics said favored titillation over substance. Given the historic representations of black women in American culture and, particularly, the film industry, their concerns were legitimate. Criticism of Grier focused on her roles as a gun-toting, resilient woman who disrobed as part of her characters' plan for seeking revenge. However, these same critics appeared unwilling to consider the difficulties African American actresses faced in the film industry.

Chapter 1 has provided a summary of the obstacles confronting African American actresses prior to the 1960s in having to play roles that greatly diminished African American womanhood. Nonetheless, film scholars such as Donald Bogle suggest that in spite of the limited material presented to her, McDaniel owned the role by injecting her own persona on mammy — a trait that many African American actresses adopted to earn a successful living in the film industry.

In a 1976 interview with Pam Grier, film critic Mark Jacobson suggested that moving from servitude and seductress roles to what he termed "tough mamma"[5] roles might have been a step forward for African American actresses. There were valid concerns about Grier and other actresses removing their clothes to play roles written to stimulate audiences and focused on gratuitous violence rather than a social message. It is significant that critics would blindly dismiss Grier's roles because of their violence and weak plotlines while ignoring the fact that she developed strong characters. It is more useful to construct critiques allowing that, while her roles were unchallenging, she molded them into something.

Thirty-one years after her first starring role, Grier is still labeled as *the* blaxploitation actress. Carrie Rickey wrote, "[A]part from Barbra Streisand and Ellen Burstyn, Grier was the only bankable woman star during the early '70s."[6]

Grier's own background may have played a part in bringing underdeveloped characters to the screen and prompting audiences to find redeeming qualities in these characters that countless African American cultural critics found offensive or degrading. Yet, in her role as a driven woman who was capable of holding her own among men and who used violence as a response to rather than for the sake of violence, Grier brought new characters to the screen that were different from those of her predecessors.

As an African American woman, Grier's experience allowed her to shape the direction of her characters despite the fact that white writers wrote under-developed characters that were difficult for many black actresses to identify with. In her first leading role, Grier used her own working-class Denver background and the African American women in her family to portray an independent heroine who was capable of handling her own among men and not afraid to respond to violence with violence against those who harmed her onscreen family.

Grier grew up in a military family and spent nine years living on Air Force bases in Europe before her family settled in Denver, where she received a rude awakening. She commented:

I spoke English with an accent and liked having tea at four o'clock in the afternoon. We lived in a very rough neighborhood. I wasn't very big then, and I had to fight all the time. You had to fight for your lunch money or act like you didn't have any. After living on Air Force bases, this was quite a shock.[7]

Coming from a long line of sturdy African American women, Grier used her strengths to fight her way into an industry that was not known for giving many opportunities to African American actresses.

I make no apologies for the women I created. Actually, I *re*created. When I grew up I knew a certain kind of Black woman who was the sole support of her family and who would, if you disrespected her, beat you into the cement. She was the glue that held her family together, got them through. I admired her greatly. I still do. And she still exists. I brought that lady to the screen — played her to the bone.[8]

Grier's first films featured her in minor supporting roles, but this changed in 1973 with her portrayal of a nurse who seeks revenge on those she feels are responsible for her sister's comatose state from a drug overdose. When *Coffy* hit theaters, audiences had not seen an African American woman character like her before. The character and Grier created controversy, partly because of the derisive remarks directed at blaxploitation movies in general and partly because many critics felt that her character presented black women in a negative light. They reacted strongly to the lack of redeeming cultural qualities in these movies, and some felt that Grier's *Coffy* was a return to the past in the portrayal of African American women. They felt that her roles reinforced cultural myths of African American women as overly aggressive and sexual.

Like McDaniel, Grier received roles that were continually challenged by the NAACP and other AA organizations who felt the genre would make it difficult for the inroads African Americans had made in the 1960s. Concerned with the depictions by actors, Junius Griffin and others took every opportunity to publicly denounce blaxploitation and the actors who starred in the genre.

Hattie McDaniel once stated that she would rather play a maid onscreen than one in real life, yet she recognized that these roles were not meant to present African American women as multi-faceted women with families and careers. When roles were scarce, McDaniel herself worked as a domestic. But the danger of accepting such roles was that, while blacks clearly understood that McDaniel's onscreen character did not reflect African American womanhood, white audiences did not make that distinction. They truly felt that McDaniel was mammy while critics felt that Grier was Coffy and clearly not representing African American women in a positive light. Thus, criticism of African American actresses for their portrayals of characters that did not present black women in a flattering picture did not begin with blaxploitation movies and had been a serious dilemma for black actresses for many years. One needs only to refer to the discussion in Chapter 1 for an understanding of the dynamics at play.

"They Call Her Coffy and She'll Cream You"[9]

In the first scene of *Coffy*, audiences see a woman who will stop at nothing to exact revenge on people who hurt her family. Grier's character wears a dress that highlights her cleavage, and she feigns drunkenness to dupe a person whom she believes is responsible for her sister's condition. As soon as he takes Coffy upstairs, she pulls out a shotgun and kills him. Then, she forces another man to shoot himself up with heroin before she goes to work as an operating nurse at a local hospital. A forceful character like this had not been seen before, but the responses from urban African American audiences were overwhelmingly positive. In an interview with Marc Jacobson, Grier said:

> I saw one woman in a 42nd Street theater smack her boyfriend's arm as Pam was icing half the Roman army in *The Arena*. The woman said, "See fool, I'm going to get myself together like her, so next time you think you're superman, watch out."[10]

Despite short filming schedules and minuscule budgets, Grier's movies earned millions at the box office. *Coffy* earned $8 million, and *Newsweek* labeled Grier "Queen of the B's." Because of AIP's history of exploitation movies, it is no surprise that the shooting schedule was completed for *Coffy* in less than a month and that the budget for the movie was low. Clearly, this is reflected in the characterization and plot of the movie. Nonetheless, Grier's steely onscreen persona gives legitimacy to her heroines. Even magazine article writers were forced to acknowledge that, despite the quality of Grier's movies, she had "an extremely valuable asset — star quality."[11]

Generally speaking, few African American actresses in blaxploitation movies "possessed the acting talent of a Cicely Tyson or a Ruby Dee."[12] Where Grier's acting talent might have lacked depth at times, she demonstrated that her acting was definitely above the material she was given.

Coffy moves effortlessly from shooting drug dealers and users to working in a hospital and caring for patients. Her heroine does whatever it takes to obtain her ultimate objective: to find the people responsible for the drugs that left her sister in a vegetative state. Yet, Coffy is not without feelings of remorse or guilt for her revenge-seeking ways. For example, she experiences a pang of a conscience after visiting her sister with her friend Brown, a police officer. When Coffy defiantly tells Brown that "the law is in for a piece of the action," he suggests that solving the drug problem is not as simple as killing those responsible for harming her loved ones. He becomes the voice of reason by forcing Coffy to think carefully before making decisions that she may later regret.

Pangs of conscience are part of Coffy's personality make-up. However, Grier's other heroines (*Foxy Brown*, *Friday Foster* and *Sheba Baby*) do not possess similar traits. Since *Coffy* was the first of Grier's action heroines, she was not as polished or sophisticated as her later heroines. Coffy is Grier's grittiest heroine in terms of emotions and her physical persona. Her growing self-confidence as an actress translated to more sophisticated onscreen heroines despite under-developed plots. More importantly, the success of the movie gave Grier a voice that allowed her to shape the direction of her characters in her later movies. She noted, "Coffy has given me a chance to really express myself as an actress. It was the first picture in which I was allowed to really act."[13] Grier recognized that to grow as an actress meant taking roles that were less than fulfilling, but provided an opportunity for more exposure towards gaining mainstream consideration for other parts.

Responses to Criticism

Although AIP disliked her open vocal concerns, Grier brought in a lot of money for the studio. She said, "They don't like me, but they want to work with me because I make them money. They don't like it that I talk about the cheesy way they work.... They think I am being ungrateful because they discovered me and made me a star."[14] Grier had specific ideas about articulating a strong image in her films and moving out of blaxploitation:

> I think it's time to move on now.... I have an audience, and if they allow me to move on, as an actress, I will take that audience that I have developed with me and do something meaningful, something they can enjoy.[15]

"Meet your maker": Coffy (Pam Grier) prepares to fire the first of many shots against those she holds responsible for her sister's drug overdose.

Grier approached her films with AIP with the same zeal that African American actresses in mainstream productions did. Of her image in blaxploitation movies, Grier stated, "I played those parts because they had women in positions of power."[16] In an interview with *Los Angeles Times* writer Dennis Hunt, Grier stated, "[I]t was a good positive image for black women."[17] Yet, she was also aware of the repetitive storylines that AIP produced and added, "I was happy when those films stopped ... the films became redundant, and I don't like being redundant."[18]

In a 1979 interview with *Essence*, Grier said, "I created a new kind of screen woman, physically strong and active, she was able to look after herself and others."[19] She further suggested, "If you think about it, you'll see she was the prototype for the more recent and very popular white Bionic and Wonder Women."[20] Grier's assertion was correct in that her heroines served as the early prototype for other heroines, particularly on television and, later, in popular cinema.

In 1974, Teresa Graves became the first African American actress to have a starring role as a police detective in *Get Christie Love!* While she was not the first actress to have a role in a leading action-oriented series nor the first African American woman to have her own series (that honor belongs to Hattie McDaniel, Louise Beavers, and, Ethel Waters in *Beulah*, and, later, Diahann Carroll in *Julia*), she was the first actress to move into a position of authority in a law enforcement drama role. After this series, television producers created more roles that focused on women as police officers, private detectives, or super-heroines out to save the world.

In spite of criticism, Grier provided a face and voice to a new type of heroine that was subsequently appropriated by the action genre, and that was significant. Her heroines (in particular her early portrayals in *Coffy* and *Foxy Brown*) redefined African American beauty, sexuality, and womanhood, and subsequently led to alternative images of African American actresses onscreen.

When she was very young, Grier doubted her capacity to truly act because "the examples that were being put in front of me were all about physical and aesthetic beauty. I didn't have a sense of myself yet or what beauty meant to me. It didn't fit with my upbringing to look at one person and see them as more beautiful than the next."[21]

Grier noted that the 1970s

> ... was a time of freedom and women saying that they needed empowerment. There was more empowerment and self-discovery than any other decade I remember. All across the country, a lot of women were Foxy Brown and Coffy. They were independent, fighting to save their families, not accepting rape or being victimized.... This was going on all across the country. I just happened to do it on film. I don't think it took any great genius or great imagination. I just exemplified it, reflecting it to society.[22]

Physically, Grier's looks were unconventional for an industry that historically categorized and typecast African American actresses based on their physical make-up. The film industry decided the types of roles that African American actresses could portray. If Grier had been an actress from the 1930s to the 1950s, she would have been unable to find acting roles. Instead, she would have been forced to leave Hollywood and continue an acting career in Europe because her features could not be easily categorized. In the early 1930s, Josephine Baker left Hollywood because of similar problems. Ironically, Baker became a headliner in Paris where ideas about race and beauty differed. There, audiences found her pretty. In Hollywood, Baker was "unconventional."

The 1960s changed the landscape by which African American women were judged and thus transferred this to the screen by first presenting highly visible images of empowered African American women such as Angela Davis, who displayed an alternative image of black femininity. The 1960s found many African Americans praising the multifaceted aspects of black beauty by championing natural hairstyles and attire that reflected pride in their African ancestry.

As noted in the introduction, Cicely Tyson was one of the first black actresses to enjoy success with her short Afro and beautiful brown complexion that in another era would have led studio executives to typecast her as a mammy. Tyson played a number of roles that defied typecasting and as such created a multi-dimensional African American woman. By the time Grier appeared onscreen, the appreciation of the vast array of black femininity was reflected in many black women characters, particularly in television.

In her films, Grier's heroines redefined sexuality, womanhood, and beauty by portraying empowering, liberated, assertive heroines who, in the words of Alan Ebert, "took no shit from The Man."[23] Ebert noted that "there was no softness or vulnerability to the Black women Pam Grier portrayed. She was tough, physically and emotionally.... The Pam Grier character could and did wield a gun much the way some men carry their weapons with a swagger and without conscience."[24]

In these films, Grier deliberately uses the sexual stereotype to her advantage, reclaiming and transforming black female sexuality. It is a technique that black women blues singers adopted in the 1920s and 1930s onstage when they sang about the sexual relationship between black men and women. Scholar Hazel Carby has suggested that female blues singers "articulated a cultural and political struggle over sexual relations: a struggle that is directed against the objectification of female sexuality within a patriarchal order but which also tries to reclaim women's bodies as the sexual and sensuous objects of song."[25]

Director Cheryl Dunye (*The Watermelon Woman*, 1997) defended Grier's use of sexuality by presenting the body as a metaphor for a political instrument. "Black women are stripped of power, and the last thing that happens is that they still have control over their physical bodies," Dunye wrote in an essay for *What It Is, What It Was: The Black Film Explosion of the '70s in Words and Pictures* by Gerald Martinez "in that kind of sense, the display of the body is a final act of resistance. Basically, that's the kind of characters that Pam played, stripping away the hoky narratives, she basically left without anything but her own physical body and brain."[26]

Grier's heroines similarly used their sexuality as a vehicle for controlling her circumstances. For example, when Coffy first appears onscreen, she is wearing a skimpy, short dress and high heels; audiences are led to believe that her heroine is a prostitute. However, she quickly changes this perception by forcing a drug dealer to inject himself with a lethal dose of heroin as revenge for selling drugs to her sister. The high heels and cleavage-baring dress were used as a disguise to exact vengeance.

It quickly became clear that this was a new heroine for African American women and audiences in general. While some black women responded favorably to Grier's characters, others cringed. According to Ebert, they "were embarrassed to think the image of the Black woman at that particular time in history was wrapped up in Pam Grier."[27]

Similarly, as Foxy Brown, Grier is introduced to the audience as she relaxes in bed with her boyfriend, a familiar female image. Suddenly, however, she jumps out of bed, puts a gun in her bra strap and rushes to the aid of her brother. Grier creates characters that surpassed stereotypical limitations imposed on film women, without denying their sensuality. Intimacy was shown as a loving act between a man and a woman, without stereotyping.

In the 1960s, the Afro hairstyle became a powerful symbol for many, insofar as it came to represent liberation. Black Nationalism offered one alternative image of black femininity by praising women who wanted to return to a natural hairstyle rather than submit to the Eurocentric beauty standards of long straight hair, delicate physical features and lighter complexions. The Black Panther Party showcased many women wearing Afros and the media attention that the charismatic Angela Davis received helped make "Black is beautiful" popular in the African American community.

The Afro represented an alternate construction of black femininity well beyond simply a hairstyle — one that empowered and uplifted many African American women. Many African American women most clearly

"Tender moments": Coffy (Pam Grier) and Brown (Booker Bradshaw) share a brief moment before she embarks on her revenge plans.

identified with the Afro, which symbolized empowerment and a discarding of Eurocentric notions of beauty.

Film scholar Cedric Robinson suggested blaxploitation movies, particularly *Foxy Brown*, "appropriated and re-presented Angela Davis."[28] He was not the first to suggest that American International Pictures appropriated Davis' image for blaxploitation movies. African American actress Lynn Hamilton, who was best known for her role as Donna on the television series *Sanford and Son*, stated when she auditioned for roles, "producers were constantly asking if she could play an Angela Davis type who did not mind disrobing before the cameras."[29] It is unfortunate that some producers sought to capitalize on Davis' strong presence in a negative manner.

An outspoken intellectual who served time in prison for her convictions in the late 1960s and early 1970s, Davis' Afro symbolized an emphasis on natural beauty and alternate image of black femininity. The fact that any film studio would consider the image of a highly visible woman who represented empowerment for many African American women and re-appropriate it in an exploitative matter was troubling. Yet, bringing a variation of that image to the screen enabled audiences outside of the urban markets to see the beauty of black women as more varied and nuanced.

Integral in creating an alternative image of black femininity was depicting the diversity of African American beauty onscreen. When African Americans began appearing in motion pictures, studios wanted to convey a certain image of black womanhood through stereotypes. For a number of years, white actors regularly portrayed African Americans in blackface. However, when African American actresses appeared for the first time onscreen, they portrayed mammy or the exotic other based on their physical characteristics while Aunt Jemima and Sapphire appeared later as more stereotypes of black femininity. As discussed in Chapter 1, the physical make-up of Aunt Jemima was similar to that of mammy while Sapphire's physical traits were nondescript.

Early black actresses such as Nina Mae McKinney, who became synonymous with the first onscreen Jezebel in King Vidor's *Hallelujah* (1929), and, later, Fredi Washington in the 1930s received roles that limited them to this character based on their light skin, wavy hair, and Eurocentric-looking features. And it is already known what roles dark complexioned actresses portrayed.

"Don't Mess Around with Foxy Brown"[30]

In *Foxy Brown*, Grier intentionally changed her hairstyle frequently, reflecting the changing definitions of beauty associated with African American women. In the opening movie credits, Grier moves with ease from a short bob, patterned after Dobson's Cleopatra character, to long, flowing, straight hair and finally to an Afro. It was clear that Grier was gaining a voice in the development of her heroine as she insisted on costume and hairstyle changes for Foxy Brown.

Director Jack Hill believed that her costume and hairstyle suggestions did not fit the role. However, Grier fought and won the battle to change Foxy's clothing attire and hairstyles. Later, Hill stated: "Pam had much more control because now she was a major star. That is why she is wearing all these glamorous outfits and makeup and stuff, which I thought wasn't really right for the movie at all."[31]

Just as Grier's characters represented a different option of African American beauty, they also redefined womanhood. The roles of Coffy, Foxy Brown, Friday Foster, and Sheba Shayne reshaped black womanhood. In a sign of the social and political progress African Americans had achieved by the 1970s, a protective, almost maternal instinct balanced the tough exteriors of these women. For example, in each of Grier's films, a family member or a close friend is severely injured or killed, and this becomes the catalyst for her to seek her own brand of justice.

In Foxy's repeated physical defense of her brother, Grier demonstrates that strong African American women maintain and transform traditional feminine traits. "Nowadays, you don't have to lose your femininity to be powerful; you maintain it. You can have high IQs, study, take martial arts, whatever.... It's very different than male power. Just maintain that female power always,"[32] Grier suggested.

Foxy's concern for her brother despite his drug use parallels many black women's positions in the family as nurturers, caretakers, and, at times, disciplinarians. Another example of Grier's characters as nurturers, caretakers and disciplinarians occurs in *Coffy*, when she visits her sister, who is in a vegetative state from a drug overdose. She also served as nurturer and caretaker in *Friday Foster*, where she took care of a younger brother while solving a series of murders in the fashion world.

In *Sheba Baby*, Grier portrayed Sheba Shayne, a private detective who comes home at her father's request to help him keep his loan business from falling into the hands of local molls. Thus, in each of these movies, Grier's characters adopted maternal and disciplinarian roles with their loved ones.

"I got my womanhood from my society, from my community, by listening to people, from being taken care of by the wonderful women in my family, by learning from people, by giving and taking,"[33] Grier said. "It all pays off. It comes from somewhere. I know I'm a messenger."[34]

Grier's early heroines display less human emotion than her later characters. Coffy and Foxy Brown were tough women who only displayed their vulnerability in certain poignant scenes. Their reactions to violence came only when they or their family members were threatened; then it became retribution and, in a few cases where the law was unable to assist, vigilantism.

On posters, Coffy was presented as a muscular, curvaceous woman highly adept at handling a gun. The posters for the movie show Grier as a bell-bottom-wearing, belly-displaying woman who appeared secure in her femininity while using weapons traditionally associated with masculinity. In contrast, Foxy Brown wore evening gowns, and the movie posters showed her with a gun, long flowing hair and in evening attire, which suggested she felt comfortable both wearing formal frocks and carrying a gun.

The image of Grier's heroines began to change with *Foxy Brown*. The producer and director made an attempt to link her image to that of Angela Davis, particularly in a crucial scene where she makes the argument for getting justice for "all the people"[35] in front of a neighborhood committee whose aid she wants to enlist. By 1975, her heroines' hairstyles shifted to free-flowing in *Friday Foster* or "coiffed hair."[36] Producers may have attempted to physically soften Grier's later heroines to expand audience interest in a waning genre or as a fashion statement of that particular timeframe.

From Bad Momma to Photographer

Despite the attempts to play up her femininity, Grier's heroines maintained their tough demeanor. For example, Friday continued to try to solve a series of murder attempts on a black billionaire even when the assailant who later tried to kill her was systematically killing her friends.

"Avenging Fox": In her final confrontation with the person responsible for the deaths of her boyfriend and brother, Foxy (Pam Grier) runs into the same henchman who vows to take care of her once and for all.

Sheba tells her former boyfriend, "I know you think I'm doing a man's job, but I'm not going to sit on the sidelines because I'm a woman."[37] This was typical of Grier's heroine, who refused to stand by waiting for others to find out who killed or maimed their loved ones. Instead, she took matters into her own hands when the law could not, or would not, move quickly enough.

Coffy only shows her vulnerability in scenes with her sister and when her friend is severely beaten and left in a coma. Similarly, Foxy took a confused prostitute under her wing and helped reunite her with her husband and child. Although her brother angered her by refusing to stay out of trouble, she was always there to protect him when he needed her most. Indeed, she eventually avenges his death.

"Smile Friday Foster": (Pam Grier) works as a fashion photographer who becomes entangled in a plot to murder the first black billionaire and must solve the murders accumulating in the fashion world.

Friday Foster protected her little brother while solving a crime, and Sheba vowed vengeance on those responsible for her father's death. In each movie, Grier adopted a maternal, instinctive nature to protect her loved ones and friends while masking this nurturing personality underneath a tough demeanor.

Despite attacks for contributing to popular interests in blaxploitation movies, Grier was aware that the genre did not represent the African American community. In a February 1976 interview, she admitted "most of her pictures were trash, but credited them with allowing a lot of blacks to break into movies for the first time and feed their families. Moreover, Grier was not shy about her feelings towards AIP, saying:

> AIP's policy is to give the niggers shit. They don't like me, but they want to work with me because I make them money. They don't like it that I talk about the cheesy way they work or that I say the movies that I did for them were jerk jobs. They think I am being ungrateful because they dis-

covered me and they made me a star. Nobody but me made me what I am today.[38]

By 1976, Grier was exercising more control over her onscreen image. She added, "[B]efore I do another film for AIP, I'll have control over score, direction, and it will be spelled out in my contract who I can fire."[39] As noted, African American actresses had little input into their characters, storylines, direction, and other aspects of a movie. Instead, if they voiced strong reservations about their character or the script, they were promptly fired. In his book, Bogle recounts the story of Louise Beavers, who found a word in the script objectionable and, while she ultimately won the battle, she had to appear before the studio executive several times and pronounce the word as "punishment" and to underscore her insignificance as an actress.[40]

By becoming a major box office draw in blaxploitation movies, Grier gradually gained more control over her career and could openly voice concerns. However, after the phenomenon ended, she found it difficult to get mainstream acting opportunities precisely because of her outspokenness.

In a 1997 *New York Times* article, Grier stated, "Foxy and Coffy and the rest were heroines of the women's movement. They showed women how to be assertive and self sufficient, not passive victims."[41] She described her feelings towards critics who accused her of demeaning black women by stating in a 1979 *Essence* interview:

> It hurt me that some people thought I was ridiculing the Black woman or putting her down. It also hurt that some folks thought I was the person I played. Why would people think I would ever demean the Black woman? I was tried and convicted without being asked to testify in my defense. Sure, a lot of those films were junk. But they were what was being offered. They provided work for me and jobs for hundreds of Blacks. We all needed to work. We all needed to eat.[42]

Interviewer Alan Ebert elaborated by suggesting, "Pam Grier is saying without saying that you take what you can get if you want to survive."[43]

Yet, ironically, there was a time in Grier's career where she wanted to distance herself from "The Queen of Blaxploitation." She stated in 1981, "I wish people would forget about those old movies. I'd like them to think of me as an actress capable of playing anything."[44]

Of her heroines, Grier argued, "Coffy, Foxy Brown, Friday Foster, et al. were reflections of African American culture in the '70s and not 'blaxploitation films.'[45] My films didn't exploit the black audience; they mirrored it. All these movies were reflections of African American religion, music,

"Forcible Restraint": On assignment in her job as a fashion photographer, Friday (Pam Grier) is uncomfortably collared by a security guard (Carl Weathers) when she tries to enter a restricted area in the airport.

art and popular culture."[46] As a reminder of bringing her experiences as an African American woman to her heroines, Grier added:

> One thing people forget is that my man would always protect me. It was only after he was killed, or whatever, that I stood up for myself. That was

the underlying message of these movies; that women can be self-sufficient and don't have to fold like a house of cards in adversity. Remember in my own family's past, the pioneer women were all Foxy Browns. If the mule dropped dead, these women were out in the fields in the harness pulling the plow.[47]

Of her first heroine Coffy, James Robert Parish and George H. Hill wrote: "91 minutes of gore, mayhem, and raw sexuality is more like a stinging nightmare. And as one producing film company American International knew, its contract star Pam Grier was perhaps the only one in Hollywood who could carry off the demanding assignment.[48] This lead character is intriguing, even baffling. She is one moment righteous and pure, the next a lady with her own brand of heated bedside manner."[49] This is an accurate summation of Grier's early heroines and the casual attitude displayed by her characters towards sex. In response to Grier's heroines' attitudes about sex, Tanya Kersey-Henley says, "[T]he treatment of sexuality was no different from the way we see it treated in action films today with female stars like Angelina Jolie. It was cutting edge back in the 1970s."[50] Yet, African American women, particularly actresses in film, have always been held to a higher standard. Unlike actresses in general, a black actress unfairly must always be conscious about the types of roles she chooses because of the inherent racial attitudes held by many about black women's sexuality. It is a burden for African American actresses since they should not carry the pressure of representing all African American women. However, this has never been the case in the film industry and Grier received the most scathing critiques by critics in the black community for her roles.

Critics failed to understand that Grier was not in charge of writing the scripts, choosing directors and producers for her film. What she gained after *Coffy* was more leverage in developing her character for *Foxy Brown*, but that is the extent of the control she had. By taking these roles, her objective was to create her own production company so that she could produce the types of films she wanted. It is significant when discussing Grier's heroines to place them within the social, political and cultural context in which they belong. George Alexander argued, "[T]o be fair we must look at the roles and the films in the context of the time in which they were created."[51] None of the films were made by black people. As film scholar Jacqueline Bobo noted, "[T]he films were created for a particular purpose — to make money.[52] That was the precise objective of blaxploitation movies and, frankly, economics plays an integral role in deciding what types of films are produced. Within the limitations of what she could do as an actress, Grier was able to exact some agency as her movies became more successful and she became more vocal in her criticism about how American International Pictures treated her. Ultimately, when the genre ended, Grier found herself without a contract with AIP and it took some time to reestablish herself in the film industry because of her vocal commentary about AIP and also, because studios did not know how to cast her beyond the Coffy image. Despite the flaws inherent in her movies, Grier became a pathfinder herself in the early 1970s by exploring cinematic stereotypes about which parts blacks could and couldn't portray on screen. She pretty much originated the action hero role of a strong, independent black woman who prevails against the long odds of a society indifferent to her suffering.[53]

In reference to her image, Grier said, "I just happened to be the first one that these filmmakers Roger Corman, Jack Hill, Sam Arkoff and AIP, found to portray that image."[54] Bishetta Mishett has this to say about Grier's image:

> Pam Grier was a pioneer in creating the image of the black action heroine. She learned how to act by acting in these early films. She was a take-charge woman who did not serve as a Mammy or as a vamp or whore. She had a steady boyfriend whom she loved and she had purpose and drive. Sadly, the men in her life disappointed her (Coffy) and she handled him as well. She killed him. When she appeared in *Greased Lightning* as the wife of black race car driver Wendell Scott, she broke this mold and was seen as a loving housewife and mother."[55]

In brief, blaxploitation provided the training ground that Grier needed to establish herself as an actress and move beyond the types of roles that made her famous. However, the genre also served as an early prototype in mainstream popular cinema for the action heroine. Film scholar Chris Holmlund wrote that in every blaxploitation film, Grier's vigilante violence — "as American as apple pie," as she says in *Foxy Brown*— is thus multiply motivated: by concern for community, on behalf of "family," and in response to personal abuse by racist whites and the occasional sell-out blacks. Grier's blaxploitation vehicles cannot easily be hailed as simply "pro-feminist" or purely "pro-black."[56] By foregrounding femininity and rethinking racism, however, they definitely disrupt conventions common to exploitation action films, whether directed by whites or blacks.[57]

After the demise of blaxploitation, many African American actresses (particularly Tamara Dobson, who had great success with her first film) could not find roles in mainstream popular cinema. Grier was one of the few to move beyond the "stigma,"[58] but she did so by leaving the industry to study her craft for a period of time before returning to mainstream cinema in the early 1980s. Unfortunately, so few film roles were available to

"Sheba stakes her claim": Sheba Shayne (Pam Grier) prepares to go after a henchman in one of many action scenes from *Sheba Baby*.

African American actresses in the 1980s that most of Grier's work during this decade was in TV or theater.[59] Yet, the shift from action heroine of the early 1970s to eclectic roles in the 1980s allowed Grier to hone her acting skills despite her inability to permanently escape her beginnings in the industry, from exploitation to blaxploitation movies. She continues to act with her biggest role in the 1990s as a flight attendant who finds herself in trouble with the law in *Jackie Brown*. Since *Coffy*, *Foxy Brown*, *Friday Foster*, and *Sheba Baby*, *Jackie Brown* was the first movie that focused on Grier as the leading character. For three decades, Grier's voluptuous look and badass attitude have "made her a model, whether as hot action babe or cool action mama for younger actresses working in action movies."[60] Film scholar Philip Green has noted that it is telling that Grier's videos have outlasted her male counterparts in blaxploitation movies, so much so that one can purchase hers on DVD or VHS as package deals.[61] She has also earned admiration from many in the hip-hop community, particularly black women rappers such as Foxy Brown who chose the moniker because she liked Grier's character. When looking at her origins and the impact of blaxploitation heroines which are applicable to today's action heroine, Grier states, "[T]hat was the underlying message of those movies; that women can be self-sufficient, and don't have to fold like a house of cards in adversity."[62] In that sense, she has proven wrong those who suggested she would no longer have an acting career when blaxploitation ended. Her comments also suggest that, despite the labels the industry attaches to black actresses, it is sometimes the case that they can raise and move beyond those labels into the realm of mainstream popular cinema.

4

Call Me Cleo

Like Pam Grier, Tamara Dobson had some exposure to celebdom before earning the role of super-heroine *Cleopatra Jones*, which brought her wider fame as an actress. Dobson began her career as a fashion model in New York. In the 1972 movie *Fuzz* starring Burt Reynolds and Yul Brynner, she portrayed the mistress of Brynner's character. This role was a far cry from *Cleopatra Jones*. Unlike Grier, she had no acting skills when she auditioned for the leading role of a glamorous, James Bond–like super agent along with 2500 African American actresses. Produced by William Tennant, written by African American actor and screenwriter Max Julien (who later starred in *The Mack*, a controversial blaxploitation movie about pimps and prostitutes), and directed by Jack Starrett, *Cleopatra Jones* offered audiences an upscale version of Grier's *Coffy* and was also "the first blaxploitation film to use martial arts as part of its promotion."[1] According to a 1975 *Sepia* magazine interview with Dobson, in order to build a mystique around *Cleopatra Jones*, Warner Brothers issued news releases stating that the Cleo character was "tough and giving everyone a hard time"[2] while simultaneously billing her as "a female James Bond, an Interpol agent fighting dope traffic, an image black people could be proud of."[3]

Warner Brothers successfully focused the attention on Cleo rather then the actress portraying her and for the New York premiere "a 20 foot high picture of Tamara Dobson dominated the sky above the theatre marquee, the largest, most glamorous sign ever erected on Broadway for a black actress, a black movie."[4] With a larger budget, in many ways a better script, and Shelley Winters, a prominent actress, playing the villain, *Cleopatra Jones* was the mainstream studio's response to AIP's *Coffy*. The role earned Dobson name recognition, allowed her entry into the first group of action heroines in mainstream popular cinema, and more control for her sequel *Cleopatra Jones and the Casino of Gold* (1975).

Sepia stated, "Tamara's name will be above the title as the sole star ... and most important she is being paid as a star."[5] Critics continually dismissed blaxploitation movies as one-dimensional portrayals of African Americans, failing to acknowledge that the genre allowed some African American actors to exercise more control over their image as illustrated by Dobson and Pam Grier.

Although there were parallels between Grier and Dobson's characters, Dobson tried to distance herself from the similarities. In her 1973 magazine article for *Ebony*, Lucy Horton wrote, "[A]n agent for Miss Dobson said that the actress refuses to appear in the same book much less on the same page as Miss Grier."[6] Additionally, she noted, "Miss Dobson also has refused to participate in the same celebrity events in which Miss Grier was involved."[7]

Grier held no such animosity towards Tamara Dobson. Dobson's disdain for Grier apparently centered on her disrobement before the cameras as part of Coffy's character. Dobson felt nudity was unwarranted and clearly sought to make a distinction between her heroine and those of other African American actresses. Dobson rebuffed nude scenes in *Cleopatra Jones*, stating, "I think it's very important for people to realize that sex is more interesting when you don't show everything at once. A girl in a one-piece bathing suit is more alluring than a girl with her belly button hanging out."[8] She added, "It's not that I am opposed to nudity in films if it's relevant. But when it's used as a vehicle to get people into the theater for $3.50 a peep, it becomes exploitation and that's not for me."[9]

Though she may not have enjoyed the comparisons, Dobson's heroine shared many traits with Coffy and Foxy Brown — independence, redefining African American femininity, empowerment and a real sense of communal justice. Additionally, Dobson's personal background was similar to Grier in that they both came from humble, working class roots. Dobson grew up in Baltimore's inner city where her mother owned a beauty salon and her father worked for the Pennsylvania Railroad station.[10]

After earning a degree from the Baltimore Institute of Art, Dobson moved to New York City to explore modeling opportunities. Initially, she experienced some obstacles; some designers and modeling agencies did not quite know how to place a 6'2" African American woman. Her height was not as problematic as her race. Guy Flatley wrote, "[I]t does come as a sur-

"All in a day's work": Cleopatra Jones (Tamara Dobson) prepares for work with a high-powered gun, sporty car and fashionable attire.

prise that in the 5'7", overwhelmingly WASP world of modeling, a girl who is 6'2" and black can rake in 75,000 a year."[11]

Dobson did precisely that before embarking on her film career. She stated, "It's true there are very few black models. You won't see them smiling out at you from the covers of major magazines. Editors blame this on the market ... but I say forget the market — we're talking about a pretty girl. I've seen ooooogly white girls on magazine covers. But black girls must be *safe*. They must have straight hair, or hair that can be pressed, and they must have Caucasian features."[12] Dobson's insight on the modeling world was applicable to the film industry. In spite of the real challenges, she was quite successful and caught the attention of producers who were seeking a counterpart to Pam Grier's heroines.

Six Feet of Dynamite

Like Grier, Dobson radiated confidence which is injected into Cleopatra Jones. In response to a strong desire to become successful in a medium that traditionally had treated African American women as second class citizens, Dobson stated, "I was determined.... I made up my mind that I would not be turned around and go back to Baltimore."[13] *Cleopatra Jones* was "filmed for 1,500,000, the picture reportedly grossed more than $8,000,000 ... or about six times its cost. By comparison the highly-successful *Lady Sings the Blues* made on a 4,000,000 budget brought in $12,000,000 at the box office world-wide ... or three times its cost."[14]

Cleopatra Jones also comes from a crime-riddled neighborhood filled with poverty and despair. She is driven to eradicate crime in her community and give younger people an alternative, with the help of her boyfriend, Reuben (portrayed by Bernie Casey), who runs a community center for young people. However, even Reuben is no match for Cleopatra when they share screen time. Dobson's character appears to dominate scenes even when the producers are attempting to create a softer image of her.

In the opening scene, Cleo dramatically strides off a helicopter to oversee the destruction of Turkish poppy fields, exuding the sexual confidence that is the trademark of her heroine. Here she is: a striking, statuesque, African American woman wearing a long fur coat, towering over the male officials whose eyes take in her every move. It is clear in this scene that Dobson's character represents the authority figure, while the male characters surrounding her are subordinates.

Cleo's authority and sexuality dominate the screen and represent a significant redefinition of racial and gender roles because her occupation (CIA operative) is one that has been traditionally reserved for white men. She flaunts her sexuality, but does not rely solely on it to help her out of tight situations. Dobson invests Cleo with an awareness of the power of her own sexuality and the self-assurance to use it to her advantage. As demonstrated in many scenes, particularly in her interactions with authority figures and criminals, Jones controls the shots from every angle. In an early scene, upon returning from Turkey, Shelley Winter's character Mommy orders two henchmen to kill Cleopatra at the airport. Sensing trouble, Cleopatra outwits and kills both before police officers appear on the scene. When they appear, she is sitting on a suitcase poised as if to say, "All in a day's work."

In a review, critic Mary Mebane stated, "[O]n the surface, *Cleopatra Jones* is about a black distaff James Bond who drives a fancy car equipped with a submachine gun in the door, wears smart clothes, is a karate expert, and travels all over the world as a United States secret agent, destroying the poppy wherever it is found."[15] Yvonne Tasker, author of *Gender, Genre and the Action Heroine*, also compared Dobson's Jones to James Bond.[16]

Writer Chris Norton takes the Bond comparison a step further by sug-

"Mommy meet Cleo's hand": Cleo (Tamara Dobson) uses her martial arts finesse to put Mommy (Shelley Winters) out of business for good.

gesting, "[L]ike Bond, Cleo is not a stealthy character who tries to infiltrate the underworld by losing her identity."[17] In comparing her to Bond, Norton notes, "Bond seldom tried to hide his identity, often using his real name during introductions, and all Bond films rely on his being recognized as 007."[18] Cleo too never goes undercover. She relies on her flamboyance and her ability to be recognized to disrupt the plans of her enemies. Like Bond, Cleo drives a flashy car outfitted with hidden compartments which hold machine guns and various weapons.

When examining the fashions of James Bond and Cleopatra Jones, Norton writes, "Cleo's outrageous outfits are also analogous with Bond's dinner jackets and playboy wardrobe. Her three foot hat brims and flowing fur robes are treated with respect and awe within the film, just as Bond's refinements are looked upon as the height of good taste."[19] However, Norton also asserts that "Cleo is not simply a black James Bond. While the Cleopatra Jones films have co-opted Bond, they avoid a total fusion of her character with that of Bond"[20] and in a sense serve as a "critique of Bond ideology."[21] It is interesting to note that Mebane, Tasker and Norton's comparison of Cleopatra Jones to a popular iconic image like James Bond, despite his troubling treatment of women, suggests that there was indeed something beyond her fulfilling a male fantasy role as has been argued by film scholar Donald Bogle.

However, Professor Frances Gateward takes exception to this comparison: "Referring to Cleopatra Jones, played so winningly by Tamara Dobson, as a female James Bond, dramatically minimizes the significant cultural value of the character, while simultaneously falls into the trap of using a male standard as the basis of comparison."[22] In fact, the only similarity between the two characters is that they are both international agents of espionage. Where Bond, at least in the classic film adaptations, was used as an agent of Cold War ideology, fighting on behalf of the capitalist West's hegemony, Jones sought to protect the African American community from the scourge of heroin addiction, which was presented not as a local problem of drug dealing, but as a product of a global capitalist system beyond the control of average working African Americans.[23]

Gateward adds:

> The globetrotting British agent operated in the realm of the elite dressed in tuxedos, playing baccarat with the famous "shaken-not-stirred" martini in hand. European capitals were presented with glamour and sheen, while the developing world was a place of both exoticism and danger. And I would remind readers, that the same treatment was given to Harlem in the horrible, exploitative *Live and Let Die*, which grossly appropriated the success of the black action films. While abroad, the locals in Bond films only function as villains, sexual conquests, or as support for the superior White hero."[24]

Clearly, critics disagree on Cleopatra Jones' comparison to James Bond, but it is troubling to make such comparisons in light of Bond's misogynistic tendencies towards women and further problematizes the way African American women are portrayed in film even when they are the heroines. On one level, Cleo may have fulfilled a fantasy for men; however, on another, she appealed to some African American women because she *was* a significant departure from the mammy and exotic other or tragic mulatto.

Similar to Grier's heroines, Dobson's Cleo was revolutionary in that audiences had not witnessed a take-charge African American heroine operating largely in a patriarchal occupation structure that put her at odds with previous occupations available to African American characters. Although the 1960s began to see a diverse range of occupations for African American characters, it was not until the 1970s that African American women in film and on television were shown with a degree of regularity as authority figures in law enforcement agencies. Despite the fantastical elements of Cleopatra Jones such as gunning down men who have been hired to kill her at the airport, and physically forcing a man to turn over evidence by manhandling him and throwing his dope stash away, there were attributes of Jones that made her appealing to audiences, particularly some African American women. Strength, fearlessness, the ability to maintain a cool demeanor in the face of danger, and independence were characteristics that Jones exuded onscreen in part due to Dobson's ability to bring these attributes to a role that was largely one-dimensional.

The social and economic mobility in which Jones traveled would have also made her an appealing heroine to those segments of the African American community, particularly women, who were redefining their roles in American culture during the 1970s after the tumultuous historic and cultural era of the 1960s. Mebane took the notion of Jones as a revolutionary film a step further and wrote that *Gordon's War* and *Cleopatra Jones* "reflect the mood of the seventies in another way, they show the *strengths* in the black communities."[25] The abuse and the disparities in prison sentences concerning crack cocaine and powder cocaine within the African American community is well-documented and is a significant problem that African American leaders still grapple with in the twenty-first century.

In the 1970s, heroin and cocaine were destroying the community, and Mebane suggested that *Cleopatra Jones* dealt with the harsh realities of impoverishment, drugs and crime in a realistic manner unlike other blaxploitation movies. Many scholars disagreed with her premise and dismissed Dobson's character as another one-dimensional heroine in a genre noted for its lack of cultural and artistic merits, but the character was indeed innovative for African American actresses. Donald Bogle suggested that Dobson's heroine was merely replacing the old stereotypes of Jezebel and mammy with a new stereotype of "the macho goddess."[26] He also noted that Dobson's Cleopatra and Grier's heroines were "high flung male fantasy ... who lived in fantasy worlds — of violence, blood, guns and gore which pleased, rather then threatened, male audiences."[27] African American women would not be able to relate to such heroines, but they could not relate to mammy or the tragic mulatto either.

Perhaps some African American women could not relate to Cleo if they were strictly looking at her as the female James Bond. For that matter, audiences in general would be hard-pressed to relate to James Bond as anything but a superhero because of the elements associated with his persona. However, Cleo's attributes extended beyond the materialistic trappings of a penthouse, sports car, high fashion and exotic occupation. Instead, the deep devotion to helping her troubled community, relationships with those who never left the community and the independence that she reflected as a woman making choices in all aspects of her life would have appealed to some African American women.

It is important to look beneath the surface of the character to see that some of the virtues that Dobson's character possessed onscreen were, in fact, virtues found in strong, independent African American women leaders. A 1973 *Ebony* article stated that "for black women's libbers who have sat through the growing procession of Shaft, Superfly, Nigger Charley and other assorted celluloid sensations of male derring-do with growing impatience for an idol of their own, Warner Bros. has come up with a gorgeous, 6 foot 2, 38–26–39."[28]

Reviews and Responses

In her review of *Cleopatra Jones*, Mebane wrote, "Cleopatra Jones portrays the relationships between black men and women as supportive and lasting."[29] It is one of the few blaxploitation movies where African American men and women appeared on equal footing, with the heroines leading a little because of their position as heroines. In response to the criticism from certain segments of the African American community (particularly women) who were "dismayed by Tamara's image as a karate-chopping, pistol popping terror,"[30] Dobson stated "[Y]ou go through phases until you find the right situation where a character works for you. A lot of tits and ass movies were made, ballbuster films, exploitation pictures. But, I don't care what anybody calls it. Doing Cleopatra Jones gave me a chance to work. I loved Cleo. She was not only gracious, but strong, clever, intelligent and sexy."[31]

In spite of the criticism heaped on the genre, Tamara Dobson and Pam Grier offered an alternative image of African American femininity. Clearly, for African American actresses who carried action storylines, blaxploitation movies offered something very different from earlier stereotypes of black women in film. Mebane, one of a handful of black movie reviewers when *Cleopatra Jones* was first released, recognized the unique characterization of such a heroine, particularly for African American women, onscreen.

It is not clear whether Dobson was cognizant that Cleopatra Jones (similar to Grier's earlier heroines) would become the prototype for the action heroine that became synonymous in later mainstream popular cinema. Although she did not create the heroine, she brought her to life on screen and in doing so demonstrated that African American actresses, when given the opportunity, could be tough, independent, feminine *and* beautiful by dismantling the film industry's preconceived notions of African American femininity.

By 1973, African American actresses who did not possess the physical characteristics of the mammy or the exotic other were receiving recognition where previously they would have found themselves unable to find acting roles, which I noted was historically a problem. It appeared that the industry attempted to capitalize on the Black Pride movement from the 1960s and varied images of African American femininity. Of course, this sudden interest can be viewed as solely a monetary interest by giving African American audiences characters beyond those portrayed by Sidney Poitier, but also a legitimate attempt by some studio executives to recognize the talents of African American directors, producers, writers and actors.

One month after the release of Grier's *Coffy* in 1973, *Cleopatra Jones* arrived in theaters. The response from audiences and many reviewers was overall extremely positive. Tapping into the Black Pride movement, the irony of using the name Cleopatra to convey a character who was strong physically, but equally feminine and highly independent, was not lost on the urban market. As the queen of Egypt, Cleopatra's role as a leader is etched in historical artifacts and in what *Ebony* calls "black women's libbers,"[32] it appeared that some African American women could identify with the personality traits of Dobson's character and as such were impatient for a heroine to call their own. Thus, while critics of blaxploitation denoted a lack of cultural and artistic endeavor in Dobson's *Cleopatra Jones*, some audiences, particularly African American women, may have thought differently and harbored harmless fantasies of playing a strong character such as Jones.

From the moment that she stepped off the plane, audiences knew they were seeing a new type of heroine who was in many ways groundbreaking. Where else could they see a tall African American woman with such finesse and an air of regality ordering the men around her to destroy poppy fields while admiring her beauty and poise? Additionally, where else could they envision a heroine who showed up at a dirt bike race in a red turban, a low-cut red blouse and spiked boots, demonstrating a coolness while chasing down another character she wanted to question. Such scenes illustrated the appeal of Cleopatra Jones for Dobson did not take the character seriously in the sense that she saw the role as groundbreaking, but rather it seemed that Starrett and writer Julien played on the campiness of Cleopatra to convey a message that glamour belied a heroine who, while living in a penthouse, driving a sports car with personalized tags, and working undercover as a CIA agent, was true to her origins and wanted to eradicate crime in her neighborhood.

If Dobson's Cleo possessed a cool demeanor, Shelley Winters' Mommy, her nemesis, was the polar opposite. In contrast to Cleo, Mommy constantly berates those around her, particularly her henchmen. Shortly after Cleo emerges onscreen, a few scenes later, the audience is introduced to a volative Mommy, who shrieks when she finds out that Cleo has ordered the poppy seeds destroyed. She screams that "black bitch"[33] while sporting a red wig, belittling the men around her who serve as little more then a sounding board and, at times, physical board for Mommy to release her frustrations. While it is interesting to see that in both of Dobson's movies, her nemesis are women, the contrast in personalities is striking. Both Winters' Mommy and Stella Stevens' Dragon Lady in *Cleopatra Jones and the Casino of Gold* are stereotypical representations of lesbians. Mommy is presented as a lecherous woman who cannot keep her hands away from the women around her and leers at them while barking orders to her henchmen.

As was the case with Grier's earlier heroines, the male characters are made to appear very inept and unable to perform the tasks that are traditionally associated with masculine qualities. When Mommy's men are ordered to kill Cleo at the airport, they botch the job and she disposes of them quickly and efficiently. In fact, Cleo manhandles every man whom she comes into contact with, particularly when she is attempting to break the case and informants seem unwilling to cooperate. In that sense, critics' suggestions that she was reinforcing negative stereotypes of African American women is correct. A strong argument can be made that by rendering the men around her ineffectual, she was an updated version of the Sapphire stereotype, the black woman who possessed a fiery tongue, reminiscent of Sapphire on the old *Amos 'n' Andy* television series.

Yet, like Grier's Coffy, Foxy Brown and Friday Foster and to some extent Sheba, Dobson's Cleo adopted a softer stance when surrounded by people she had a deep attachment to — particularly her boyfriend.

For the most part, *Cleopatra Jones* received positive reviews upon its release, but the sequel's reception opened to savage reviews. *Cleopatra Jones and the Casino of Gold* (1975) was disastrous on many levels when it appeared in theaters. By that time, interest in blaxploitation movies had waned, particularly when studios discovered that urban audiences would pay to see movies outside of the genre. Moreover, the massive proliferation of blaxploitation movies with little thought to characterization and storylines soon reduced the genre to formulaic with over-the-top caricatures of every

"Beautiful, but deadly": Dressed to kill figuratively and literally, Cleo (Tamara Dobson) prepares to enter the dragon lady's lair.

stereotype imaginable. In many of these movies, African American men became pimps, drug peddlers and corrupt politicians who extracted money from the community they served. While African American women became prostitutes who eagerly peddled their bodies, Caucasians were presented as bigots, gay women were butches and men effeminate. Few were spared the indignations and misconceptions about race, gender, class or sexuality in the genre.

What was once deemed a radical departure in filmmaking for African Americans had by 1975 become a subject of ridicule, so much so that even African American actors in the genre when attempting to distance themselves from the movies.

Lackluster Sequel and Negative Reviews

For these reasons, *Cleopatra Jones and the Casino of Gold* was not successful and arguably may have played an integral role in Dobson's inability to move beyond a character that in 1973 seemed like a breath of fresh air for many African American audiences, particularly women. The bad publicity that Dobson received may also have affected her career adversely. At this point, Dobson was the star of the movie and received top billing, yet Cleo shared a lot of screen time with an Asian character played by actress Tammy Lee. Without knowing Tennant's intention in the creation of this new partner, the subtle message appeared to be that Cleo was no longer the tough, independent heroine of 1973. Now she needed the assistance of someone to help her solve a crime whereas, in the first movie, everyone took a backseat to her.

Ironically, allowing Dobson more input on shaping Cleo may have been a detriment. Similar to Winters' Mommy, Cleo's wardrobe was extremely flashy. The outfits Dobson wore in the movie did not seem overly extravagant. In contrast, Cleo's fashions in *Cleopatra Jones and the Casino of Gold* bordered on the absurd and she became a larger-than-life figure — a comical caricature to whom audiences could not relate on any level. If the argument in 1973 was that African American women could not identify with her, in 1975, Cleo had undergone a drastic transformation from action heroine to a persona who was reduced to comedic status. The costumes, lackluster plot, and addition of a partner diminished Cleo and moved Dobson's character further away from her ground breaking status as of one of the first action heroines in mainstream popular cinema

In spite of the softening of her later characters, Grier was able to keep some semblance of the tough-minded, empowered, independent woman who is physically adept at taking care of herself and those around her, but Dobson's Cleo was unable to maintain similar attributes. Yet, some reviewers felt that Cleo had maintained her iconic status as an action heroine in the sequel. Kevin Thomas, a reviewer for the *Los Angeles Times*, wrote, "[O]f more interest as sociology than art, this Warner release is a time-capsule as a women's lib fantasy—scarcely ever has there been a tougher, steelier woman than Cleopatra on screen."[34]

Whether or not it was warranted, Dobson received bad publicity before the release of the sequel. She admitted to "having had a rough time during the three months she was in Hong Kong because of the weather and a communications gap" between the locals on set and herself. Because of the troubles, she stopped speaking to Bill Tennant, the producer of the first *Cleopatra Jones*, and the first director was replaced.[35] Yet, Warner Brothers believed that the sequel would be as successful as the first movie and rewarded Dobson with top star billing, a higher salary and spent over $500,000[36] to promote the movie. Though the *Sepia* interview suggested that *Cleopatra Jones and the Casino of Gold* would be successful, it was a box office failure and suffered harsh reviews.

Reviewer Derek Elley of *Films and Filming* wrote, "[T]he real start of the picture, when she is on-screen, is T'ien Ni, outclassing Dobson in both personality and grace—whether in blue jeans, bath-robe or spectacular white cheongsam."[37] Todd McCarthy wrote, "[T]he lack of a romantic angle makes Cleopatra Jones too cool to engender much audience warmth or identification, especially in this sort of genre piece."[38]

Cleo works with a partner, Mi Ling Fong who assists her in closing Stella Stevens' Dragon Lady drug operation while simultaneously rescuing two friends from the old neighborhood who have the misfortune of crossing Dragon Lady's path. It is the rescue of her two friends that leads Cleo to Hong Kong in the first place. While there appeared to be some divide among critics as to whether or not the sequel was better, the box office gross for the movie was less then stellar. In fact, *Cleopatra Jones and the Casino of Gold* performed poorly and Dobson appeared in only two movies after 1975, returning for awhile to her fashion roots before disappearing from public view altogether.

Stevens' Dragon Lady was not as charismatic as Winters' Mommy. Both villainesses reinforced negative stereotypes of lesbians. Mommy was too unfeminine, lecherous in her affectations towards other women by always surrounding herself with model types and placing her hands on their buttocks; Dragon Lady was the extreme opposite—a cool, collected, glamorous blonde who was affectionate towards other women, but also lecherous at times. Additionally, like Mommy's henchmen, the men who worked for Dragon Lady were inept at taking care of business.

It is uncertain as to why Tennant incorporated a partner for Cleo for it was clear from the first movie that Cleo did not need assistance despite the cultural barriers she would have faced traveling abroad. It was to the detriment of Dobson's character to add a counterpart even with the plausible storyline because one of Cleo's greatest attributes from the first movie was her adeptness and cleverness to outwit her nemesis. Her attire distracts from her action heroine status, particularly when Cleo is juxtaposed against her partner Mi Ling in their fighting sequences with Dragon Lady's henchmen and the villainess herself.

Unlike the dramatic entrance of *Cleopatra Jones*, in *Casino of Gold*, Cleo's initial appearance is more understated, with only her clothing attire and makeup underscoring her significance as the heroine. She arrives in Hong Kong, on a mission to save her two friends from the neighborhood whom have gone undercover as to obtain information on Dragon Lady's drug business. After learning of the kidnapping of her two friends, Cleo arrives wearing a plaid suit with a hat and enough eye makeup to remind the audience that she is Cleopatra Jones, a fashion model–undercover secret agent.

In her first fighting scene, Cleo is caught off guard by several men as she is attempting to find information on her friends. In typical Cleo fashion, she single-handedly takes care of them with plenty of karate chops while getting hit a few times as she exchanges blows with them. As she is about to receive a fatal knife wound, Mi Ling arrives and kills the last henchman. This scene demonstrates *why* Dobson's character was so appealing in the first movie. By adding karate chops, the studio could appeal to the audience segment that showed a growing interest in martial arts movies, particularly with the arrival of Bruce Lee's *Enter the Dragon* (1973). *Cleopatra Jones and the Casino of Gold* was more violent as the director combined martial arts with machine guns. Thus, Cleo uses more ammunition in the sequel then she does in the first. There are plausible explanations as to why she uses more guns in the sequel. One possible explanation is that by 1975 the proliferation of detective movies was so great that the studio felt they had to cater to a segment of the audience who craved gratuitous violence. Secondly, to really make Cleo the female version of the James Bond required the use of more handguns. Also, using more handguns may have demonstrated that while Cleo had a preference for martial arts, when necessary she was not averse to using ammo to achieve her goal. Dobson's character carried and used a handgun in *Cleopatra Jones*; she used it more frequently in the sequel.

Her counterpart, Mi Ling, is perfectly capable of holding her own against the villains and in fact helps Cleo out of precarious situations a few times. In the sequel, Dobson is clearly more physical, performing a variety of karate chops and using a machine gun when necessary. The fighting

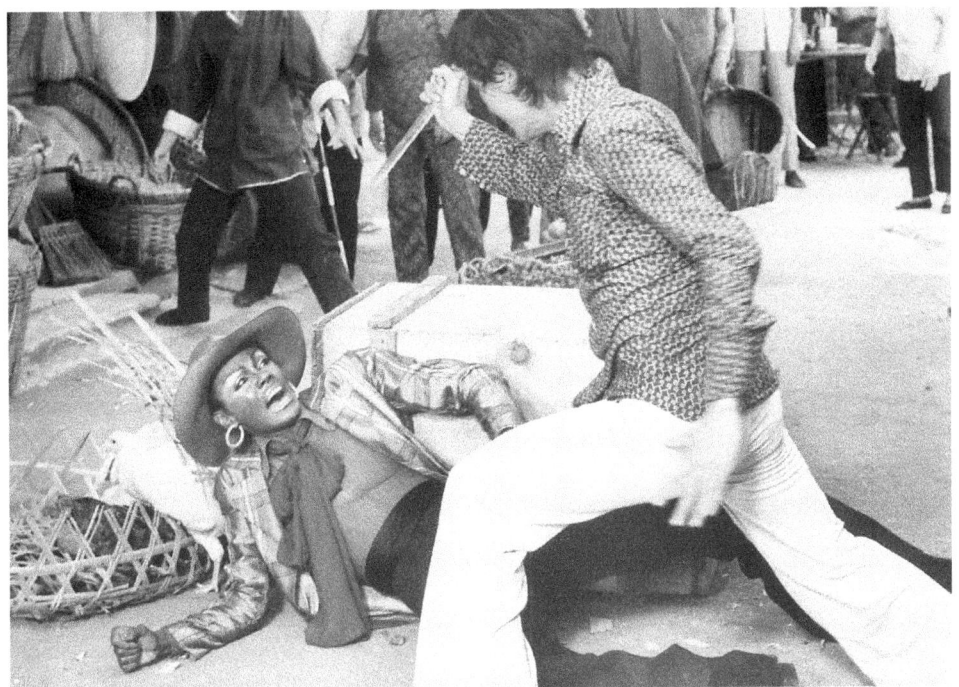

"Trouble in Hong Kong": Cleo (Tamara Dobson) battle villains in Los Angeles and halfway around the world in Hong Kong.

sequences are more elaborately staged in *Casino of Gold* than *Cleopatra Jones* and in fact a better demonstration physically of Cleo's action heroine status. The missing element is Cleo's boyfriend and the communal concern for the old neighborhood. Although she arrives in Hong Kong with the task of finding her two friends from Los Angeles, the sense of helping the community is not the focus in this movie.

On the other hand, the fighting sequences are dazzling and her nemesis, Dragon Lady, is more toned down then Shelley Winters' Mommy. Stevens portrays a calculating villainess who, instead of getting angry at her cohorts' ineffectiveness, decides to eliminate the problem herself. The first and final confrontation between Cleo and Dragon Lady is orchestrated on the same level of the sequence in *Cleopatra Jones* between Cleo and Mommy. The final Cleo-Mommy confrontation occurs in a junkyard where Cleo easily prevails via a few karate kicks whereas in *Casino of Gold*, Dragon Lady presents a formidable foe to others, but is quickly disposed of by Cleo.

Still, Dragon Lady is more formidable then Mommy in that she orders her henchmen to take care of people, but has no qualms about eliminating the competition herself if necessary. This is illustrated in one scene where she dons a hat, with a black scarf underneath, pants and a shirt and enters a "ring" surrounded by sharp blades carrying a sword to battle another nemesis — Jimmy Chen. After a little bit of a struggle, she disposes of him with ease and returns to her casino in a gown. This scene, as well as the scene with Cleo and Mi Ling battling and effectively handling henchmen, illustrates how women, at least in these films, have the upper hand as the men around them seem ineffectual at resolving conflicts. On one level, that is why these particular films are so interesting: because they represent one of the few times where women in general (action heroines in particular) are either on equal footing or, in some cases, a step ahead of their male counterparts. The trait that the Winters and Stevens villainesses share is that they control the biggest heroin operation in their respective locations. Mommy is based in Los Angeles while Dragon Lady owns a casino that is actually a front for her operation in Hong Kong. In keeping with blaxploitation movies, particularly those centered on Grier and Dobson, the main villains appear to be women, especially in Grier's best effort in the genre (*Foxy Brown*) and both of Dobson's features.

As previously noted, reviewers did not give *Cleopatra Jones and the Casino of Gold* excellent ratings. Some critics looked at it favorably, but most were less than kind. Todd McCarthy noted "a somewhat cartoonish quality characterizes the otherwise tiresome parade of kung fu fights, swordplay, gun battles and car chases, indicating that a tongue-in-cheek attitude may have been intended, but the resultant entertainment dividends are minimal regardless."[39] Despite a poor review, McCarthy credits Tamara Dobson *and* Stella Stevens. He noted, "[A]ny impact the film makes can be attributed to the leading women."[40]

In spite of the material provided to them, Grier and Dobson had the ability to take a character written and created by white producers and make her marketable as well as give the action heroine a persona that was later repeated several times on television shows as well as in popular movies.

Like Grier's later heroines Sheba Shayne and Friday Foster, Dobson's sequel is less interesting and, in many ways, less revolutionary then her 1973 movie. Part of that can be attributed to the fact that by 1975, audiences' appetite for blaxploitation movies had waned considerably. The genre was ending, which spelled an end to the careers of many African American actors including Tamara Dobson. Also, while Dobson made have had more control over Cleo's persona, the costumes and outlandish eye makeup took away a part of Cleo's personality in the first movie because now she did not appear to be a woman that many African American women could relate to on any level. Although the characteristics of an independent, empowered, career-oriented woman with the ability to physically handle men or women and a demeanor that made Cleo appealing in *Cleopatra Jones* remained very much part of Dobson's heroine in the sequel, it was not enough by 1975; studios were no longer producing blaxploitation movies in quantity and were in fact moving towards another genre that would displace blaxploitation altogether — the martial arts movie. The sequel clearly "diminished the potential of a towering Tamara Dobson in Hollywood."[41]

In addition to the reasons listed above, film scholar Jennifer DeVere Brody notes, "In the two years between 1973, when *Cleopatra Jones* was released, and 1975, the release date of *Casino*, racial as well as sexual politics changed."[42] Black Feminist criticism had become a critical practice sanctioned by and produced in the academy, and so-called black feminist practice flourished.[43] The explicit, self-named political movement known as "black feminism," whose existence was essentially inchoate in the early 1970s, began to be articulated clearly after 1972, as did an explicitly black lesbian feminism.[44] In essence, by 1975, black feminism had grown as a theoretical framework in which African American women could voice and critique the images of black women in American culture. Although I have previously noted that I am using some elements of black feminism to analyze the images of black action heroines, many black feminists in 1975 would have had similar concerns about the portrayal of African American women in blaxploitation movies as did other black intelligentsia. Their problems with heroines such as Dobson's would extend to seeing Cleo portrayed as a one-dimensional character created by a black screenwriter, but with little agency of her own. I tend to disagree with such an assessment and believe that although Dobson herself might not have had full control over how her onscreen heroine was portrayed, by the second film, she had enough of a voice to outline which direction Cleo should take. And, as Brody writes, "Dobson did her own makeup."[45]

Dobson's Demise

After the disastrous sequel, Tamara Dobson appeared in a small role with Redd Foxx in *Norman ... Is That You?* (1977). By 1979, she had returned to her modeling roots and only made one more movie in the early 1980s before disappearing from Hollywood and what appears to be the fashion world as well. An outspoken Grier had more range as an actress and was able to slowly build a career outside of the blaxploitation genre. Those

African American actresses who found themselves typecast because of blaxploitation films were unable to earn a living in movies or television. It was unfortunate for Dobson, who began with such promise in a role that defined her and yet confined her as an actress. Ironically, the role of Cleo made her a star and served as a groundbreaking role for African American actresses. It also became a vehicle with which women in general redefined the action narrative that had for years been strictly confined to white actors.

However one chooses to critique the studios' motives, it was apparent that while the mammy, the exotic other, Aunt Jemima and Sapphire images were still on display, an alternative image of beauty representing neither category had emerged thanks in large part to the civil rights movement and African American women in the forefront of the movement. By the 1970s, hairstyle options for African American women were limitless, and arguably Dobson's choice of style could have been simply a fashion statement rather than a political critique. Nonetheless, she altered the traditional movie portrayal of African American female beauty by presenting a character for the film community and beyond to see and for the African American community to emulate. Dobson's Cleo and Pam Grier's heroines continued to expand pre-existing definitions of beauty and change old, widely accepted screen stereotypes created for black women. An added dimension for both Grier and Dobson was their ability to "become stars, without the benefit of studio promotional machinery, by playing the kinds of roles no white woman ever played."[46] Gateward sums up Cleo's style well when she adds, "Though Jones was never presented as a member of the under or working class—given the car she drives and her fabulous, ever-changing wardrobe, she still sees herself as part of the community, moving easily in the environs and interacting with the citizens."[47] This was the essence of Dobson's heroine.

5

Love That Woman and Watch the Dynamite

Of the African American actresses who portrayed action heroines, Teresa Graves was the *most* recognizable because of her previous work on television. Unlike Pam Grier and Tamara Dobson, Graves was able to reach a larger audience because her character Christie Love appeared in an ABC movie of the week that was turned into a television series (*Get Christie Love!*). Additionally, Graves had the distinction of being the first actress to have a successful television series that focused on a woman detective. As noted in the introduction, the formula wasn't new and had been tried with little success in the 1950s and 1960s. I concur with Philip Green's assessment that Graves' character was "the most unexploitative use of a black hero or black heroine."[1] I have included her as part of the discussion on blaxploitation action heroines, however, because by the time her television series appeared in 1974, the genre was showing signs of strain. Unlike the other actresses, Graves had significant input into her character's development from the beginning. (Grier and Dobson later achieved a greater voice in the development of their respective characters and storylines because of the success of *Coffy* and *Cleopatra Jones* respectively.)

Although *Christie Love* only lasted one season, it spawned many successful television series that centered on women as detectives or working for a private detective agency with the most famous being *Charlie's Angels*, closely followed by Angie Dickinson's *Police Woman* and many more.

Of the action heroines in blaxploitation films, Christie Love was the

"Here's the plan!": Christie (Teresa Graves) and her boss (Harry Guardino) go over plans to infiltrate and break up a drug ring.

most accessible because Graves portrayed her as a woman just doing her job as a detective without the secret operative of a Cleo and without the revenge motif of Coffy and Foxy Brown. Clearly, all of the action heroines had their strengths and weaknesses. To effectively play to a movie-going audiences required a fleshing out of the character that would be limiting in a television setting. To be fair to each actress, the comparisons of who was a better action heroine is not at issue since each heroine had attributes that made her unique from her counterparts and yet, all shared characteristics. Regardless of the weak storylines and under-developed characters, the heroines shared two familiar motifs. First, each actress brought her experiences as an African American woman and actress to her heroine whether she intentionally set about doing so or not. Second, Grier, Dobson, Graves and Bell's heroines shared a sense of helping their community whether that meant working within the law as was the case with Cleo and Christie Love, or outside of it as Coffy, Foxy Brown, Sheba Shayne and Diana "TNT" Jackson did.

Before her television series, Graves performed for one year in 1968 on Rowan and Martin's *Laugh In*, a comedic television series that often offered social and political critiques via comedy sketches. According to a press department biography, Graves was born in Houston, Texas, but moved to Los Angeles with her parents and older siblings when she was five years old.[2] After *Laugh In*, she made a special appearance on one of Bob Hope's specials and developed a nightclub act in which she became a top single attraction.[3] Additionally, she appeared frequently on game and talk shows while also performing in nightclubs. Prior to *Get Christie Love!*, Graves "did a pilot with Flip Wilson that never aired and another pilot—*Keeping Up with the Joneses*—that never sold."[4]

Graves appeared in two blaxploitation films, one with Fred Williamson titled *That Man Bolt* and another, *Stone*. These roles were designed to change Graves' prevailing image from sass to sex.[5] In the film *Vampira* she played Countess Dracula opposite David Niven's Count Dracula. As the countess, Graves wore a number of revealing outfits that displayed a lot of cleavage; this embarrassed her later, after she became a Jehovah's Witness. Introduced to Jehovah's Witness by her sister Peggy, Graves converted shortly after her series began. In an interview with *Ebony*, Graves said, "she started Bible discussions with Peggy originally with the intention of disputing her arguments but ended up being won over herself."[6]

In November 1973, the actress-singer-comedienne was signed by producer David Wolper for the title role in *Get Christie Love!*[7]; it is not inconceivable that television producers may have gotten the idea for a movie and subsequent series about a woman detective from seeing the success of *Coffy* and *Cleopatra Jones*, both of which were released in 1973 within a month of each other.

Graves was not the first choice to portray Christie Love in the television series. The December 1974 issue of *Ebony* noted, "[T]he role was originally offered to Cicely Tyson, but when she bowed out at the last minute with a foot injury [and subsequently took the role in *The Autobiography of Jane Pittman* for which she won an Emmy], the show was almost abandoned until somebody remembered Teresa."[8] Graves brought a sense of light-heartedness to Christie Love in part because of her own comedic background and also because such a trait may have been better suited for a television feature rather than a theater-length movie.

Richard Roundtree's *Shaft* (1971) became a television series after its theatrical release and was unsuccessful for many reasons, among them the lack of cool persona exuded by his Shaft theater counterpart. Turning *Get Christie Love!* into another blaxploitation film specifically for theaters would not have worked for similar reasons. Graves' bubbly personality as Christie may not have sustained movie-going audiences. In addition, as an action heroine, Christie was not as violent as Grier's Coffy and Foxy Brown or as sophisticated as Dobson's Cleo. She was a "superhip policewoman"[9] in the words of series executive producer David Wolper. Thus, it is not inconceivable that television producers such as Wolper saw the success of Grier and Dobson's heroines and decided that an action heroine for the small screen would work as well.

By the time the series premiered, Graves was deeply immersed in her religious faith and refused to perform scenes that involved wearing suggestive clothing or scenes requiring a violent response to another character. In the *TV Guide* issue of November 16, 2002, after Graves' tragic death in a housefire, Wolper recalled "her coming to his office and giving him a list of what she would no longer do as Love, including knock off bad guys or sexually entice men."[10] Her stance was a far cry from the television movie in which Christie appears in the first scene wearing a short skirt with a matching blouse, a wig and fur coat, working undercover as a prostitute.

Graves was extremely committed to her faith and had stipulations written into her contract such as the ones noted by Wolper that called for work to end at "5 p.m. ... two days a week to attend Jehovah's Witnesses meetings."[11] Whether or not the restrictions in her contract played a role in the demise of *Get Christie Love!* I do not know. According to *Ebony*, the show was made on a relatively low budget and offered nothing really new in its genre, with the exception that Graves was black and a lady. *Christie* depended virtually entirely on the drawing appeal of the star.[12] While the movie showed a more physical Christie Love, by the time the series aired, Graves had requested that the producers tone down the violence.

In her contract, Graves stipulated that Christie refuse to "kill anybody on the show, never tells a direct lie (although she may assume undercover identities) and utter no profanity."[13] These stipulations may have played a part in the series' demise. When interacting with her superiors or criminals, Christie was more relaxed and light-hearted than her film counterparts. Yet, in the initial movie, she displayed many of the violent attributes and some of the superhuman strength of Grier and Dobson's heroines by delivering karate kicks that rendered others powerless and wrestling a gun away from a man twice her size (he ultimately fell to his death in the scene). She stated, "It was a little much. Of course, there's got to be some violence. But I really don't like the word."[14]

"You're under arrest, Sugah" (a line taken from the movie *Get Christie Love!* starring Teresa Graves and Harry Guardino). Christie (Teresa Graves) strikes a pose with badge in hand.

Even without Graves' stipulations, she would not have had the flexibility enjoyed by Pam Grier and Tamara Dobson on the big screen. Still, a detective show without *any* violence, particularly when competing against other shows starring actors whose characters incorporated violence into the storylines, did not help Graves' series and contributed to the decline in ratings and subsequent cancellation in 1975.

I have noted the growing disenchantment with blaxploitation despite the fact that Pam Grier's biggest film at the time was released in 1974. Studios often seize on a novelty and mass produce it to the point that audiences no longer care about the characters or the storylines. Television audiences like film audiences may have grown weary of seeing African American actors in roles that differed substantially from previous typecasts, but lacked depth. Richard Roundtree's Shaft is an excellent example of a character who succeeded in film, but was unsuccessful on television for a number of reasons. Audiences may have enjoyed seeing a cool character on the large screen, but tuning in every week to watch the same formula (especially with a sanitized version of Shaft which was created to make the character more palatable to television producers) did not work. Teresa Graves' Christie Love did not suffer the same fate for the character was created for an ABC television movie before becoming a series and received enough interest from the television audience to warrant producing a show around her. However, like Shaft, Christie Love was not interesting to an audience who had seen big-screen versions of the same characters. The more vocal Graves became about the direction of her character, the less exciting Christie Love became until the series was almost comical.

Ironically, the same audience that may have been tired of these types of storylines responded enthusiastically to white actresses playing detectives. To my knowledge, there have not been studies done to determine the racial and ethnic groups that tuned in to watch these particular series. It would certainly be interesting to see whether Angie Dickinson's character appealed to African American and white audiences alike. It does appear that with Aaron Spelling at the helm, Dickinson's series (as well as the succession of series that followed in the 1970s and later) featured characters created with more care. This was not the case for Teresa Graves. Instead, producers operating on a low budget had no time to invest in creating an interesting, dynamic character that happened to be an African American woman in a position of authority.

An African American woman playing a detective on a television show was revolutionary given the historic representations of African American women on film and television. For many years, the only roles on television available to African American actresses were those of a servitudinal nature until the 1960s when the landscape of television changed with the appearance of Diahann Carroll as a nurse in *Julia*, Nichelle Nichols as Lt. Uhura on *Star Trek* and Gail Fisher as Mike Connors' executive assistant on the detective show *Mannix*. Further underscoring how pivotal Graves' role was in opening doors for actresses to play detectives and in showcasing African American actresses in roles beyond the stereotypes found on such television shows as *Good Times* with Esther Rolle, she was nominated for a Golden Globe as Best Actress in a television drama in 1975.

In television ads promoting the series, Christie Love was billed as "beauty, brains and a badge"[15]— a billing that would become a staple in selling television audiences on a detective series that focused on women in starring roles. Famous television producer Aaron Spelling relied on captions similar to Graves' *Christie Love* series to promote his highly successful *Charlie's Angels*.

Yet, in 1974 Christie Love was the only woman detective series on television and, in spite of critics' dismissal of the series and the fact that it only lasted one season, it was remarkable to see an African American heroine portraying a role that traditionally would have been played by a white actress. Unlike Grier and Dobson's heroines, Graves provided her heroine with a comedic edge, particularly when Christie found herself in potentially dangerous situations. Her catchphrase "You're under arrest, sugar" became a trademark of Christie Love whenever she apprehended criminals. Despite the insistence on less violence, Graves' heroine was quite likable. In reference to her heroine, Graves stated, "I liked her a lot. She took care of business, but she was still sassy. She was cocky at times. She was emotional. Yet she was vulnerable."[16]

Although critics were never keen on the movie, they became even less enthusiastic after the series shifted from too much violence to a "lessening of the show's original bite."[17] One television critic wrote, "[I]t has all the humor of *Shaft* and all the devil may care breakneck action of Mary Tyler Moore."[18] Yet, this criticism was typical of most blaxploitation films, including the ones made for a television audience.

Television Series

The television movie's plot was similar to that of Dobson's Cleo. Christie worked for law enforcement as a detective whose task was to track down the major drug dealer who is responsible for crippling the city with his brutality. Christie worked undercover and encountered a henchman whom she disposed of with the same grit and brawn that her film counterparts used. Similar to Pam Grier's Coffy, Christie is first seen dressed as a prostitute who is soliciting males with the express purpose of hoping one of them is a serial killer who has been menacing the city. Like Cleo, Christie worked in a system that was historically unfriendly to all women, let alone African American women. Yet, Christie was quite proficient and able to do something her male counterparts were not and that was arrest the serial killer by herself.

While her superiors were less than pleased with her performance, they could find no real problem with Christie because she was quite efficient and they soon realized that her race and gender were secondary to the ability to perform her job as a detective. In that regard, the respect from her peers is similar to that of Cleopatra Jones. This is not to say that she never encountered resistance from her peers, yet at the end of the television pilot, there was grudging admiration for her work from a gruff superior who never seemed comfortable around Christie Love, but grew to respect her detective skills. Graves' comical retorts (such as "I guess you know this means no tip"[19] in one scene from the movie where she faces danger from an assailant) also offered a refreshing change from the grim portrayals of Grier's heroines.

A common theme that brought Grier, Dobson and Graves' heroines together is their cool and sometimes aloof demeanor even when faced with physical danger. Christie lived in a modest apartment, not a posh penthouse, drove a Volkswagen convertible and reinforced the professional opportunities open for all women in 1974, particularly African American women. When African American women appeared on television, much like their film counterparts, they often portrayed servitude roles that changed thanks to Nichelle Nichols' Lt. Uhura on *Star Trek* and Diahann Carroll's *Julia*, but continued to show up on television in various incarnations during the 1970s.

Similar to Grier heroines, Graves' Christie used her wits to fashion a weapon out of things that might seem harmless at first glance. For example, Christie often carried a very large purse that happened to come in handy when she was attempting to catch henchmen. The pilot episode has Christie taking on six hoodlums bare-handed and winning, but this cartoonish aspect was toned down as the series got fully under way.[20] It was not unusual for Cleo or Coffy and Foxy Brown to perform such stunts that may not have seemed outlandish to a movie audience. However, a television audience may have expected more realism and perhaps producers thought it best that Graves' character was softer than her film counterparts for the added layer of realism and credibility. As indicated earlier, Graves was a devout Jehovah's Witness by the time the series began and would have insisted that producers do away with as much violence as they could for a detective show.

Audiences may have been able to relate more to Graves' heroine than Grier's and Dobson's because of her regular everywoman style along with the humor Graves injected into the character. Christie, more so then any of the other heroines, epitomized an everywoman of the 1970s who was enlightened by her career choice. While a few of her cohorts and superiors may have had trouble with the fact that Christie was a woman, she had the ability to diffuse potentially volatile work situations because the males around her did not want to work with a woman. A typical episode plot might involve "the investigation of a wino's murder. Christie is paired with a surly partner who doesn't think women should be on the police force."[21] By the end of the show, Christie had solved the crime and won the admiration of her superiors and her partner.

Unlike Grier's and Dobson's heroines who battle villainesses, the villain in *Get Christie Love!* (the telemovie) is a male although Christie does encounter resistance from his girlfriend. The contrasts between Christie and Helena Vargas is telling as Vargas is portrayed as a fragile butterfly while Christie is independent, works for a living and does not have the luxury of lounging beside the pool every day. After a few rocky moments, the two women forge a friendship and Helena comes to admire Christie's empowerment. This is in contrast to Grier and Dobson's heroines who did not form alliances with other women unless they had to protect them from others. Thus, Christie's friendship was another example of how the heroines in film and television differ. Graves' character may have appealed to many women beyond race and class.

Since the episodes of the television series are unavailable, there is no way to know whether or not her character remained consistent with the telemovie. However, reviews and articles indicate that the "sexier, more provocative Christie"[22] appeared before her full immersion as a Jehovah's Witness. There is little doubt that the immersion interfered with her character and television series. Although *Get Christie Love!*, the television series and the pilot, did not receive a warm embrace from critics, it served as the foundation for which future television series starring actresses as detectives and in other law enforcement roles became a staple. In that sense, *Christie Love* was historic. But, equally important, Graves' character broke the barriers of a traditionally male-dominated profession at the time — that of a police detective when women were fighting for equality in the workplace while African Americans were still building on the gains made by the Civil Rights Movement. Christie Love belongs alongside her film counterparts, Coffy, Cleopatra Jones, and Foxy Brown if only because in her own way, she too made history and helped the action heroine move from popular cinema to television, thus ensuring the action heroine's increased visibility among audiences in general. Graves devoted her life to the teachings of Jehovah's Witness and left show business permanently after the cancellation of *Get Christie Love!* Graves' neighbors were surprised to learn after her death that she had been an actress. She did not discuss her thoughts about the road her character paved for future action heroines in television, but the impact was felt throughout the 1970s into the 1980s and 1990s and now of course is a staple.

Many scholars who focus on the representations of gender in television have extended the action heroine to also include television series in the 1990s such as *La Femme Nikita, Xena: Warrior Princess* and *Buffy, the Vampire Slayer*. In some fashion, these shows arguably also owe a tribute to Graves as well as Grier and Dobson's heroines which will be discussed more thoroughly in Chapter 7. In sum, critics may not have liked Graves' Christie Love and she was subjected to criticism similar to that which Grier and Dobson's heroines received, yet her contribution to the action heroine character remains an important and one that should not be easily dismissed.

T.N.T. Jackson

Jeannie Bell's Diana in *T.N.T. Jackson* (1974) arguably does not belong in the same category as Grier's heroines, particularly Coffy and Foxy Brown, Dobson's Cleopatra Jones or Graves' Christie Love. The arguments against blaxploitation films are readily apparent in *T.N.T. Jackson*. The movie is filmed with gratuitous violence and nudity particularly on and of women, racial slurs, profanity and stereotypes of many African American and Asian characters. These are common themes in many blaxploitation movies.

Bell's character is extremely under-developed; the plot is painfully thin and overall characterization, storylines, and technical aspects of the movie are very weak. New World Pictures[23] wanted to capitalize on AIP's success with Pam Grier and Warner Brothers' Tamara Dobson. Grier made several movies with Corman[24] before becoming a star in *Coffy*. The success of Grier and Dobson spawned several imitators such as *Lady Cocoa* (1975), *Velvet*

Smooth (1975), *Black Sister's Revenge* (1975) and *Ebony, Ivory and Jade* (1976). Yet, none of these movies were as successful which was not surprising given the emphasis on duplicating rather then coming up with a new twist on the action heroine. Of the imitators, *T.N.T. Jackson* comes closest to duplicating Grier's *Coffy*. With Grier and Dobson enjoying mainstream success, producers needed a new face within their price range. Cirio H. Santiago, the producer of *T.N.T. Jackson*, decided on Jeannie Bell, a former *Playboy* model. Sexuality is used in different ways by Grier's, Dobson's and Graves heroines; however the deliberate selection of a former *Playboy* model by producers does not go unnoticed. Using sexuality to attract a young, male audience was in keeping with the blaxploitation formula. Although an argument can be made that Grier's nudity (particularly in her earlier movies) was used to advance her cause, Bell's nudity appeared as a thought on the part of producers simply to titillate audiences rather then as part of her character. Moreover, ads for the movie underscored that Bell was a former *Playboy* model.

The plot is similar to Grier's films in that Bell's T.N.T. Jackson sets out to discover and seek revenge on the culprits who killed her brother in Hong Kong. The plot used Hong Kong as the locale, but T.N.T. Jackson was filmed in the Philippines. She attempted to infuse her character with the same grittiness and street-wise smarts of Grier and Dobson's heroines, and the sassiness of Graves' Christie Love. Her heroine is the most physical of the heroines discussed in this book, preferring the use of martial arts over a gun. The physical stunts are remarkable even though many of the action sequences are unbelievable. Yet, that was the nature of the genre and of action films in general. New World could market the movie towards two audiences: fans of blaxploitation movies and fans of martial arts films. Such a combination would have produced a bonanza at the box office if the movie were successful. It would not have been the first time that a studio tried this combination. Jim Kelly starred in *Black Belt Jones* (1974) the same year that Grier's *Foxy Brown* and *T.N.T. Jackson* were released.

T.N.T. Jackson displays martial arts prowess that even Cleo would find difficult to top and, like her other counterparts, is extremely adept at taking care of herself in tough situations. For example, when she arrives in Hong Kong, she immediately asks the taxi driver to take her to the roughest neighborhood so she can began her investigation of her brother's death. He is reluctant to do so but takes T.N.T. there and leaves. Almost immediately, she is surrounded by six men who want her suitcase. She springs into action, taking care of all six men — not necessarily with ease, but with knowledge of martial arts that leaves them baffled. Like Cleo, T.N.T. employs martial arts on a number of occasions throughout the movie and seems to have a preference for it over using a gun. Similar to the other action heroines, T.N.T. is fearless in her pursuit of retribution and does not appear bothered by where her investigation might lead her even if it means her own death. This is a trait shared by all the action heroines, particularly Grier's earlier characters who stopped at nothing in their quest for retribution.

Like Coffy and Foxy Brown, T.N.T. works outside of the law and even has a disdain for police officers which is illustrated in one scene where she discovers that the woman who is the local drug lord's girlfriend is actually an undercover agent. Upon learning this, T.N.T. vows not to help her bring the drug lord (who incidentally is her boyfriend) to justice because she is distrustful of the police. T.N.T. shares this distrustful nature with Coffy. Like Coffy and Foxy Brown, Bell's character relishes her independence and thrives on working as the lone anti-hero — a common theme in many blaxploitation movies, but especially many exploitation films in general beginning in the late 1960s and continuing through the early 1970s.[25] This trait makes T.N.T. the exception to Cleo and Christie who feel that working within the law is the best resolution for seeking retribution if necessary.

Another interesting similarity between T.N.T. and Cleo this time is the partnership (or in the case of T.N.T., an uneasy alliance) that exists between her and Elaine (portrayed by actress Pat Anderson). It is Elaine who saves T.N.T. from more henchmen who come after her when she successfully fights off the first six men. Passing by in her chauffeured car, Elaine orders the driver to stop and offers T.N.T. a ride. T.N.T. takes an instant dislike towards Elaine. It is clear that she is quite used to taking care of herself and would probably resent help if offered.

Adding to the dynamics between the two women are race and class differences. Producers go to great lengths to demonstrate the disdain Diana feels towards Elaine. Class is highlighted as Elaine appears to be a woman of leisure who enjoys fine clothes, dining and listening to her boyfriend's plans to smuggle a shipment of heroin into the country. Yet, the woman-of-leisure appearance is a façade as Elaine is really a CIA agent, which has a ring of familiarity to Cleopatra Jones.

Nearly all of the characters in the movie display martial arts finesse and Elaine is no exception. In one scene, she and Diana fend off several henchmen with karate chops. Also, before they truly know one another, they fight each other, with Diana emerging as the victor. But, upon discovering that Elaine knows her identity and has information about her brother's murder, Diana forms a reluctant partnership with her.

Diana's real bond occurs with the local owner of a Hong Kong tavern who knew her brother and agrees to help her find his killer. One of the most outlandish scenes in the movie is when she is forced to defend herself against several men — one of whom rips her nightgown, thus rendering her topless. Not surprisingly, her martial arts skills are far superior and she beats them all before outwitting them by turning out the lights and "disappearing" in the shadows. It is difficult to justify Bell's blatant nudity in this scene because (unlike Grier's *Coffy* and *Foxy Brown*) no argument can be made that her character gains information which she can use later and even then, critics would suggest that this justification is rather weak. They are correct given the prevailing stereotypes of African American women in literature, in advertisements particularly prior to the 1960s and their historic representations in cinema. Yet, the argument that Diana or the other heroines served as the predecessors to later action heroines remains because first, they demonstrated how action heroines evolved and gained more control in later popular films and, second, at least in the case of Grier and Dobson, they were very early prototypes of the action heroine to come.

The ending is rather abrupt as Diana discovers that her lover is responsible for her brother's murder, and they battle each other with karate chops, not guns. She emerges the victor which is not surprising because, in an earlier scene to prove her worthiness in joining the organization, she must battle him in a match. The final scene ends with his blood splattered all over her clothes and the credits rolling. The audience is left to wonder about the fate of Elaine, who was shown in an earlier scene battling her boyfriend (who discovered that she was responsible for sabotaging his heroin shipment). In the fight, both crash through a window and it is assumed that they die.

Although Bell's film appeared when Grier's *Foxy Brown* was released and Grave's *Get Christie Love!* appeared as a television movie, it received little attention. It is clear that despite overall criticism of blaxploitation movies, *T.N.T. Jackson* is not on the same level as *Foxy Brown*, *Coffy* or *Cleopatra Jones* and some might find it interesting that the quality of blaxploitation films actually varied in spite of the complete dismissal of the entire genre by many film critics, scholars and reviewers. Not surprisingly, the reviews of the movie were not good. Critic John H. Dorr described Bell as "an emotionless actress who talks tough and looks suitably mean."[26] Another reviewer describes Bell as "a rough-talking, hard-hitting black femme who does her Wonder Woman"[27] but also notes that "Bell lacks any sense of style, chopping."[28]

All action heroines shared similar characteristics, but they differed largely because of the actresses who portrayed them. Whereas Grier's heroines, particularly Coffy and Foxy Brown, were serious, gritty and raw, later she became more light-hearted, especially in *Friday Foster*, and presented more realistically in *Sheba Baby*. Dobson's Cleopatra Jones was sophisticated, glamorous and straightforward, but drawn in a way that made it more difficult for audiences to relate to — similar to criticism leveled at super spy James Bond. Graves' Christie Love was serious when necessary, but had a sense of warmth and humor that gave her an aura lacking in Grier, Dobson and even Bell's heroines.

Bell's Diana "T.N.T." Jackson was supposed to represent a milder Coffy, but the actress lacked the depth to create a convincing and sympathetic heroine. However, if film critics can compare Dobson's Cleopatra Jones as the "female version of James Bond," then arguably T.N.T. Jackson was an extremely raw and loose version of Bruce Lee,[29] albeit, Bell did not perform her own stunts whereas Lee did. Such comparisons are problematic when gender and race become added to the discussion.

The Actresses In-Between

Against the backdrop of blaxploitation, African American actresses continued to struggle beyond the mammy and the tragic mulatto roles so prevalent in the film industry. On television particularly, black actresses could be seen in an array of roles from Nichelle Nichols' Lt. Uhura, Gail Fisher's Peggy Fair on *Mannix* (1968–75) and Diahann Carroll's *Julia* (1968–69) that offered vastly different images of African American femininity from those that appeared in film. In reference to her role on *Julia*, Carroll stated, "My show was an absolute change. Unlike its predecessors, it was promoted and produced by two of the largest conglomerates in America — 20th Century–Fox and NBC."[30]

> I don't think any other show had that kind of production team. It was a new beginning. The main purpose for those entities coming aboard was to formulate a new image of Blacks on television. It was groundbreaking in many ways. Louise Beavers and Hattie McDaniel were maids."[31]

Julia was different from previous television shows centered on black actresses, for it was the first show to depict an African American woman in a professional position who worked outside of the home (in a hospital) while also raising her son.

The 1960s demonstrated just how many advances black actresses had made from their earlier filmic representations. Carroll loved the role because Julia was "articulate and a nurse raising her only child after her husband's death."[32] Yet, she also received her share of criticism from those who felt her character was not "black" enough and from viewers who were only used to seeing African American women in subservient roles. She said, "I was criticized by both communities. Some felt I wasn't Black enough. I ended up in the hospital twice due to stress. I'm happy I was young."[33] A key point that Carroll makes and one that bears repeating is that African Americans are not nor have they ever been monolithic. The diversity of the black community has not been fully realized in film or on television and she notes, "The producers of *Julia* were attempting to show the diversity of Blacks in American, that we were not just a composite."[34] Nichols, Carroll and Fisher were highly instrumental in demonstrating this diverseness in their respective professions on television. Fisher "did not make her appearance until the show's second season, when Mannix left the detective firm Intertect and became private investigator."[35] In 1970, Fisher was honored for her work on this series with an Emmy Award for outstanding performance by an actress in a dramatic supporting role. (She beat out Susan Saint James of *The Name of the Game* and Barbara Anderson of *Ironside*.)[36] Television offered more substantive roles for African American actresses to a certain extent — roles that they could not obtain in film.

Despite the increased visibility of African American actresses in roles beyond their historic filmic representations, mammy and the tragic mulatto remained permanent fixtures. That the 1960s was an era of social, cultural and political changes is clear, but these changes (while opening up multifaceted roles for black actresses) also proved to be challenging. That mammy co-existed in the midst of the positive images on display in television demonstrated how synonymous the image had become with black femininity in American culture. Blaxploitation heroines such as those portrayed by Pam Grier and Tamara Dobson provided an alternative image in film, but could never erase African American women's association with mammy and the tragic mulatto. To some degree, the stereotypical images were lessened at least on television in the 1960s, but they returned to center stage in the early 1970s on television and never completely disappeared in film. African Americans were simply tired of old stereotypes that reinforced derogatory images of them onscreen and were seeking a change, but the industry (while responding to the demands for new images) made sure that these caricatures remained. Mammy and Aunt Jemima in particular, while receiving a physical make-over to some extent on television and in advertising, remained a fixture in television series such as *Good Times*, where we see this with Esther Rolle's character Florida Evans, the matriarch of the Evans household who worked as a domestic for employers who were never shown. In fairness,

Rolle's character was often depicted at home addressing the issues of her own family which was a far cry from earlier portrayals. But, the two-parent household always struggled over financial anxieties while aspiring to build a better life outside of the inner city. It did not help the sitcom in that Jimmie Walker's character J. J. Evans, Jr., was portrayed as a comedic buffoon. Recognizing the damaging effects of such a character and no longer able to handle Walker's character, Rolle left the television series for a year.

The television series *That's My Momma* starred Theresa Merritt in the title role and Clifton Davis as her son. Merritt was portrayed as a modern-day mammy. K. Sue Jewell describes the 1970s mammies as "contemporary" in nature who were "frequently synthesized, resulting in an African American woman domestic whose comedic ability was displayed as she issued verbal put-downs in her relationship with the leading African American male character."[37] Jean Carey Bond notes that the media response to demands for better representation on television was to increase the visibility of traditional stereotypes.[38]

Ironically, however, the updated mammy begins to see how others view her and, in the film *Hurry Sundown* (1967), "grieves for the sorry thing that has been her life as a white folks' nigger."[39] The cognizant nature that she has been nothing more then a caricature for others while neglecting her own family is a departure from the eager-to-please mammy of the 1930s. Still, the rebirth of black films in 1971 gave us a new liberated mammy in place of the old.[40] For the first time, mammy is offering aid, advice, and comfort to a black character (Diana Sands) in *Georgia, Georgia* (1972).[41] With authority and determination, she dominates the girl's life even to singing lullabies and brushing her hair. She views the singer's dalliance with a white man as bringing shame upon the black race. The catch here is that mammy's rage, repressed in over fifty years of Hollywood films, is due for deliverance. Her ultimate release is achieved through the impassive strangulation of Georgia, the confused young black heroine.[42]

With the two sitcoms, Sapphire's traits were fused with mammies to create an "updated" version of the same derogatory images that black women had fought so hard to remove, particularly in the 1960s where, as I noted in the introduction, the diverseness of African American femininity could be found on television. The fusing of the two stereotypes were blatant. On the one hand, *The Jeffersons* presented an upwardly African American couple portrayed by Sherman Hensley and Isabel Sanford. But the Jeffersons had a maid named Florence (Marla Gibbs) who verbally sparred on a regular basis with George Jefferson. As a contemporary Sapphire, Florence always got the last word in an argument with George, who was obstinate, prejudiced and was created as the African American Archie Bunker since he shared similar personality traits with him and first appeared on *All in the Family* as the Bunkers' neighbor.

Nonetheless, the Rolle, Merritt and Gibbs characters represented a regression towards the gains made by showing black women in different occupations during the mid–1960s. Thus, there is a paradox when comparing the images of blaxploitation heroines with those of black women in general on television and in film because while actresses in some movies were creating groundbreaking characters, on television with the exception of Teresa Graves' *Get Christie Love!*, African American women were not making much progress.

In advertisement, Aunt Jemima received a physical make-over with a softer hairstyle and one more representative of 1970s fashion trends. Yet no matter what style advertisers created, ultimately an African American woman was still smiling on the cover of pancake boxes.

The Heroines' Perspective

Independent, strong heroines have appeared throughout cinematic history with Barbara Stanwyck's *Stella Dallas* (1937) and Joan Crawford's *Mildred Pierce* (1945) as two examples. However, independent African American heroines were non-existent onscreen. As noted throughout the book, the roles available to African American actresses before the 1960s were servile or seductive in nature. Multi-faceted roles simply were not available in an industry where non-black actresses often found themselves competing for plum roles with their peers. Grier, Dobson, Graves and Bell's films offered another option to the mammy, Jezebel, Aunt Jemima and Sapphire roles of yesteryear. They were meant to entertain and, clearly, studio executives wanted to profit from a segment of the audience that the film industry had ignored for many years. Thus, they created these "supermacho goddesses"[43] who provided escapism for many African American women, but also showed another aspect of African American femininity — resilience and independence.

Not enough credit is given to the actresses who realized that if they were to have a lasting career in the film industry, they had to move beyond the confines and labeling of blaxploitation actress. In an effort to wrest control over the direction of her characters, Grier notes, "I was not just going out doing blatant violence.... A lot of serious moments, which showed the motivation for the violence, were cut from her early films, so all you saw was shoot-em-up. Bang bang!"[44] Jack Hill, director of *Foxy Brown*, reveals a similar struggle: "The people at AIP had nothing but contempt for the audience they were making movies for. Not just the Black audience but the whole audience that they made movies for. They didn't understand Black pictures.... I had to really fight to keep elements in the picture that I felt the audience would respond to."[45]

While I have argued that there were more similarities than differences between Grier and Dobson's heroines in particular, the differences are worth examining. Mark A. Reid writes that the heroines of American International Pictures and Warner Brothers are "made to engage male fantasies." Both Dobson and Grier have svelte, athletic bodies that are as thinly clad as their sisters' in most action film fare. The semi-nudity of both heroines de-emphasizes their ability to physically ward off villains.[46] This is also applicable to Jeannie Bell's heroine and, to a lesser degree, Teresa Graves' Christie Love. But, I disagree that semi-nudity affects the ability of these heroines to defend themselves for Grier and Bell's characters are intent on protecting themselves at all costs and if that means displaying nudity in the process, then Coffy, Foxy Brown and T.N.T. Jackson do not mind. Also, one has to keep in mind that the nudity factor is there to appeal to adolescent males. Thus the effect is one of titillation particularly since AIP's market largely centered on this segment.

Despite the opinions of cultural critics, who suggested that black women could find little to identify with in their adolescent-male-fantasy-oriented roles, blaxploitation allowed Grier to move on to mainstream roles. The negative aspects of violence, drug abuse and weak characterizations in these action films were countered by the strength, beauty, sexuality, complexity and humanity that the heroines portrayed onscreen.

Grier and Dobson used their opportunities to play empowered, liberated women in hopes of gaining other acting roles. They particularly appealed to some African American women because their characters rejected the dominant culture's ideals of African American beauty, sexuality and womanhood. However, some critics and scholars disagree as to whether or not these heroines were actually liberating for African American women. Mark A. Reid notes that on the one hand Grier and Dobson's "films ... are appealing to the male ego that has been threatened by the rise of the women's liberation movement" and also, "equally appealing to women who waffle between liberation and the self maintenance of subservient roles." Yet he argues, "The penetrating male heterosexist gaze does more to disarm these heroines than their actions do to empower the filmic image of black women." In addition, Cleopatra Jones' empowerment derives from battles with women, the antithesis of truly feminist struggle.[47] I disagree that the archvillains' gender in Dobson's films and in Grier's *Foxy Brown* lessens their characters as empowering action heroines. By bringing their own perspectives, ideas and (more importantly) experiences to the development of these characters, Grier and Dobson were articulating a feminist stand. Their feminist stance derives from the ability to articulate and to have producers listen and, in some cases, incorporate their ideas into the storylines. For African American actresses, this was certainly a monumental achievement given the lack of a voice in the film industry. Although Pam Grier in particular did not always agree with Samuel Arkoff or other producers at AIP concerning her character, the studio realized that the success of her movies gave her certain power that she would not have had if the movies were *un*successful. These films have never received critical acclaim, but they were not meant to. They were produced to capture a niche market, and they did that extremely well for several years. Film critics and scholars have remained concerned about the genre's exploitation of African American women, but in many ways, Grier, Dobson, Graves and to a small extent, Bell's heroines redefined beauty, sexuality and womanhood for a generation of movie goers and countless black actresses who followed their lead. According to Grier, "The masses enjoyed it. They enjoyed seeing a female hero."[48]

Clearly, audiences in general respond positively to action heroines, whether they appear in popular film or on television, as witnessed by the success of Sigourney Weaver's Ripley. Whatever one's feelings about blaxploitation and the actresses involved in the genre on television and in film, the appearance of a new character for women in general that subsequently garnered its own genre should not be ignored. Grier summed it up best for Dobson, Graves and Bell when she commented in reference to her films, "My movies were the first they had done with a strong woman character, not to mention Black."[49]

6

The End of Blaxploitation

Sweet SweetBack's Baadasssss Song is widely credited with introducing blaxploitation movies to movie theater audiences, film critics and society. With its sex, violence, powerful African American protagonist who shows no respect for law, and indictment of white society, it can be considered the originator of the blaxploitation genre.[1] However, *Cotton Comes to Harlem* (1970), which was directed by the late Ossie Davis and based on black detective write Chester Himes' novel of the same name and starred African American actors Geoffrey Cambridge and Raymond St. Jacques, can also be credited with introducing both audiences and critics to the genre. On many levels, the movie was unprecedented. Van Peebles made *Sweet Sweetback's Baadasssss Song* outside of the film industry and controlled *all* aspects of the film — a feat unheard of by an African American director at the time. He spent $500,000 to make a movie that grossed over 10 million at the box office and "spawned a wave of inexpensively produced films intended for African American audiences"[2] as studios discovered this new market — young, urban African Americans — and looked for ways to make a profit following Van Peebles' success. In creating a new black hero to attract a young black audience, he drew from white popular culture and from black mythology and folklore.[3] He used some of the heroic elements which white culture had popularized in such films as Clint Eastwood Westerns[4] where the protagonist is a loner who operates on the fringes of society. Van Peebles also used elements from the mythic street hero of urban, black folklore — one skilled in performing sexually, evading the police, and fighting.[5] The *Sweetback* character and the movie itself were vilified by civil rights leaders, cultural critics and others who were concerned with the depiction of African American men and women in *Sweetback*. There was a strong desire to find other "heroes" for African Americans to relate to. With *Sweetback*'s profits, the studios seized the opportunity to capitalize on the movie's success and quickly rushed to fill the void by producing films that played on stereotypes that African Americans had been attempting to lessen if not completely erase within the film industry since D. W. Griffith's *Birth of a Nation*.

Sweetback received a great deal of attention from those in the African American community who found it revolutionary and those who held it in disdain for the portrayal of African American men as hustlers, pimps and for representing African American women as prostitutes. Huey Newton thought the movie accurately reflected the frustration many African Americans felt socially and economically, but especially politically. Newton hailed it as "the first truly revolutionary Black film made ... presented to us by a Black man"[6] and "devoted an entire issue of the Black Panther party newspaper to the film."[7] Newton praised Van Peebles, but others in the African American community deemed *Sweet Sweetback* as a step backwards for all African Americans.

Lerone Bennett, Jr., a leading cultural critic in the African American community and a writer for *Ebony*, wrote a lengthy review of the film in which he stated, "*Sweet Sweetback* is neither revolutionary nor black. Instead of giving us new images of black rebels, it carries us back to antiquated white stereotypes, subtly and invidiously identified with black reality."[8] Many in the African American community rejected the movie because they felt Van Peebles depicted the worst aspects of African American life. Despite the concerns of Bennett and other film critics such as Clayton Riley (*The New York Times*), the movie struck a chord with its intended audience. Young, urban African Americans filled the theaters. *Sweet Sweetback* ushered in a wave of films seeking to depict African American men triumphant over "the man."[9]

Released just a few months after *Sweetback*,[10] Gordon Parks' *Shaft* (1971) starring Richard Roundtree in the title role was enormously successful and demonstrated the appeal of such heroes for an urban audience. The movie brought blaxploitation to mainstream audiences. Based on Ernest Dickerson's novel of the same name, Roundtree played a modish private detective who successfully negotiates the underworld crime scene and the politics of city hall, and struck a chord with many audiences. Interestingly enough, in the novel, Shaft was a white detective, but under Parks' direction the character changed. *Shaft* confirmed that black moviegoers would turn out in great numbers to see one of their own win.[11] In addition, the movie attracted white moviegoers,[12] proving that some blaxploitation films had crossover appeal. Similar to Van Peebles' movie, Parks' also received a great deal of criticism. Riley called it "an extended lie, a distortion that simply grows larger and more unbelievable with each frame."[13]

He further noted:

> [I]nevitably Shaft will be compared to the title character in Melvin Van Peebles's cinematic triumph, *Sweet Sweetback's Baadasssss Song*. That argument is already settled for me: *Sweetback* wins in a walk. Which is, whether or not you believe a painful truth (*Sweetback*) or a soothing falsehood (*Shaft*).[14]

Comparing *Sweet Sweetback* to *Shaft* is unfair since both films were made with different messages in mind. One important factor that distinguishes the two films: Van Peebles' success came from outside of the studio system whereas Parks' movie was specifically created within the industry once studio executives saw the appeal of black-oriented films. Within less than a year after *Shaft* first began playing, it had earned MGM over nine times the film's $1.2 million production cost[15] and the score composed by Isaac Hayes won an Oscar in 1971.

Although white audiences went to see *Shaft*, "blacks were responsible for the film's success. They were obviously attracted by the title character, who in his own way was able to cope with white society in a manner that Sweetback could not."[16] Moreover, Roundtree's character was less threatening than Sweetback and racial tensions were not as pronounced in *Shaft*. Additionally, the film does not promote the same heroic values that *Sweetback* dramatized.[17] Shaft works within a white system (he's a detective sanctioned by white authorities).[18] Even though he retains a keen knowledge of Harlem street life, he also lives in Greenwich Village and has a midtown office.[19] He never socializes with Harlemites.[20] Instead, he is an habitué of an integrated Greenwich Village bar.[21] His knowledge of Harlem and residence in the Village suggests that he has somehow bettered himself without forfeiting his ghetto savoir faire.[22] Similar to Tamara Dobson's Cleopatra Jones, Shaft has the best of both worlds. He has the trust of law enforcement *and* the black community in Harlem.

The movie and soundtrack were extremely successful with the latter earning an Oscar for its composer Isaac Hayes. The film grossed millions and Hayes' soundtrack "earned $2 million,"[23] eventually reaching platinum sales. Yet, Richard Roundtree earned $12,500 for playing the title role — proving that while African Americans were making inroads in the film industry by the early 1970s, as actors their salaries were inequitable. Despite the success of *Shaft* and its sequels, Roundtree had difficulty getting a salary increase for the sequel to *Shaft* and "would have received no more than 25,000 had Parks not intervened."[24]

There is no question that *Shaft* laid the groundwork for an influx of movies focused on a black male protagonist and yet Parks tried hard to remove the blaxploitation label in an interview, stating, "[P]eople sometimes mix it up with Black Exploitation film, just breaks me to my heart."[25] *Shaft* convinced the Hollywood production forces that there was a market for black film.[26] Joel Freeman, the producer of *Shaft*, also tried to distance the film from the blaxploitation label. He stated, "*Shaft* was an action film, but it was not blaxploitation, it wasn't full of drugs, it wasn't full any of that stuff, but following that along comes *Across 110th Street* and the other bunches of porns, down and dirty, we were not the same thing.... *Shaft* had some dignity."[27] Although Parks and Freeman may have wanted to lift *Shaft* out the blaxploitation filter, many film and cultural critics would not. With more rounded characters, a stronger script and solid acting, *Shaft* was clearly better then its subsequent imitators from AIP, yet it also proved that audiences wanted black heroes badly enough to accept quantity via the proliferation of movies over the quality of strong black heroes and heroines.

Scathing critiques of the genre intensified, cumulating in 1973 with the release of a film by Gordon Parks, Jr. (the son of Gordon Parks), *Superfly*. The plot focused on a charismatic character named Priest (portrayed by Ron O'Neal) who wanted to leave the drug trade, but needed one last major deal to put his criminal life behind him for good. The movie was "made for less than $500,000, did an astounding $1 million gross in two New York City theaters alone, and grossed more than $11 million in its first two months of business."[28] Facing criticism, many black actors and actresses began to lash back. In response to the plot of *Superfly*, O'Neal stated, "[T]he plot is so old hat to every kid in Harlem. Blacks are no longer interested in perpetuating the old myths. The critics of *Superfly* want to support the myth that crime doesn't pay. But we all happen to know that crime *is* paying off for some people every day."[29] James Earl Jones, considered to be an actor on the level of Sidney Poitier by many critics, said, "If they're going to put the damper on John Shaft let them put it on John Wayne too and they'll find out that there are a lot of people who need those fantasies."[30] African American audiences wanted their own heroes, but unlike white actors, black actors have always carried the responsibility of choosing roles carefully simply because audiences seemed unwilling to separate their on-screen characters from their off-screen personas. Unfortunately, John Wayne was not expected to shoulder such a burden. Nor were many other exploitation movie actors such as Burt Reynolds, who starred in a series of early 1970s movies as a character named Gator.

The most derisive comments about *Superfly* came from the Kuumba Workshop, which published a short pamphlet detailing aspects of the film that were highly problematic. As the organization had done with *Sweetback*, Kuumba took everyone associated with *Superfly* to task for underscoring damaging depictions of African Americans. Francis Ward, author of *"Superfly": A Political and Cultural Condemnation by the Kuumba Workshop*, wrote:

> [I]t exploits one of the greatest problems facing Black people by glamorizing a dope dealer, placing an unmistakable stamp of approval on his work, and is hustled off as adventure without the slightest social or politician comment on how dope has ravaged generations of Black people — and is now striking at the heart of our very survival.[31]

More anger was directed at *Superfly* because it was an African American ad man, Phillip Fenty, who conceived the idea for a story of a man who is "exciting and provocative to the Black world: the successful cocaine-and-marijuana dealer."[32] Despite protests by African American actors who starred in many blaxploitation movies, their heroes made an impression on many young urban African Americans during a period when drug abuse was rampant in the urban community. The effects of drugs from usage to selling it to subsequent death or incarceration was highly problematic in 1973 and has escalated today. At the height of their popularity, blaxploitation movies' adoration came from the same impressionable youths.

O'Neal's Priest spurred some young African American men to dress like the character, sporting a cocaine spoon as a necklace, and many young men began straightening their locks to resemble O'Neal's in the film. However, the actor rejected the notion that some idolized Priest as a role model. As part of the character, O'Neal wore gaudy attire, drove a flashy Cadillac, lived in a penthouse and had a regular choice of women, but one main girlfriend. Concerns about the depiction of a lifestyle that was filled with crime, that debased women, and that glorified certain attributes that simply perpetuated stereotypes of African American males is similar to denunciations made by many today concerning misogynist elements in hip hop culture and, more specifically, certain types of rap music. In his 1975 master's thesis on the responses of audiences to a few blaxploitation movies, Oliver Slaughter suggested "women in Blaxploitation films are seen by critics as being shallow and displayed as nothing more than ego-builders which increase black men's fantasies."[33] Given the historic representations of African American women in film, by 1973 many critics of blaxploitation were rightly concerned that the genre would temper the gains made by all African Americans, but particularly African American women in the 1960s. (It was the 1960s that began to produce a number of prominent black women politicians.)

Noted black psychiatrist Dr. Alvin F. Pouissant summed up the sentiments of what many felt about *Superfly* when he wrote, "These recent movies for the most part reinforce negative images of black people ... despite claims that such films give the black man a chance to portray himself as he really is."[34] Critics were disturbed that movies such as *Sweet Sweetback's Baadasssss Song* and *Superfly*, not to mention countless other black action films, glorified violence and only portrayed one way to achieve the American dream — through criminal activity.

O'Neal's character "was widely recognized for making fashionable the gold necklace with attached coke spoon, and as critics have noted, for contributing to the dramatic increase in cocaine use among inner city black youth."[35] Despite organizations such as the NAACP, the Coalition Against Blaxploitation (CAB), the Southern Christian Leadership Conference (SCLC), Jesse Jackson's People United to Save Humanity (PUSH) and countless other concerned activists who protested vehemently against movies such as *Sweetback*, *Superfly* and *Shaft*, studios continued to produce cheap imitations of them.

Many of these organizations were so outraged that they held news conferences to express their frustrations and dissatisfaction. Junius Griffin, who was past president of NAACP's Beverly Hills chapter, delivered a scathing indictment of blaxploitation, the actors, directors and others associated with the genre. He pointedly told a press conference[36]:

> [W]e will not tolerate the continued warping of our black children's minds with the filth, violence and cultural lies that are all pervasive in current productions of so-called black movies. The transformation from the stereotyped Stepin Fetchit to Super Nigger on the screen is just another form of cultural genocide. The black community should deal with this problem by whatever means necessary.[37]

Oliver Slaughter notes that "many critics felt that these roles are white roles being played in black-face."[38] Slaughter is correct in assessing that "the same Hollywood minds that made millions of dollars while excluding blacks are now using blacks to replenish the dying coffers of Hollywood producers."[39] Although a few African American actors and directors managed to make the transition to mainstream popular movies, this was not the case for the vast majority of actors.

In response to outrage expressed by community activists, some actors and musicians suggested that the violence mirrored what was happening in the inner cities at the time much like the same argument is used today to defend certain aspects of gangsta rap. Singer-composer Curtis Mayfield, whose soundtrack for *Superfly* grossed millions, stated: "I don't see why people are complaining about the subject of these films ... the way you clean up the film is by cleaning up the streets. The music and movies of today are about conditions that exist. You change the music and movies by changing the conditions."[40]

While organizations sought to counteract the derogatory images present in many black action movies, their protests did not spur studios to change characterizations in these movies. Instead, faced with impressive box-office receipts, studios tried to replicate the formula of *Sweet Sweetback*, *Shaft* and *Superfly* by inundating audiences with the same formula, but a poorer quality of story development.

Studios such as AIP began looking for their own versions and "took the framework created in *Shaft* and manufactured films that were appealing because they had no boundaries."[41] In *Shaft*, one does have the feeling that there were some things that Shaft just wouldn't do.[42] In contrast, AIP was not interested in producing movies with any redeeming values, instead relying on heroes who fulfilled "a long missing black fantasy that the public loved."[43] The formulas for AIP black action films included an empowered black woman protagonist, a strong black man as protagonist, corrupt law officials (mainly white), gratuitous violence, sex and nudity, mistreatment of women, stereotypes of gays, a character with a connection to Black Nationalism and many other problematic motifs that contributed to the outrage expressed by several organizations, critics and even some actors.

Despite these images and the fact that audiences were cognizant of the formula, AIP was highly successful and, with the exception of *Cleopatra Jones*, *Get Christie Love!* and *T.N.T. Jackson*, all of Grier's films during this period were produced by AIP.

The people who bore the brunt of criticism were the actors and actresses, not the studios. The most successful performer in blaxploitation films during 1973 was Pam Grier.[44] When she became a star, disapproval of her movies intensified and Grier found herself having to defend why she chose these roles. The advertisements for her movies did not help as they proclaimed "She's the GodMother of them all.... The Baddest One Chick Hit-Squad that ever hit town!"[45] More then once, Grier stated that her roles represented positive images for women. Critics believed that Grier and Dobson's heroines represented a step backward for black women and saw Grier in particular as "presenting a distorted image of them as sexually aggressive and violent."[46] However, Tanya Kersey-Henley suggested, "[I]f you look at what Grier was doing, she was a vigilante — the good woman going after the bad guys."[47]

Dobson also came under scrutiny for *Cleopatra Jones* and employed a similar line of defense by stating that her character was empowering. She escaped some of the criticism as she chose not to do nudity in *Cleopatra Jones* and *Cleopatra Jones and the Casino of Gold*, but nonetheless, she received her share of knocks for participating in blaxploitation movies.

Through the age of controversy against the genre (particularly black action films centered on violence, the glorification of a criminal life and the worries that young adults would emulate characters such as Priest, Sweetback, Coffy and many others), African American audiences responded enthusiastically. Critic Joy Gould Boyum reported that a predominately black audience watching one of these movies in mid–1974 cheered and applauded every assault on whites.[48]

The pressures on African Americans working in blaxploitation movies were significant, and yet, during no other time in cinema history had so many actors, actresses, technicians, directors, producers, writers and composers received the opportunity to work in the film industry. For African American actors, negotiating this dilemma was difficult. Had Grier and Dobson chosen not to take roles in their respective movies, there is a strong possibility that they would not have been able to find acting roles. As it is, before graduating to AIP, Grier appeared in a variety of low-budget films that offered little in the way of gaining exposure to a wider audience. At the very least, blaxploitation movies provided her with an outlet in which she might be able to move into roles of substance. More importantly, she became a top box office draw in the genre which would in turn prove to be beneficial years later. Grier, like many actresses in the genre, wanted to move beyond the role that made her famous. Yet, despite the progress made politically, socially and economically for many African Americans, the 1970s was still a time of continual change and the film industry reflected that. Historically, acting opportunities were not plentiful, particularly for African American women, and many could not portray the depth of Cicely Tyson's character in *Sounder* (1972), nor were they considered for such a part.

Gordon Parks was understandably proud that *Shaft* "opened up a lot of doors for black people" including the gaffer, the wardrobe mistress, and the film editor.[49] Some might refer to this as a small step in the progress to earn a living in the film industry, but it was a step that could easily open avenues for other opportunities. But, the box-office windfall did not filter down to the actors. Very few African Americans who starred or portrayed supporting roles in blaxploitation movies reaped huge financial rewards for their contributions, thus in this particular context, the term blaxploitation is extremely applicable. It was a precarious situation for Grier, Dobson and other actors. Taking roles in a genre that was doomed from the start assured criticism from African American organizations and yet, if they held out for other types of roles, there was a real risk of not being able to pursue acting as a livelihood (particularly for Dobson who had no acting experience prior to *Cleopatra Jones*). Teresa Graves' situation was different because she began her career in television and primarily as a singer-entertainer; therefore, she had other options when her television series ended. Increasing interest in her faith and an insistence on many changes to the series to reflect that meant a slow transition from the industry to another rewarding career in the ministry. However, for every actress who found other aspects of the film industry or left Hollywood altogether, there were those such as Dobson and Bell who had great difficulty finding roles when the genre faded.

Dispute remains about when blaxploitation actually ended, but for Grier, Dobson, Graves (although she was on television and did not participate in blaxploitation movies) and Bell, 1975 marked the end of their respective careers. Grier knew that AIP was using her as a "Black sex goddess"[50] and hoped that her box office draw would give her a voice and enough power to form her own production company. She was vocal about Hollywood in general noting:

> The people in Hollywood don't understand where I am coming from. They don't understand where I have been. They have lived in Beverly Hills for too long, and they don't know from nothing because they are not exposed to anything.[51]

On other occasions, she voiced dissatisfaction with the studio's treatment of her and other actors; this outspokenness played a part in Grier not getting a lot of roles over the next several years after 1975. Dobson and Graves also gave input into their characters and in some ways, this also hurt their careers. For Dobson, the behind-the-scenes tension between her and the director in *Cleopatra Jones and the Casino of Gold* (and other aspects of the film) earned her a difficult label as media reports focused on what was happening behind the cameras rather than in front of it. Graves' producers were more accommodating to her requests of toning down her character, but as a result the show lost its pizzazz and became a comedy, which was not the intent of the producers. Bell's acting talents were more limited than the other actresses and when studios ceased producing blaxploitation movies, this marked the end of her acting career. Thus, the difficulty of moving out of the genre and into mainstream roles proved to be an obstacle that few actresses could overcome.

Some studios may have met with organizations such as CAB and the NAACP to discuss the negative stereotypes, violence, and sex that were common motifs in the sub-genre, but did little to change the storylines to reflect more sensitivity. Aware of the racial accusations hurled at his studio for their part in blaxploitation movies, Samuel Arkoff noted,

> Because of the times—a period in which public schools in cities like Boston were desegregated and some black militants were resorting to violence—all of us making these black action pictures felt we were treading in a delicate area. Nevertheless, as sensitive as we tried to be, the black films in general, including our own, came under repeated attack."[52]

In 1973, there were few highly visible African American studio executives. Even the most racially-sensitive white studio executives failed to understand or overlooked the multi-faceted nature of the African American community when making these movies; the studios were concerned about profits rather then making a political or social statement. In fairness to Arkoff, he met with the Coalition of Blaxploitation to discuss their concerns; however, an incident involving a car set on fire in AIP's parking lot made the studio rethink a meeting with the coalition particularly when they "refused to condemn the actions of their brothers."[53] Instead, the studio used the actors themselves to justify the production of blaxploitation movies. Despite her own treatment by AIP, Grier became one of "AIP's biggest supporters."[54]

Some might view this as a little hypocritical on Grier's part, particular since she experienced difficulties with AIP. Yet, it was her earnings as the top draw for AIP (particularly in 1973) that allowed her to ultimately form her own production company so that she could produce the types of films she wanted to make under her own terms. And even her steadfast support of AIP did not stop Grier from criticizing them or the industry in general for relying on mass production rather then developing strong characters with compelling stories.

Grier recognized early on that these films were very profitable for studios, but the genre could not survive as African American audiences grew weary of formulaic story lines and the lack of multi-dimensional characters. She commented:

The white people who control this business thought Black exploitation films would make money, first of all and they thought these were the kinds of films Black folks wanted. So they said, "Give the niggers what they want."[55]

To give a clearer perspective of how profitable blaxploitation movies were for AIP, "in 1970 [the studio] had a total film revenue of $22,370,213 which was up from the $20,509,744 of the previous year."[56] By February 1973, after a year of making and distributing Blaxploitation, the revenues jumped nearly 20 percent to $424,500,043.[57] At a time when some studios were recovering from a dismal fiscal market and regaining their footing with blaxploitation, AIP (which did not share a similar financial crisis) continued to earn profits by exploiting the current trends in American culture. It was the same strategy used since Arkoff and Jim Nicholson founded the studio in the 1950s and one that ultimately proved disastrous for blaxploitation movies. As the tide turned against the genre in favor of martial arts movies and mainstream films, the studio stopped producing them and actors such as Grier and Fred Williamson found themselves dumped unceremoniously by AIP.

The decline of blaxploitation movies began in 1974 and with it the decline in the careers of Grier and Dobson. Although *Foxy Brown* was a major hit, it was clear that audiences were beginning to disengage themselves from Grier's heroine. What may have been unique in 1973 for onscreen African American heroines such as Coffy and Cleopatra Jones was in danger of becoming passé by 1974. The release of William Friedkin's *The Exorcist* (1973) had enormous appeal across racial boundaries with movie audiences. The appeal was such that studios began to note that a large segment of African Americans wanted to see multi-faceted images beyond blaxploitation movies. To compete, AIP and other studios were forced to bill actors in order to draw in audiences. Blaxploitation continued to be successful for studios, but it was declining at a steady rate. It took three of blaxploitation top actors to create 1974's highest grossing blaxploitation film.[58] *Three the Hard Way* paired Jim Brown, Fred Williamson and Jim Kelly as old friends who unite to save the black population from genocide at the hands of a racist industrialist.[59] This was one way in which AIP could regain African American audiences; however, three top stars meant higher salaries, thus cutting into the profits of the studio, particularly one that was used to producing movies cheaply and quickly.

As studios looked for ways to regain the audience for blaxploitation movies, other films that centered on strong black protagonists performed well at the box office. One such film, *Claudine* (1974), starred Diahann Carroll as a single mother of six children who attempted to make a better life for them while trying to break the welfare cycle. She fell in love with a character portrayed by James Earl Jones who had troubles of his own and was unsure of whether or not he wanted to marry a woman with six children. The film earned Carroll a Best Actress nomination. The previous year, *Sounder* (1973) earned rave reviews from critics while audiences responded favorably to the depiction of an African American sharecropper family struggling through the Great Depression. The film starred Cicely Tyson and Paul Winfield. Both *Claudine* and *Sounder* proved that African American audiences wanted to see films that did not focus on a black hero or heroine, but rather focused on family in the midst of adversity. They also demonstrated what should have been clear — the audience in the African American community is not monolithic.

While these films were heralded as positive depictions of African Americans, they too are stereotypical in their representations. For example, Carroll's character is a widowed woman with six children in an apartment tenement who constantly has to hide her boyfriend and gifts from the caseworker who visits the home. At a time when the African American community was still reeling from the effects of the Patrick Moynihan Report, one could easily make the argument that portraying an unmarried African American woman with six children on welfare contributed to the myth of large numbers of African American women "in the system." Tyson's character wore headscarves and plain clothing for her portrayal of a sharecropper's wife and while the role called for such a costume, viewing an African American woman onscreen in such garb conjured up images of the Mammy even though that may not have been the director's intent. Although some might see both films as invoking stereotypes, a more accurate assessment is that they presented another aspect of African American film — that black movies were more diverse than what audiences saw in blaxploitation movies — that there was both a desire to see other images of African American life depicted onscreen and a desire to see black heroes and heroines in action-driven plots. Thus, films like *Claudine* and *Sounder* offered viable options to the violence, sex and profanity that embodied many blaxploitation movies.

An important factor here is that in the early 1970s, many films were produced with African Americans in mind, something that had not occurred in cinema's history. In the past, Hollywood had regularly ignored the African American audience, but the 1960s and early 1970s, they needed this audience and began to make movies with them in mind. For African American actors and actresses, this meant more acting opportunities than their predecessors and a chance to star in movies that were written specifically with them in mind.

In another era, Grier, Dobson, Graves and Bell would not have been able to earn a living as an actress because their physical features did not fit Hollywood's casting system for African American actresses. Unable to play a maid or a seductress, they would have found themselves as outsiders in an industry that had already rendered African American actresses as invisible and marginal. Blaxploitation movies were a stepping stone to gaining acting credentials and experience in the industry with the hope of moving onwards. Dobson and Bell found that when the genre ended their acting careers stalled. While not part of the blaxploitation explosion in film, Graves benefited from it as television producers used the idea of a strong African American action heroine as a springboard for a series. Graves' decision to leave acting was by choice rather then being forced out by a trend that faded as quickly as it appeared. Grier continued to act sparingly in movies that held little mainstream appeal. It was clear with her later heroines in *Friday Foster* and *Sheba Baby* that blaxploitation had ended and AIP, still attempting to profit from it, simply remade her character who became less gritty, more glamorous and less interesting then her predecessors. Dobson found herself in a similar situation and after *T.N.T. Jackson*, Bell did not appear in any other films. When studios no longer found Grier and Dobson's heroines fashionable, they discarded them; in fact AIP released Grier after *Sheba Baby* and moved on to the next trend. After her series ended, Graves left and no mention was made by critics and scholars that *Get Christie Love!* was instrumental in spawning successful imitations. Since she left acting, Graves was quickly forgotten.

In spite of one-dimensional characters, there is no doubt that it provided entertainment for audiences thirsty for their own Clint Eastwood– and Charles Bronson–style heroes. Fred Williamson stated:

> [A]t the time we made our movies, heroes were needed more than they are now.... You'd see on the news, Blacks getting beat up, dogs being sicced on them, firemen spraying water on people. This was one of the things that motivated me to make action movies with Black heroes in the first place."[60]

Different heroes and heroines and new ways of defining African American femininity are what the blaxploitation gave audiences. While mammy and the exotic other remained integral to defining African American women's filmic representations, they existed alongside strong heroines who, regardless of critics assessments of their value, were indeed valued by audiences seeking a change. Tapping subconsciously into the powerful imagery of African American women who had made inroads in the political arena during the 1960s and 1970s may have served as the "inspiration" for AIP and other studios to create African American heroines who physically and perhaps, in some ways in terms of their personality, resembled such leaders. Another explanation is simply that AIP wanted to make sure they profited from the success of *Shaft* by replicating many blaxploitation movies that focused on heroes and heroines simply to attract an urban audience. Given AIP's status as a studio that focused exclusively on exploitation films, this seems more plausible.

Regardless of the motives, the movies were successful enough in bringing Pam Grier into the spotlight for audiences beyond blaxploitation movies. Fred Williamson also managed to maintain his success by appearing in a number of movies outside of the United States. In the mid–1990s, Jim Brown enjoyed a brief resurrection in Tim Burton's *Mars Attacks!* (1996). All three actors had appeared in *Original Gangstas* (1989), a movie that was a take-off of their earlier roles in blaxploitation movies.

Grier and Williamson continue to maintain a level of success in Hollywood, with Quentin Tarantino going as far as to make *Jackie Brown* (1997) specifically with Grier in mind. It was Grier's comeback movie that introduced younger audiences to her iconic status in blaxploitation movies while audiences who remembered her from the era received the opportunity to relive those days again. For years after the end, Grier sought to distance herself from the films that cemented her status as Queen of black action movies, yet recently she has appeared more willing to discuss those earlier years. Given the way she was treated by the studio when her movies were no longer profitable and the harsh criticism she received within the black community for starring in these movies, it is understandable why Grier tried to separate herself and move on. Yet, despite her attempts to reinvent her acting career, Grier's heroines had become ingrained in American popular cinema and received notice outside of the African American community. Grier's powerful female character, previously unseen in blaxploitation films, garnered the movie a lengthy discussion in *Ms.* magazine.[61]

While Grier and Williamson have managed to continue well beyond what many thought would end their acting careers, others did not. One has to question whether or not the lack of success for many actors from the period is due to the blaxploitation label or talent. Though critics disliked Grier's movies, she honed her acting skills in these movies. Clearly, as an actress she was not on the level of a Cicely Tyson; nonetheless she brought a certain amount of believability to her heroines that made her personable onscreen. That in and of itself is the main reason why she was able to move beyond blaxploitation when many other actresses experienced difficulty gaining entry into mainstream roles. For every successful actor there are many stories of many who did not make it after the demise of the genre. Gloria Hendry, another successful performer in the period with films such as *Black Belt Jones* (1974) and *Black Caesar* (1972) commented, "Some of us became bag people, some of us killed ourselves, some of us dropped out totally, and despondent, some of us pulled in and became very hateful. Some of us went to drugs and went to alcohol. It's awful."[62] She added, "When the films stopped, it was a double-edged sword because they were so right but when you see the baby going in the wrong direction and you see the baby trying to walk but doesn't know how to do it, you don't beat the baby, you nurture it."[63] In essence, while critics within the African American community were correct to voice concern about the depictions of African Americans in blaxploitation movies, meeting with studio executives and focusing on ways to bring more minorities into the system as decision makers would have helped. Lashing out at actors and actresses assumes that they have the power to institute change in the film industry when this simply is not the case, particularly in the early 1970s. Today, some African American actors such as Denzel Washington and Eddie Murphy may have the leverage to get a film made, but it continues to be a struggle and will remain so until more African Americans play an integral role in the boardrooms of the studio system. Still, there is no guarantee that good black films will be made — for like any business, the film industry is concerned with profits and if there is not a substantial market to warrant production of a certain type of film, studios will continue to replicate what is successful at the expense of characterization and plot.

In their haste to capitalize on this new audience segment, studios rushed to produce many black-oriented films with little regard for developing a cultural aesthetic for black films. Not surprisingly, the very market to which blaxploitation movies catered matured and soon grew weary of the formula. This is not unusual since the film industry seizes the moment in many cases and once a certain type of movie is successful, replicates the formula to the extent that audiences tire of seeing sequels.

Secondly, Hollywood had regained its financial footing with a number of successful films outside of blaxploitation and executives discovered that the demand for films such as Francis Ford Coppola's *The Godfather* (1972) and sequels, William Friedkin's *The Exorcist* (1973) and Steven Spielberg's *Jaws* (1975) moved beyond racial lines as audiences of color rushed to see these films. Finally, the criticism of blaxploitation movies was caustic and primarily directed at the actors who held little power in the studio system. Moreover, "it seems nothing more than an unsubstantiated myth that the black community per se rejected the black action films as being spurious, repetitive, and filled with anti-social behavior."[64] At their most flagrant, these black action films, peopled with hoods, pimps, and easy-living folks, are no different from the formula Charles Bronson, Sylvester Stallone, and Chuck Norris action features which continually get made and remade today.[65] Yet, Bronson, Stallone and Norris would never be held to the same standards or carry the burdens that black actors did then and now.

In spite of criticism by the African American intelligentsia, black audiences wanted to see heroes that differed from the asexual, non-threatening characters of Sidney Poitier in the 1960s. Many wanted to see "black players in major film releases playing major roles in stories revolving around them"[66] and saw character such as Sweetback and Shaft along with Coffy and Foxy Brown as "cathartic not repulsive."[67]

Finally, once studios regained their financial footing, they abandoned blaxploitation and in the case of AIP moved on to other movements such as martial arts. As Pierson notes, it was "not a quick death,"[68] but rather a gradual decline in interest from African American audiences and by 1975, many studios were producing blockbusters that appealed to audiences across racial boundaries. The interest and subsequent careers of those involved in the blaxploitation had ended. As interest waned, what could those actors who were not on the level of Grier and Williamson do? The ease with which studios discarded black actors when they no longer had a need for a Grier, Dobson, Richard Roundtree and Fred Williamson is disheartening, and it is easy to see why some became embittered with Hollywood. What is surprising is that the same intelligentsia that railed against the actors did not continue to press the film industry to offer more African Americans opportunities as actors, directors, producers and technicians. The films that came after *Sweetback* were Hollywood's version of what African Americans wanted to see.[69] As African Americans put down their money to consume these images, the profits went into the pockets of whites.[70] The fact that most of the profits from these films ended up in the hands of whites was a further justification to label the films exploitative.[71] The blaxploitation films only served to solidify the common perception that African Americans were dangerous, prone to violence and sexually lustful.[72]

The tragedy of the blaxploitation era and its demise is not so much that the people involved in making these films were forced to work under formidable constraints of time, money and genre, but that they could not then further their artistic development under constraints that were, at least, different, if not less strict.[73] Unlike their counterparts who appeared in "white exploitation,"[74] black actors and actresses were unable to make the transition to mainstream popular cinema largely because of the label itself and the controversy surrounding the genre, but equally important the very structure of the film industry which did not lend itself to producing movies that allowed black heroes and heroines from blaxploitation to cross over. Ironically, many of the more successful action-oriented films (particularly in the 1990s and the new millennium) have centered on African American actors such as Denzel Washington, whose ability to portray characters in many genres makes him more marketable, and Wesley Snipes, whose first *Blade* movie (1998) cemented his status as an iconic action star. In addition, Danny Glover's role in the *Lethal Weapon* series and Will Smith's roles have also increased the visibility of African American actors as action heroes. Washington, Smith and Snipes have had great success in the genre and while their characters differ from the action heroes of the 1980s (Sylvester Stallone, Arnold Schwarzenegger, Bruce Willis, and Mel Gibson), all have proven that if the story captures audiences' interest, the film will be successful. Interestingly enough, the same has not proven true for African American actresses who attempt to duplicate their male counter parts in action movies. Blaxploitation was the fertile ground for black action heroines, but despite the progress made by African Americans on the social, political and cultural landscape of the 1960s and African American women during this era, it did not help Pam Grier, Tamara Dobson and Jeannie Bell become "mainstream" stars. Once it became apparent that "blaxploitation was the fixed star [around] which all black American cinema in the seventies was forced to revolve,"[75] actresses found themselves with the same predicaments that plagued their predecessors in from the 1930s to the 1960s — typecasting and limited opportunities.

7

Aliens, Terminators and Outlaws: The Mainstreaming of the Action Heroine

Sexy, curvaceous, and seductive, the black action heroine of the 1970s blaxploitation films had a definite physical type. She was a come-hither, beguiling siren who used her wiles to ensnare the bad guys. There was an engaging element of surprise as this member of the "softer sex" would unleash her lethal capabilities. Audiences enjoyed that unexpected empowerment of the female character.

These black action heroines blazed trails for actresses seeking meatier lead roles in genres previously denied to them. After the acting careers of Grier, Dobson, Graves, and Bell subsided, audiences began to see the emergence of a new action heroine, both on television and the big screen. She could not be viewed as an "everywoman" and was, in many ways, similar to Dobson, particularly in her characterization as a superwoman who performed physical tasks effortlessly in her zealous efforts to save humankind.

Riding the popular wave started by blaxploitation movies, television introduced the transitional action heroine who, while a bit homogenous, appealed to somewhat wider, ethnic-majority audiences just beginning to embrace the idea of women in non-traditional roles. With the women's liberation movement rising to the cultural forefront came opportunities for actresses to portray more than June Cleaver stereotypes on television and more than damsels in distress in film. Indeed, the early 1970s represented an exuberant time for actors who were earning roles that were both independent and interesting.

Beginning in 1975, an influx of TV action heroines appeared in a number of drama series focused on women as police officers, private detectives, or even as super-heroines. The female characters in many of the 1970s television series starring women can be described as action heroines. While *Charlie's Angels* outlasted the other women detective series, television audiences were slowly witnessing the same phenomenon that had occurred in film — the rise of a take-charge female character who was not afraid to engage in physical combat, if necessary, but who throughout it all maintained her femininity.

Film historians have pointed to Martin Scorsese's *Alice Doesn't Live Here Anymore* (1975), starring Ellen Burstyn, and *Klute* (1971) with Oscar winner Jane Fonda as a prostitute, as movies where women were autonomous, strong heroines. I am not particularly certain that the Burstyn or Fonda characters were truly liberated, but they represented a departure from the heroines of an earlier decade and, in some ways, particularly in Burstyn's film, the heroine seemed more real in that her circumstances and her struggles were believable. These were the types of roles that prevailed in film, while television was a little ahead of studios, placing female protagonists in central, action-driven storylines.

Somewhere during the evolution of the mainstream action heroine, a powerful physical metamorphosis took place. The most obvious change was race. As the genre of blaxploitation gradually disappeared, so, it seemed, did the black action heroine. Taking her place in mainstream cinema were white actresses and, in some instances, Asian performers (though mostly in martial art films) who ironically were creating groundbreaking action heroines long before mainstream, Hollywood films discovered the character. Along the way, a striking physical contrast of an entirely other sort emerged.

In his commentary, *How to Fight Like a Girl: The Roles of Women in Action Movies*, Jason Meyer introduces the term "gender-suppressed heroine"[1] in describing the latest manifestations of the action heroine. Meyer observed, "In an attempt to empower a female character, she is often simply stripped of female characteristics. This allows justification for female violence in that the action heroine simply doesn't appear that feminine."[2]

Gone were the fertile, rounded figures that seduced earlier blaxploitation audiences. Soft, ample curves were replaced by sinew and musculature. Anthropology scholar Jeffrey A. Brown, in his Spring 1996 *Cinema Journal* article titled "Gender and the Action Heroine: Hardbodies and the *Point of No Return*," posited that the newest action heroine was basically a boy in girl's clothing, on par with the obvious female impersonator.[3] The thick

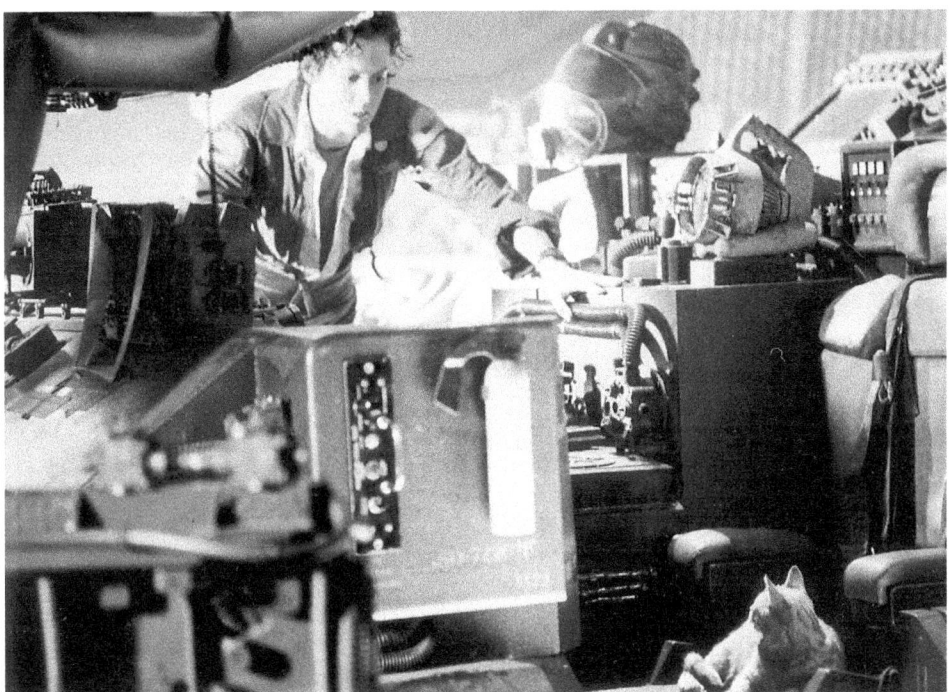

"Here, Jonesy!": Ripley (Sigourney Weaver) tries to catch Jonesy before Mother Alien has him for dinner.

waist, boy's hips, no bosom, overlaid by combat boots and ammunition clips, worked for many critics to efface femininity altogether.[4] The first woman to make it into the boys' club was Sigourney Weaver's Ripley in *Aliens* (1986).[5] Brown writes, "*Aliens* exchanged the horror conventions of its predecessor for those of the action genre and developed the already tough character of Ripley into the striking image of a muscular, gun-toting heroine who was alternately dubbed by the press 'Fembo' and 'Rambolina.'"[6]

Weaver's initiation into the boys' club, coming many years after the trailblazing performances of blaxploitation actresses Grier, Dobson, Graves, and Bell, was different in that the *Alien* series was a widely distributed, mainstream phenomenon. The traditional male-dominated action films gradually had begun introducing more female characters, not only to broaden potential audiences but primarily to validate the heterosexuality of the male leads, as well as contradict the genre's homoerotic subtext as it applied to buddy relationships.

Weaver's emergence as a strong, not overly sexualized, self-reliant action heroine in the *Alien* movies signified an evolution in the direct purpose of women's roles in mainstream action movies. Previously, women were present to support the action hero, to be objectified in a number of ways to service the action plot. In her book *Spectacular Bodies: Gender, Genre and the Action Cinema,* Yvonne Tasker notes that it is "almost cliché" in male-dominated action movies for the hero early on to have had a wife, lover, or female family member assaulted, raped, or killed, setting up the violence-justifying motive of avenging the grave injustice.[7] Women in these movies, further, were objectified as love interests for the male lead or objects in need of male protection.[8]

"It is, perhaps, no surprise then that the heroines of the Hollywood action cinema have not tended to be action heroines,"[9] Tasker asserts. They tend to be fought over rather than fighting, avenged rather than avenging. In the role of threatened object, they are significant, if passive, narrative figures."[10]

The idea of a stand-alone, fully substantive action heroine in mainstream (the operative word here is "mainstream") popular cinema really had not materialized until Weaver entered the realm of action movies with a role that become synonymous with the action heroine. *Alien* was one of the first action blockbusters to have a female protagonist, and, just as importantly, the character of Ripley was one of the first blockbuster action heroines.[11]

As has been noted, the action heroine was not outwardly revolutionary by this time. Nonetheless, when discussions turn to action heroines, Ellen Ripley is the name that comes to mind for many people. The character was so popular that she remains one of the few action heroines to have a series of action dolls made. (Although many of the television series also had dolls.)

Weaver's Ellen Ripley was presented as an athletic woman who wore no makeup. Yet there was no mistaking that, even without the makeup and clothes, Ripley retained her feminine characteristics, as evidenced in the last scene of *Alien* (1979), where she dresses down to her under-garb while cradling her cat.

Critics differed on that count, however, as Meyer has contended that Ripley "wanders sexless"[12] through an environment in *Alien* that is highly sexualized, as corridors of the alien ship itself resemble "vaginal portals."[13] Furthermore, Meyer writes, "[T]he belly bursting alien is phallic in appearance as well as perversely in action. The face-sucking alien co-opts a male stomach as a surrogate womb, raping and feminizing men."[14]

The transformation of Ripley from emotionless company agent to passionate Mother Warrior occurs gradually over the course of *Alien* and *Aliens.* In the first film, Ripley is not the commander in charge and follows the orders of Tom Skerritt's character, Dallas, in seeking out life in space. However, upon discovering that this particular extraterrestrial life form is hostile and intent on taking over the crew, Ripley is thrust into the spotlight as the "go-to woman." When the alien kills Dallas and others start to fall victim to the creature, it falls on Ripley's shoulders to save the remaining members by destroying the alien.

Throughout the movie, her colleagues reach a heightened state of panic. However, almost robotically, Ripley maintains a level head and keeps the crew members from succumbing to complete hysterics. The contrasts between Ripley and another crew member, portrayed by Veronica Cartwright, are striking. On the one hand, Ripley remains cool and very much in control, despite the fact that this alien life force is killing off the crew. At the same time, Cartwright's character begins to fall apart and suffers a near emotional breakdown before she, ultimately, is killed by the alien.

This juxtaposition of types is symbolic of the basic female struggle to achieve independence, both on and off screen. It represents conflicting stereotypes that, eventually, would lead to a deliberate transformation of female stereotypes in action movies.

A clear difference between Ripley and her earlier prototype action heroines in blaxploitation is the degree and method of constructing sexuality. In blaxploitation movies, producers used sex as a way to reach audiences by showing Grier and Bell in nude scenes. In *Alien*, Ripley's gender never was specified in the original script.[15] Emphasis was on Ripley's character rather then her feminine attributes until nearly the end of the movie. And while, there is a glimpse of affection between Ripley and the character of Dallas, audiences never saw emotions develop further than passing glances at one another.

In blaxploitation films, the action heroine was an unconstrained, but overtly sexual African American woman with a social and political message. As noted in earlier chapters, Bogle calls these heroines "macho goddesses"[16] that comprised a convenient hybrid of female stereotypes. Bogle suggests, "[N]arratives featuring the black female fighter resort to both the use of comedy and the fetishistic representation of female power."[17]

"Whilst the phrase 'macho goddesses' acknowledges the complex blend of masculine and feminine elements at work in this stereotype, it is worth exploring this hybridity a little further,"[18] writes Tasker in *Spectacular Bodies*. "It is, in part, the blackness of these heroines which opens up, through notions of black animality, the production of an aggressive female heroine within existing traditions of representation. Black female stars who have played action roles, such as Tamara Dobson, Pam Grier, and Grace Jones,

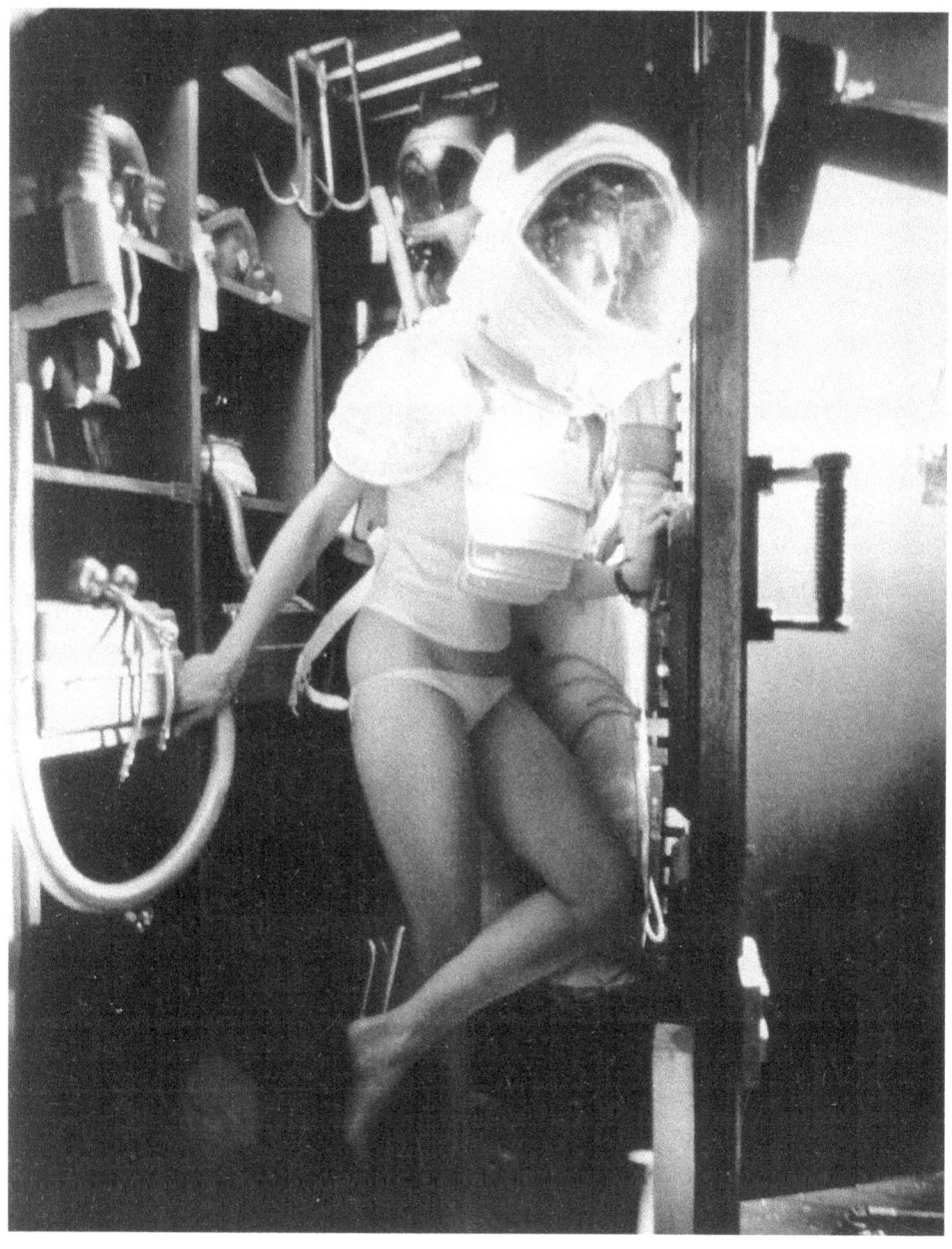

"If it's a battle you want, it's a battle you'll get": Ripley (Sigourney Weaver) puts on her gear to face Queen Alien for the final showdown.

"I have you, Newt!": Ripley (Sigourney Weaver, left) protects Newt (Carrie Henn, right) against the army of deadly extraterrestrials that has overrun an Earth colony.

often function as 'exotic' creatures within the narrative. For her role as Zula in *Conan the Destroyer* (1984), Grace Jones is literally given a tail. The meaning of the emphasis placed on animality in Grace Jones's film roles is, however, complexly linked to the ways in which her image itself has addressed the stereotypical physicality and sexuality attributed to the black woman."[19] Thus, empowerment in blaxploitation is replaced by presenting an African American action heroine as animalistic signifying a return to black women as the "other" in mainstream action films.

The positioning of Jones in *Conan the Destroyer* is further complicated by her insistence on using her features deemed exotic by some to play on this animalistic look for her role. This leaves one to question whether Jones was a willing participant being used by the studio to portray a certain type of character that many black actresses might not portray or whether she was fully aware of the problematic imagery conjured up in the minds of audiences, particularly those who remember negative filmic images of the past. Ultimately, however, there is more speculation as to how Grace Jones could have signaled a transformation for black action heroines in her own action-oriented film.

In *Alien*, the character of Ripley became a woman who was out to save mankind from destructive forces, whether man-made or extraterrestrial. Whereas she managed to maintain her femininity, as embodied by Grier and Dobson in particular who wore outfits that emphasized their physical attractiveness, fashion was not integral to the character in later, mainstream action heroine movies like *Alien*.

The emphasis on fashion by the studios did not detract from Grier and Dobson's action heroine status. If anything it enhanced it, particularly when viewing their characters as representing an alternative definition of African American femininity. They were certainly different from roles prior to the 1970s.

Even though Ripley became the protector of her crew aboard the space vessel *Nostromo*, whose computer mainframe Ripley addressed rather ironically as "Mother," she is detached and analytical, hardly the warm, maternal figure one might expect.[20] "The gender-suppressed nature of her presentation is part of what made Ripley a marketable action heroine,"[21] Meyer asserts. Grier, Dobson, Graves, and, to some extent, Bell's heroines, were what Bogle calls "Woman as Protector, Nurturer, Communal Mother Surrogate."[22] These categories appear to fit with later action heroines as well. Ripley's innate toughness is retained in the *Alien* sequel, *Aliens*, but is softened with the introduction of her added role as mother figure to the young girl, Newt. Action heroine movies often turn to a time-honored sub-

"Hold on to me!": Ripley (Sigourney Weaver) helps her comrade-in-arms Hicks (Michael Biehn) when he is wounded in an encounter with one of the aliens.

ject and motivator — motherhood,[23] Meyer notes. "Few action heroines can wholly escape maternal imagery, simply because movies seem at a loss to deal with female-perpetrated acts of protection without labeling them maternal."[24]

The use of motherhood themes to motivate and justify the "unfeminine" (by Western cultural standards) aggression and violence necessary to achieve objectives important to the action heroine is a logical and effective device.

As *Aliens* opens, Ripley is a woman searching for meaning and purpose in a life forever altered by the horrific alien experiences that have both hardened and humbled her. As motherhood is used as a device to justify her uncharacteristically male-like action heroine aggression, Ripley further is excused from the violent insanity of her situation by her initial and open reluctance to even "go there" by returning to the site in the first place. Because she is, naturally and at her core, a more conventionally female, peace-loving individual, Ripley's first instinct is not to get involved in a proposed rescue mission on the alien planet.

"It is decisively concretized when she finds Newt,"[25] Meyer explains. "As soon as Ripley scoops her into her arms and starts cleaning her off, a new character emerges. Ripley's maternalism is reserved only for the very needy—Newt as sole survivor fits the role. Ripley takes on leadership of the Marines only when they are on their last ropes." Like the motherhood role, Ripley's leadership of the Marines also was assumed in response to desperate circumstances and the acceptance of those around her amid those circumstances. Throughout it all, Ripley's deep character shined through, and she rose to every challenge.

Another strong female character in *Aliens* comes in the persona of Private Vasquez, a somewhat "dike-ish"-looking, muscular woman with tightly cropped hair. Portrayed by actress Jeanette Goldstein, Vasquez enacts what Tasker calls "the female action persona of the 'ball-busting' woman."[26]

"On waking from hyper-sleep," Tasker writes, "[Vasquez] immediately starts doing pull-ups in front of the screen, and in a notorious scene responds to a male colleague's question, 'Ever been mistaken for a man?' with the reply, 'No, have you?' before slapping the hands of her buddy within the unit.... All this posing and verbal horseplay dwells on, and comically works over, the problems of the figure of the tough woman in the male team. In order to function effectively within the threatening, macho world of the action picture, the action heroine must be masculinised."[27]

Ripley's creators made her character more palatable, more acceptable to mainstream audiences, primarily because of her culturally predominant female preference to avoid conflict. So long as she was the "reluctant warrior," she could still retain some of her femininity, albeit lean and mean.

In addition, it often is important to establish a male love interest for the successful action heroine to assuage mainstream audiences — and sell movie tickets. Due to the homophobic nature of most mainstream audiences, many narratives overtly seek to establish the heterosexuality of action heroines by providing a nominal male love interest or by linking the action heroine to notions of a fierce maternal instinct,[28] Brown states.

In *Aliens*, Ripley finds a personal connection with Corporal Hicks, who becomes the ranking officer of the Marines as, one by one, they are killed off or injured. Hicks "follows Ripley's commands as his own,"[29] Meyer wrote. "There is a romance of sorts between them. He teaches her how to use the weapons; they develop a bond. At the end, she tends to him with a gesture of nurturing love. Her leadership of the platoon is filtered through his—Ripley leads and is listened to only when she plays wife to Hicks, the Marines' Good Father."[30]

Ripley's leadership of the Marines was fully adopted only after the supporting characters perceived her in the "wife" role to Corporal Hicks. Furthermore, Ripley's adopted motherhood was confirmed when Newt ran up to her, arms wide, calling "Mommy!" It's as if a woman could not command respect on her own merits; such respect, it would seem, is directly connected to the role a woman plays and its attachment to traditional, sentimental femininity.

Meyer divides the action heroines of mainstream films into two categories: maternal and spectacular. The maternal action heroine, as portrayed by Weaver in *Aliens,* had some personality traits that fit the action heroine of blaxploitation movies. That is to say, she was concerned about others, went to great lengths to rescue loved ones or those she cared a great deal about, and fought at all costs to save her family or, in Ripley's case, her adopted daughter and what was left of her space crew.

Other images of Ripley in *Aliens* clearly paralleled themes in conventional, male-dominated action films. A prime example, Meyer noted, is "Ripley in her power loader exoskeleton, face-to-face with the Queen Alien — the movie's other Mother Warrior. Ripley takes on the Queen Alien woman-to-woman, a renegotiation of the mano-a-mano and man-to-man showdowns of the mainstream action genre."[31]

Tasker finds the exoskeleton veneer of the power loader particularly symbolic. The sheer bulk of the loader gives Ripley physical stature. In this striking image, the heroine directly enacts a fantasy of physical empowerment, one which is usually reserved for the hero,[32] she suggests. Her relative powerlessness, her physical vulnerability, is played with so that Weaver's femaleness additionally eroticizes this fantasy of power through the transgression of gender boundaries.[33]

"Whether intentionally or not, recent action films challenge both cinematic and cultural assumptions about what constitutes natural or proper female behavior,"[34] Brown stated. The same can be said of stereotypical female physicality. For some audiences, the conversely muscular and maternal heroine could be confusing. "In the world of action films," he added, "to be mannered is to be feminine, and to be feminine is to be perceived as weak."[35] Therefore, it has been almost necessary to add muscles and brawn to the action heroine, presumably to derail society's preconceived notions of feminine weakness and make the heroine more convincing and somewhat believable.

Brown has contended that the masculinizing of the modern, mainstream action heroine was seen by many early on as the equivalent of "gender cross-dressing" or assuming the role of "man in drag."[36] An implication exists, however, that, over the years, the constant reinforcement of the hard-bodied action heroine gained wider acceptance and even contributed to a culture change as more audiences began to embrace the well-toned, healthy woman as preferable to or even more attractive than the softer, voluptuous body type.

Tasker's *Spectacular Bodies* analysis concurred: "The critical suggestion that the action heroine is 'really a man' ... represents an attempt to secure the logic of a gendered binary in which the terms 'male' and 'masculine,' 'female' and 'feminine' are locked together.... However, the action heroine has also, in the last 20 years, undergone a significant redefinition in western films."[37] One of the most extreme examples of the masculinized action heroine and "Mother Warrior" came several years after *Aliens* with Linda Hamilton's portrayal of Sarah Connor in *Terminator 2* (1991).

The character of Sarah Connor already had been established as a toughened-by-hard-knocks figure in the first *Terminator* (1984), which could be described as a sort of female action heroine "coming-of-age" movie. Hamilton garnered more attention in the sequel than she did in the original primarily because her physique had changed to the point where "academic circles and women body-building magazines"[38] were pointing to her as a possible model and empowerment for women. Arguably, Hamilton received a great deal of publicity for the *Terminator 2* precisely because she added muscle for the role and more importantly, this could have been an attempt on her part to transform herself from the role she portrayed on the television series *Beauty and the Beast*. However, according to Meyer, Hamilton's role as Sarah Connor was a "cult figure since *The Terminator*."[39] Whatever the case may be, it was clear that Hamilton, as Weaver before her, transformed the action heroine landscape again. About two-thirds of the way through *Terminator*, Connor reaches a dramatic turning point when the character of Kyle Reese, sent back from the future to protect her, is mortally wounded, and she must take control. Her character achieves a near 360-degree transformation into toughness and determined self-reliance.

"Addressing him as 'Soldier,'" Tasker writes, "[Sarah Connor] takes up the role of a commanding officer who harangues a tired platoon in order to save them, a role familiar from many Hollywood war movies. It is after this proof of her transformation, and Kyle's death, which follows soon after, that Sarah finally terminates the Terminator. Kyle must die since, like the male hero, it seems that the action heroine cannot be in control of an adult sexuality."[40]

Like Connor, the character of Ripley in the *Alien* films is transformed — however reluctantly — into a true and heroic soldier-warrior. While Ripley remained, for the most part, physically consistent (lean and lanky though

"You're about to be terminated": Sarah Connor (Linda Hamilton) has fashioned herself into a tough warrior to protect her son and herself in the impending war between man and the machines.

not overtly muscular) throughout the *Alien* series, audiences saw a clear and dramatic physical transformation in Connor between *Terminator* and *Terminator 2*. Connor had survived the traumas of *Terminator* and become brutally educated — and perhaps cynical to the point of virtual paranoia — in the sequel. After psychological professionals certified her premonition of the coming war with the machines severely delusional, they placed Connor in an insane asylum, where she continued to prepare for this mechanized Armageddon. Meanwhile her son, John — the future leader of the human resistance — indulges his rebellious adolescence while living with the well-meaning but imperfect foster parents he'd been placed with after his mother's institutionalization.

T2 opened on the striking musculature and near catatonic concentration Connor embodies while exercising in her hospital "cell." In a single, raw moment onscreen, Hamilton conveyed to audiences arresting intensity, calm determination, and near clinical detachment at the prospect of her mission ahead. It was a powerful opening message.

"Her first scene gives us her wedge-shaped, muscled back far more than her face, and then the face is obscured by her straining biceps as she chin-ups,"[41] Meyer observed. "Sarah Connor is one of the most visually striking action heroines anywhere. Her visual presence easily rivals any other Action Hero or Heroine."[42] That's a powerful statement, for sure. One of the most physically striking action heroes, male or female. The standard for many years in the action genre had been exclusively male.

"As one of the most dominant genres of popular cinema since the early 1980s, the action film has done much to construct the body of the male hero as spectacle,"[43] Brown states. The well-displayed muscles of such heroic icons as Sylvester Stallone and Jean-Claude Van Damme have worked within a narrative space that presents masculinity as an excessive, almost hysterical performance. Indeed, the spectacle of the muscular male body has become the genre's central trademark, a feature that has allowed Arnold Schwarzenegger to catapult from professional bodybuilding to the highest-paid movie star on the planet.

In *T2*, it was Hamilton's chiseled physique that received the spotlight

"It's hasta la vista time" (a line taken from the movie and spoken by Arnold Schwarzenegger's Terminator). John Connor (Edward Furlong) and his mother, Sarah (Linda Hamilton), square off against a seemingly unstoppable killer cyborg.

despite the presence of her co-star, the longtime bodybuilding icon and former Mr. Universe Arnold Schwarzenegger, whose body was actually concealed by full biker leathers throughout most of *T2*. In fact, the two characters were the opposite of what would be expected by the audience, with Schwarzenegger's cyborg T-101 Terminator taking on the softer, parental or care-giver role to John Connor while Sarah Connor assumed the role of gritty soldier, protector, and strategist.

"That a cyborg Schwarzenegger can be read as the more feminine role,"[44] Brown wrote, "is an indication of how over-determined our cultural notions of appropriate gender behavior are. *Terminator 2* is a film preoccupied with discrediting surface appearances; nothing is as it seems."[45]

In addition, the more sophisticated T1000 cyborg's "fluid ability to transform his body constructs him as a feminized monster,"[46] Tasker observed. Perhaps, reflective of the rising pro-fitness era in which *T2* was made, American cultural perceptions about the ideal female body were shifting. The soft curves presented as defining the ideal female form in the 1950s has shifted to an emphasis on muscle tone in images of the 1980s and early 1990s. Nonetheless, "the muscular female body raises a different, if related, set of issues."[47]

"Whilst the muscleman produces himself as an exaggerated version of what is conventionally taken to be masculine, the female bodybuilder takes on supposedly 'masculine' characteristics," she continued "Muscles as a signifier of *manual* labour become appropriated for the decoration of the *female* body. Both figures draw attention to and redefine a bodily understanding of gendered identity."[48]

And while Connor's character in *T2* appears outwardly "pumped up" and physically strong, virtually unstoppable, the film turns elsewhere to expose her traditionally "female" vulnerability. Tasker suggests that this diversion attempts to identify an inherent contradiction between the "naturalized" and the "manufactured" body, something she dubs "masculinity."[49] In other words, although the "butch-*femme*" character of Sarah Connor defies conventional visual images of femininity, deliberately selected emotional flaws in her character seem to serve as reinforcement of proverbial feminine weakness.

"There is never anything awkward or faltering about her prowess, the single exception being her inability to gun down the inventor of SkyNet once his family rushes to protect him," Meyer observes in his extensive analysis of the action heroine. Everywhere else, Sarah Connor is visually a romanticized soldier of fortune hero, surpassing Rambo, Martin Riggs, and so many others, forceful, super-competent, and even graceful.[50]

Nonetheless, Connor was a flawed action heroine, with moments of vulnerability, irrational thinking, and paranoia. This may have been a device to bring her otherwise stoic character down a notch and make her a little more palatable to the mainstream audience that might not accept a totally invincible, all-conquering action heroine.

"Sarah is never fully vindicated by the movie; the same sorts of blindness perpetrated by the doctors are created by the narrative so invested in the concept of the male hero," Meyer wrote. "Nowhere is being a woman truly vindicated."[51]

Perhaps it is a basic societal conflict between the traditionally active male and passive female that denies absolute vindication to the action heroine. In her essay, "Visual Pleasure and the Narrative Cinema" (1975), Laura Mulvey contended that old sexist conventions die hard.

"Classical cinema conventionally portrays man as the bearer of a voyeuristic gaze and woman as its object,"[52] Brown stated. Men, Mulvey goes on to argue, are the agents that propel the narrative while women stop it; men act while women are passive. For Mulvey, the sexual difference demarcated by the active/passive split mark the cinematic gaze as a masculine look that objectifies women as spectacles to be looked at.

"But the modern action heroine is far from passive. She fights, she shoots, she kills, she solves the mysteries, and she rescues herself and others from dangerous situations. In short, she is in full command of the narrative, carrying the action in ways that have normally been reserved for male protagonists."[53]

A common representation of the voyeurism intrinsic to women in action films was evident in *Point of No Return* (1993), starring Bridget Fonda as the protagonist assassin Maggie. On the one hand, the movie echoed earlier blaxploitation movies that preserved the curvaceous, seductive woman heavily contrasted by her militaristic deftness in handling big, manly firearms. On the other, it incorporated gender masquerade elements common to newer action films.

"Maggie's initial rugged aggressiveness is tantamount to the action heroine's performance of masculinity,"[54] Brown states. "Maggie is physical and self-reliant, murdering without remorse and capable of overcoming Bob and holding him hostage as she tries to escape the agency in an early scene. This early Maggie is persistently violent and physically unkempt in old jeans and a man's undershirt. The same type of black undershirt is worn by Stallone in the *Rambo* series, Bruce Willis in *Die Hard*, and such muscular/masculine women as Linda Hamilton in *Terminator 2* and Rachel McLish in *Aces: Iron Eagles III*. This black undershirt, which has become the standard costume of the genre, is functional for its ability to reveal the hero's body. The shirt is, quite literally, a muscle shirt, putting the hero or heroine's pumped-up body on display."[55]

Brown asserts that the black undershirt not only supported Maggie's aggressive behavior but also signified her "cross-dressing" as well as placed her in context with previous actors of the genre. Later in the film, Brown continues, Maggie's black cocktail dress appears as an almost "frilly version of the undershirt.... The masculine undershirt is reconfigured as a feminine dress, and the feminine body is equipped with a masculine gun."[56]

During the movie's training scenes, Maggie uses the element of surprise to dominate her opponents. "In these training scenes, we get a glimpse of Maggie's ability to exploit her opponent's perceptions of her as a weak female,"[57] Brown notes. Owen Gleiberman, in an *Entertainment Weekly* review, observed: "She's hardly an icon of physical menace in this era of iron-pumping maidens,"[58] which allows her to cunningly disarm her opponents.

"Throughout the film, it is this image of a frail, pretty, slip of a girl that allows Maggie to catch her enemies off guard,"[59] Brown says. The character of Maggie ably depicts masculine behavior that is not totally divorced from the feminine. For Maggie, femininity becomes a means to empowerment rather than a hindrance to it. Her play with gender roles becomes another weapon in her arsenal.[60]

Unfortunately, the voyeuristic nature of Hollywood movies, as relates to women as objects, may be construed in action films as a fetishization of violence. Some men's perception of Maggie's character as a "Terminatrix," Brown asserts, "is just the type of playful, demeaning slippage between the heroine as a self-reliant character and a sexual object that undercuts the effectiveness of the more progressive aspects of mainstream popular cinema's negotiation of gender."[61]

Brown argues, however, that, in a sense, the action movie genre is "an equal opportunity offender" because heavily armed, brawny male bodies are used onscreen "in fetishizing shots at least as often as the female form."[62]

In *Tank Girl* (1995), Lori Petty, playing the character Rebecca, turns the tables on standard gender action formulas by challenging assumptions that women are objects to be looked upon while men are the subjects doing the looking. Her character basically turns fetish to folly, using humor, power, and an overt, ravenous, male-like libido to defy sexual stereotypes.

"Rather than Mother, she plays mentor and partner; rather than genderless, she plays a self-motivated woman who actively pursues relationships and is unashamed of her sexuality,"[63] Meyer observes. She is not a sex object, but she is an unashamedly sexual being. She makes jokes about sex and plays out sex fantasies with her lover but without being confined to the sex object role. Her control, individuality, and appearance forbid it.[64]

Meyer noted that, while Rebecca uses her sexuality as a means to an end, "the movie doesn't seem to use her sexuality to merely titillate the audience."[65] The female road movie *Thelma and Louise* (1991) introduced new sexual themes, including a suggestion of lesbianism among the title characters. Some saw *Thelma and Louise* as a feminist reworking of a male genre, the road movie, with women taking the place of the male buddies familiar to viewers of popular Hollywood cinema. Yvonne Tasker writes in *Spectacular Bodies*, "[F]or others, the film represented an interrogation of male myths about female sexuality, an admirable commentary on rape and sexual violence."[66]

Tasker observed that the women-with-guns image depicted in *Thelma and Louise*, some would argue, basically rendered the female protagonists "symbolically male."[67]

The film locations — traditionally male spaces or domains, like bars and the great outdoors — further suggest this masculinization of *Thelma's* female buddy characters. In essence, she says, "The road comes to signal a certain mythicized freedom."[68]

That freedom is so powerful that, by the end of the movie, both protagonists have achieved such a liberating sense of independence and self-worth that returning to their previous lives is, quite literally, inconceivable.

The mainstreaming of the action heroine in popular cinema can be seen as a delayed response to the feminist movement. It also reflects a departure from old formulas. Many interpret this, albeit cautiously, as progress for women even though the film roles often propagate competing images and stereotypes. Themes sexualize the female body or present violence in contrasting perspectives. "Feminism has proposed a rather different understanding of violence against women in relation to institutionalized male power, often expressed through metaphors of physical strength versus weakness,"[69] Tasker writes in *Spectacular Bodies*. "In thinking about women in the action film more specifically, we should consider that if women on the screen are excessively sexualized, then so is the violence to which they are subject. This returns us to the frequent repetition of images and narratives associated with rape.... The development of muscles as a sort of body armour signifies physical vulnerability as well as strength."[70]

To wit, Tasker asserts that, throughout the contemporary action genre, "images of bodily penetration abound." *T2* is a prime example as the T1000 cyborg stabs the heroine Sarah Connor with an arm transformed into a

"Bosom buddies": Frustrated with their lives, Thelma (Susan Sarandon) and Louise (Geena Davis) enjoy their newfound freedom and embrace their liberation from the constraints that have been tying them down.

blade. Whilst such images obviously draw on figures of penetration, they also bring up, once more, themes of the vulnerability and invulnerability of the body. Also, there is another interesting dynamic in *Terminator 2* centered on the physique of the two terminators. Where Schwarzenegger is buffed and looks like an imposing figure, his nemesis T1000 is, as Stephanie Mencimer notes, "the new prototype for the modern action movie… [C]ompared to the T1 [Schwarzenegger], T1000 [Robert Patrick] was smaller, faster and smarter."[71] Mencimer suggests that it is Patrick's character that serves as a model for action heroines.

Still with the success of the action heroine in all of Weaver's *Alien* films, but noticeably *Alien* and *Aliens, Terminator 2* and *Thelma and Louise*, Hollywood did not achieve the kind of box office success that Weaver had with another female protagonist in an action-oriented movie until the new millennium. There were other action heroines films such as Geena Davis' *The Long Kiss Goodnight* (1995) and Demi Moore's *GI Jane* (1997); however, their characters did not receive the reception of Ellen Ripley, Sarah Connor and Thelma and Louise. Mencimer suggests that the reason action heroines like

"Outlaws and loving it": Thelma (Susan Sarandon) and Louise (Geena Davis) are on the run after a weekend getaway goes awry.

Davis's characters did not do well is because "women playing real action figures who menace real men still don't sell."[72] In the opening scene, Davis does something unbelievably unladylike: She kills Bambi, snapping a deer's neck with her bare hands. That scene alone probably sank her movie.[73] Men may have accepted women as action figures, but only when those action figures are a cross between Gidget and Bruce Lee.[74] The point that Mencimer as well as other film critics have suggested is that action heroines cannot be too masculine. While fighting criminals or engaging in battles, action heroines must be (according to those who follow the genre closely) able to retain their femininity because if they appear too threatening, if men would be afraid to sleep with the leading lady,[75] then action heroine films will not perform well at the box-office.

It is ironic to say that on the one hand, action heroines are liberating and offer viable alternatives of femininity in general, and then suggest that they must keep an aura of femininity in order to pique the interest of male audiences. Yet, I believe this is true. When looking at the blaxploitation heroines, studios always made certain to include, at least in Grier's films, a nude and sex scene to emphasize her femininity. However, we should also remember that American International Pictures produced her films and as noted in Chapter 2, as a studio that specifically catered to a certain market and demographic, the nude and sex scenes had less to do with retaining femininity and more with drawing in a particular audience.

There are differences between the action heroine of blaxploitation and her mainstream counterpart with considerable attention on how femininity is presented through Weaver, Sarandon, Davis, Hamilton and many other action heroines in mainstream popular cinema. While Pam Grier and Tamara Dobson especially wore clothing that emphasized their femininity and sexuality, later action heroines (particularly Linda Hamilton's Sarah Connor) adopted traits that had been traditionally associated with masculinity in the guise of developing a more muscular physique. Yet, though their physiques may have differed from Grier and Dobson's heroines, the qualities remained the same. Many of today's action heroines beginning with Weaver and continuing into the early 1990s possessed a nurturing trait whether or not the characters were actually mothers. In the cases where they were not mothers, they acted as surrogates protecting the world, the community or their loved ones and this is a trait shared with blaxploitation heroines.

The future of action heroines in popular cinema will depend on whether audiences still respond favorable to them. Also, it will take an actress who can turn an interesting storyline and character into a hallmark such as Weaver's Ellen Ripley. Although some scholars argue that creating unique action heroines with the depth that Weaver possessed (particularly in *Aliens*) might only happen with more women writers and directors, it depends on the actress and the material that she has at her disposal. Some actresses can create believable action heroines precisely because their acting skills are strong. Weaver is one such actress and both Susan Sarandon and Geena Davis were extremely convincing in their roles as Thelma and Louise.

In addition, the studio has to want to create strong heroines that appeal to a spectrum of audiences in terms of demographics, race, gender and class (this will be discussed further in the last chapter). A major reason why Weaver's Ripley remains *the* representative of mainstream action heroines is that the *Alien* series combines "the icons of the action narrative with borrowing from the horror genre." Thus, in addition to a deeply developed character and storyline, particularly in the first two *Alien* films, Ripley appeals to those who like action and horror. The blending of the two genres means a diversity among audiences who might only be attracted to action movies or horror films without thinking of the possibility of both.

The action heroine has cemented her place in mainstream popular cinema in large part due to Sigourney Weaver and the actresses that followed her with varying degrees of success. In the early 1990s, the genre had a great deal of success, but in the twenty-first century, the action heroine has suffered perhaps from a lack of originality, particularly in film. For now, suffice to say that the more interesting action heroines appear on television because as a medium television seems willing to take chances that the film industry will not. In sum, action heroines have evolved a great deal since blaxploitation and other earlier prototypes on television, but feminist critics are right. Women are still only allowed to be violent within certain parameters largely proscribed by what men are willing to tolerate.[76] To be sure, what men will tolerate has certainly changed a good deal. However, in the old action films, at the end, the male hero always walks away from a burning building looking dirty, bleeding, sweaty yet vindicated. (Remember Bruce Willis' bloody feet after walking through broken glass barefoot in *Die Hard*?[77]) None of today's action chicks come near that level of messiness.[78] The violence is sterilized, they rarely mess up their hair, nor do they really fight — or perhaps gun down — significant bad guys, like say, Rutger Hauer or Wesley Snipes do; that would seriously upset the balance of power.[79] Often they end up sparring with other women. This is even true of Ellen Ripley who battles the mother Alien Queen. With the exception of Grier's *Foxy Brown*, her nemeses are male. Their motives are always pure and they never use unnecessary violence the way Arnold and the boys get to.[80] In essence, these traits account for the success of the action heroine in the twenty-first century. All in all, expanding action roles for women in Hollywood, if nothing else, signal a trend in which the action heroine is evolving from pure object status and relative passivity toward center stage and real action. It remains to be seen whether or not this evolution will or can continue.

8

Metamorphosis of the Black Action Heroine

> I venerate the armed woman as a transcendent symbol of independent female power — from ancient goddesses like ... the knife-wielding Hindu Kali to the pistol-packing babes of *Charlie's Angels*[1] — Camille Paglia

This work has been concerned with icons of African American womanhood, actors who have broken barriers, stereotypes and the old model of women as wives, child bearers, maids and sexual creatures on celluloid. No one can doubt that as an ethnic group and as Americans, we are very proud of all our people who have contributed to the culture, arts and sciences of this country, and in so doing, have commanded the attention of the whole world on who we are. Clearly, the contributions of African Americans have been great and at the same time, their contributions have been largely dismissed in an industry that is focused on superficiality and not talent as it relates to black actresses. To be sure, Hattie McDaniel, Louise Beavers, Lena Horne, Dorothy Dandridge, Josephine Baker and many other earlier African American actresses struggled immensely in film more because of their race than gender. Roles that empowered and demonstrated the multifaceted aspect of being a black woman were scarce for these actresses and the challenge continues today. Even so, all of the actresses above and many more who were not mentioned, but have earned their rightful place in the history of cinema, took what was available to them small and insignificant as it might seem to some while demeaning to others and created a special place that can no longer be ignored. Film historians (most notably Donald Bogle) have done an excellent job of detailing the struggles of early African American actresses and it has always been a contention of this book, while I may not have explicitly stated it, that McDaniel, Beavers, Horne, Dandridge, Baker, Fredi Washington, Nina Mae McKinney and many others played an integral role in the growth and evolution of black actresses particularly as black audiences in the 1960s demanded changes in how representations of blacks in film were constructed by the industry.

Through each chapter, I have demonstrated how vital African American actresses were in the portrayal — not the creation, but the portrayal of a character that has since become a staple in popular cinema. No longer are black actresses relegated to the periphery and marginalized as they have been; their contributions to an important character in feminist film studies deserve to be at the center of the discussion if one is to continue on the relevance of the action heroine and the relevance of blaxploitation in cinematic history. The action heroines who have peopled the pages of this book include: Hattie McDaniel, Louise Beavers, Dorothy Dandridge, Lena Horne, Josephine Baker, Diahann Carroll, Gail Fisher, Nichelle Nichols, Cicely Tyson, Pam Grier, Tamara Dobson, Teresa Graves, Jeannie Bell and many others. At this juncture, the point is clear: these women wrought a transformation in:

- perceptions of the black female film artist;
- the diversity of roles black women would soon come to play;
- box office success;
- stereotyping not only with regard to the roles they would play, but also with the reception of the who and how of what they had to offer; and
- the workplace which is now quite different.

I include McDaniel, Horne, Dandridge, Beavers, Baker and other early African American actresses because whether the film industry and audiences recognized it or not, and despite intense criticism for her portrayals of a stereotypical character onscreen, McDaniel embodied the traits both in her professional and personal life that Grier and Dobson in particular, unknowingly drew on to portray their characters in the 1970s. Also, these actresses made it possible for the success of many African American actresses now. Moreover, there is a fellowship among the actresses because all received stinging indictments from some within the black community and outside of it for their onscreen roles.

It is not an over-simplification to say that the political climate that characterized the country played out in their workplace, but to say that no affirmative action tempered the minds and behavior of the studio executives and crews is no exaggeration. In the very words of Pam Grier we learn: "The people at AIP had nothing but contempt for the audience they were making movies for. Not just the Black audience but the whole audience that they made movies for. They didn't understand Black Pictures...."[2] That sums up how some studios feel today towards audiences. Fame certainly has costs associated with it. However, Grier's disclosure concerns more than a difficult workplace; in a medium where the actresses had to portray emotions worthy of the action of the film, those capital investors who banked the profits did not have the presence of mind to promote a psychology to optimize the benefits to those who bore the weight.

This is yet another instance where the cost of gains in terms of a national legacy cannot, nay should not, be glossed over. Grier was at the pinnacle of her career in blaxploitation movies when she was obliged to negotiate between studio executives, producers and directors. Though her talent is validated by giving the action heroine in mainstream popular cinema a face, we can only imagine what the difference would have been had she worked with a Spike Lee, Tim Reid or John Singleton. What would Grier and Tamara Dobson's heroines look like helmed by these directors or with the type of script Sigourney Weaver had in *Alien*? We can only surmise that with the right director and script, Grier and Dobson's heroines would have altered the landscape of the action heroine in ways that were more sophisticated than they were allowed to do in blaxploitation movies. Clearly, the political, social and cultural climate has changed from Grier's *Coffy* to the present. It can be summed up by the following:

> ... Hollywood has long sought to attract black audiences since the 1970s when black exploitation movies proved lucrative. There were the films about middle class values such as *To Sir With Love* starring Sidney Poitier. But those films fell out of vogue with the civil rights movement and were replaced with another batch of black exploitation films like *Superfly* and *Shaft*. "It never got a chance to fulfill itself. It got shut out before a lot of talent could really come out of it," actor Fred Williamson says.[3]

They did inspire a new generation of black filmmakers. When Hollywood saw the dollar signs come from John Singleton's *Boyz N the Hood* ($56 million), it was eager to repeat the success with similar films. Black filmmakers remain optimistic that a new genre of black films, depicting universal themes, will appeal to moviegoers of all colors.[4] Some changes are apparent, not least among them the fact that talent embodied in black actors and filmmakers is being recognized for what it is. That is not to say that the present is divorced from the problems described by Grier, but the inroads that are being made by blacks give cause for hope. Given the inherent problems that African American actresses have faced then and continue to face now, one wonders about the appeal of a black action heroine in popular cinema today. There appears to be an independent consensus among scholars (I have underscored this in Chapter 6) that studios have never grasped the concept of creating a black film and the response of black audiences. Even among scholars of black film, there is not a consensus on what a black film means; thus it is difficult to expect the film industry to create such a film if there is no agreement on what it encompasses. It is not unreasonable then to assume that should a new black action heroine emerge, the character could face similar problems to her blaxploitation predecessors' unless studios are willing to develop a storyline, character and supporting cast that mirrors the depth of Sigourney Weaver's Ellen Ripley. I am not suggesting that studios create an African American Ellen Ripley, but time and thought should go into the creation of a new black action heroine that would add more layers than what audiences received from the blaxploitation heroines.

In general, action heroines are at a crossroads in mainstream popular cinema as the interest and excitement in seeing such characters is waning. Nowhere is this more apparent than when one critiques the recent action heroine films at the box-office. Arguably, it seems that for the most part, moviegoers are not as interested in action heroines as they were in the early 1990s. Jessica Alba's character Sue Storm in *Fantastic Four* (2005) did well this summer; however, she was a member of an ensemble. Also, part of the film's success may have been due to the fact that those who were fans of the comic book and also watched the cartoon version would want to see its incarnation onscreen. Jennifer Garner's *Elektra* (2004), a spin-off from the successful *Daredevil* movie starring Ben Affleck and Garner, failed to generate interest from audiences when it was released. But, at least one critic offers clues as to why it received mediocre reviews and audiences avoided it. In her article "Seven Mistakes Superheroines Make: Why the latest action-babe flicks flopped," Christina Larson writes, "Elektra another comic-book adaptation, might turn heads in her tight-laced scarlet bustier, but her personal magnetism doesn't measure up."[5] She's a gloomy assassin who suffers from nightmares, insomnia, and OCD.[6] Plus, she hates her job but can't—or won't—figure out what else to do with her life.[7] In essence, Elektra lacks charisma and audiences usually do not respond to a character who seems frankly dismal.[8] Larson suggests that teenage girls would not find Elektra appealing, but an action heroine's popularity lies in the ability to reach a spectrum of audiences — not one particular group. Although the blaxploitation heroines catered to a specific demographic and were highly successful, a new action heroine (particularly if she is African American) must be universal. Unfortunately, the film industry only believes in the power of black audiences when it is trendy, witnessed by the emergence of blaxploitation and the gangsta' movies of the early 1990s.

In addition to the performance of *Elektra*, Halle Berry's *Catwoman* was a $90 million financial disaster. I agree with Larson's assessment of why this movie did not ignite audiences upon its release, but I also remember that the film was not heavily marketed. In fact, the studio, director and Berry went out their way to state that there was no resemblance between her Catwoman and the Catwoman in the 1960s cultish television show *Batman* or the film versions of *Batman*. Consequently, perhaps, audiences were not interested in the movie, and because the studio did not make a strong effort to market the movie by connecting it to popular culture. For example, marketing dolls and other merchandise with a popular fast food chain may have proved useful in piquing curiosity among theatergoers. But, critics make an excellent point about the dominatrix costume of Catwoman and this certainly would cause fast food restaurants to reconsider since the appeal of marketing a film to such a target must lie in creating a family-oriented friendly environment. Larson also points to the director's idea to have Catwoman "latch on to a female mentor who lives alone with three dozen cats"[9] and to have her complain, "I was a professor for 20 years, until I was denied tenure-male academia"[10] as a turn-off to audiences. One of the secrets to a flop action heroine movie is to "wear fetish clothes,"[11] according to Larson. The sequels to *Charlie's Angels* and *Lara Croft: Tomb Raider* were unable to inspire the same enthusiasm for similar reasons.

What Hollywood didn't seem to realize is that the first crop of warrior women won a following because they were strong, smart, and successful in addition to being sexy. These were the ingredients in blaxploitation heroines, which were subsequently co-opted by mainstream studios when Ellen Ripley made her grand entrance and not only became, but remains the standard by which the film industry, film critics, film scholars and audiences measure the action heroine.

Despite the setbacks, the action heroine remains an integral part of the action genre and producers continue to make movies centered on the character. To this end, studios are looking for ways to reenergize the action heroine. Berry is remaking Pam Grier's *Foxy Brown*. It is unclear if the remake

"Cat on a ledge": Patience (Halle Berry) as Catwoman, in a throwback to the 1960s campy *Batman* television series starring Adam West and Burt Ward, patiently waits and prepares her strategy.

will be made since there has been little press about it, and whether it would have any similarities to Grier's original is not now known. An update is likely to fail; it has been tried by John Singleton and Samuel L. Jackson in *Shaft* (2000). Blaxploitation was a moment that extended beyond filmic representations and encapsulated a specific dynamic in the early 1970s for African Americans that cannot be duplicated.

The true test for Berry and the studio will be to reinvent Foxy Brown as a new character fabricated from the social issues and icons of the time, one who pulses to the beat of *this* generation. Adoption of this formula will ensure that an assembly line model which most moviegoers feel no empathy for will not be made. While this pragmatism solves the box office problem, it duly expresses the feeling and expressions of the age as most good art does. Those who are nostalgic for Grier's version will inevitably be disappointed, but Halle Berry should make the character her own rather then invite comparisons to the original.

Film scholar Frances Gateward suggests that the "future of female

8. Metamorphosis of the Black Action Heroine

"Here's the plan.": Lara Croft (Angelina Jolie, left), Hillary (Chris Barrie, center) and Bryce (Noah Taylor, far right) outline plans for recovering a stolen key that leads to a valuable talisman.

action heroes is untenable at this moment."[12] She notes that "recent blockbuster action films featuring women have been damaging pointing to a key that is integral to the development of a new black action heroine — African American directors."[13] When given the opportunity to helm big-budget genre films, directors have done so without casting any African American women in central roles, such as *The Italian Job* (2003, directed by F. Gary Gray) and *2 Fast 2 Furious* (2003, directed by John Singleton).[14] Clearly, directors do not always have the last word in casting decisions, but having an African American actress in one prominent action-oriented role would offer a glimpse of a new black action heroine. Gateward also suggests that part of the reason why black actresses have not received roles as action heroines is because there is a "current trend of Latinas dominating roles that were traditionally cast as African American."[15]

I do not believe that an African American actress can restore the action heroine to her blaxploitation roots nor do I think a new black action heroine should return to the genre. As I have argued throughout the book, blaxploitation was a particular moment in cinema when the political, social and cultural climate was in place to allow the creation of the genre. I concur with Professor Eric Pierson's assessment of the genre as such. Despite an overwhelming dissatisfaction with blaxploitation movies, they captured a time that cannot be regained. More significantly, it was a time when the largest number of African Americans were employed in the film industry on all levels. Since 1975, the number of roles for African American women has remained consistently low while roles for African American actors have become more visible with Denzel Washington, Will Smith, Martin Lawrence, Wesley Snipes and Eddie Murphy leading the way. It is worth noting that Murphy for a long time was *the* quintessential black superstar and that is reflected in a number of very successful action-oriented movies he made — particularly *Beverly Hills Cop* (1984) and sequels, *Another 48HRS.* (1982) and *Trading Places* (1985).

Ironically, action hero status for black actors has increasingly grown, while African American actresses continue to languish. One cannot help but note that while African American actors' as action heroes have increased and become more visible, the same is not true of white actors as action heroes, which has markedly diminished in recent years. The film industry simply "overreached"[16] with action heroines similar to what they did with action heroes. As evidence of that, Christina Larson points to actors such as Steven Seagal, Sylvester Stallone and Arnold Schwarzenegger who were "getting a little grayer, a little slower, and a whole lot less popular at the Cineplex."[17] Yet, Denzel Washington and Wesley Snipes have portrayed action heroes that have appealed to audiences in the same way Seagal, Stallone, Schwarzenegger and Bruce Willis' characters used to. The willingness of audiences to "accept" (I want to use the word "accept" in a loose context) black actors as action heroes suggests that in some ways, it is not race that keeps black actresses from receiving a similar reception. I believe gender also greatly influences the visibility of black action heroines and while race is certainly a factor, at issue is the marketability of action heroine movies and whether audiences *want* to see these types of movies.

For many reasons (largely inherent in the structure of the film industry which goes back to earlier depictions of and treatment by studios regarding African American actresses), they are not cast in action-oriented roles as the lead. One can point to historic racism in the film industry that prevents African American actresses from achieving a smart role such Weaver's Ellen Ripley. But, there are other variables to consider. First, the action heroine needs a make-over. The character has languished in movies in part because studios have relied very heavily on sex and action to market their respective films. It is difficult to argue for a resourceful, empowered woman,

"All geared up": Jinx (Halle Berry), wearing camouflage, prepares for her final battle scene.

particularly an African American woman, when the roles in the action heroine genre in general have become formulaic to the point that audiences do not want to see them.

Moreover, actresses in general face ageism which is another issue, but certainly one that appears to be contradictory when examining the roles available for actors and actresses beyond 45. For African American actresses the amount of roles are small to begin with and when one adds age, then the choices are scarce. Halle Berry is approaching 40 and Vivica A. Fox is already 40, which is an obstacle in a youth-obsessed film industry. The film industry continues to be discriminatory in terms of race and age. Ironically, Wesley Snipes, Denzel Washington and Samuel L. Jackson are well past the 40 mark and continue to appear as leading actors in action-oriented storylines. In this case, I would argue that gender trumps race as the actors above prove that, regardless of age, studios find action heroes more appealing then seeing actresses portray action heroines beyond a certain age.

The biggest challenge then lies in finding a studio that is willing to develop a black action heroine with a solid script and good director. To do

"A lovely but deadly 'fish'": Jinx (Halle Berry) emerges from the water with her gear and ready to take on all challengers.

this and also appeal across the audience spectrum, the new black action heroine must be more universal with a storyline that reflects this universality. It would be difficult to create a black action heroine with the same attributes of Pam Grier and Tamara Dobson's heroines. Studios are less willing to cater to a particular market and demographic because financially they do not need to. Grier, Tamara Dobson, Teresa Graves (to some extent) and Jeannie Bell were focused on family and community and were not attempting to save the world. These heroines' objectives were centered on issues relevant to their world and reality. To regain her racial roots, the action heroine must be developed in a way that appeals to a range of demographics and focuses on issues that are global in nature since films tend to mirror what is happening in society.

In the early to mid–1990s, audiences could see some semblance of a black action heroine particularly in movies such as *Strange Days* (1993), a science fiction film where Angela Bassett portrayed a woman who was trying to help Ralph Fiennes' character regain his memory in a dystopian futuristic world very similar to Ridley Scott's *Blade Runner* (1982). Also, Jada Pinkett-Smith as Niobe in the *Matrix* trilogy could be considered an action heroine despite the fact that her roles in the two sequels were limited and her character was not as developed in comparison to action heroines in general. The same is true of Bassett, though there was a time when I believe (given the right script and character) Bassett would have made a formidable action heroine. The 1996 film *Set It Off* has four characters that come close to demonstrating black action heroines, yet, the two most interesting characters in the movie are Queen Latifah's Cleo, whose name could be a reference to Cleopatra Jones, and Vivica A. Fox's Frankie. Latifah, Fox, Jada Pinkett-Smith and Kimberly Elise are action heroines for different reasons. Elise's character's main motivation for robbing a bank is to steal enough money to regain custody of her child. Pinkett-Smith's character became involved after her brother was mistaken for a robber and shot, and she was distraught over his death, but disgusted with the system. When he died, she felt there was nothing else to live for as her parents had died when they were quite young and she took over the mother role and did whatever she could to ensure that her brother would have the opportunity to attend college. Fox's Frankie thrust into bank robbing because she was wrongly accused as a teller of stealing money.

Finally, as the ring leader of bank robbers, Cleo's motivations stem from a desire to protect the other three characters, but to also support her girlfriend. *Set It Off* could be construed as an all-women version of *Bonnie and Clyde* (1967) since the characters engage in illegal activities, but do not gain the notoriety that followed Bonnie and Clyde. Moreover, the complexities of the motives surrounding the characters in *Set It Off* cannot necessarily be reduced to robbing banks as part of a larger message of anti-authoritarianism present in Faye Dunaway and Warren Beatty's classic. Race and gender are integral to the storyline in *Set It Off* and the structure of the system that spurs four women to rob a bank deserves an in-depth critique. The movie proves that action heroines do not necessarily follow a proscribed storyline in which they emerge as victors and sometimes become outlaws themselves. In this sense, the characters are truer to Pam Grier's heroines, who are not above taking the law into their own hands and exacting revenge when the system fails. Pinkett-Smith, Fox, Latifah and Elise's motives are quite similar to Grier's Coffy and Foxy Brown in that they turn against the system after it fails or victimizes them. The success of *Set It Off* did not open the doors for a sequel and I believe the studio thought the movie's success was probably a fluke. Unlike the early 1990s, where Mario Van Peebles' *New Jack City* (1991) ushered in an era of gangsta films, this was not the case with *Set It Off*.

There have been a few African American actresses who have portrayed action heroines with mixed results. Sanaa Lathan's Alexa in *Alien vs. Predator* (2004) is the most interesting. Similar to Sigourney Weaver's Ellen Ripley, Lathan's Alexa literally must save the world from two monsters, an alien and the predator, thus combining the two genres that I briefly discussed in Chapter 7. The script is implausible, the character development is extremely weak, and overall, the movie lacks cohesiveness. Having said that, Lathan's character is interesting and reminiscent of Grier in one way — her determination to protect at all costs those she has been entrusted with. The website *Girls with Guns* states, "[T]he heroine herself makes a decent impression, improving as the film goes on in much the same way as Ripley did in the original. Of course, Lathan is not Sigourney Weaver — but neither was Weaver when she started."[18] With the sequel, Weaver's character is much stronger and determined in a way that she was not in *Alien*. With the right role, Lathan could be the next black action heroine.

In the 1970s, the action heroine was indeed a new phenomenon in popular cinema. The most interesting action heroines could be found in exploitative movies because as noted in the introduction, studios who made these movies could and did take chances that Warner Brothers and Columbia would not. The action heroines who appeared on television after Teresa Graves' Christie Love were far more one-dimensional and less remarkable than even their counterparts such as Blackman, Rigg and Thorson's characters on *The Avengers*,[19] Stephanie Powers' *The Girl from U.N.C.L.E.*, Monica Vitti's *Modesty*

Blaise (1967), and Raquel Welch's *Fathom* (1967). In some cases, especially with Rigg and Thorson, they were more physical than their male counterparts. The latter two films focused on campy heroines, but ironically, as a character in a series of books, Modesty Blaise was stronger as an action heroine than the way she was portrayed in film—although admittedly Vitti portrayed her as more fun then serious. Nonetheless, the 1960s opened the windows of opportunity to view women in action narratives; however, it was not until blaxploitation action heroines became successful that mainstream studios began to pick up on the trend of a woman at the center of an action-oriented storyline.

The 1960s were clearly the decade for many changes in the film industry, particularly for African American actresses. Positioned against the Victorian ideology of the cult of womanhood, the transformation of African American women from Mammies, Jezebels, Aunt Jemimas and Sapphires appeared logical with the emergence of the black action heroine in the blaxploitation movies. But, the logical transition for black action heroines onscreen stemmed from seeing highly visible, buoyant African American women make political inroads in the 1960s.

In the *USA Today* article on action heroines, film critic Susan Wloszczyna offers insight into creating a viable action heroine that can be applied to a new black action heroine. She suggests that action heroines must be taken seriously if they are to have sustained success. It did not help Berry's Patience to be written as a heroine out to save cosmetics and not the world.[20] While saving the world may not be a plausible storyline, saving cosmetics reinforces notions of women as trivial and diminishes what could have been a new black action heroine by portraying Berry's character in this manner.[21] In reference to what the producers were thinking in creating Berry's *Catwoman*, Rob Morley of comics2film.com stated, "[T]hey went out of their way to make it girly. They went too far in pushing the femininity of the character."[22] In addition, the producers also focused a lot of attention on Berry's attire as Catwoman creating this dominatrix superheroine which may not have been the best approach for a action heroine let alone a black action heroine, given the historic sexual stereotypes in film of black women. Wloszczyna notes that another suggestion for the next action heroine is to not be overtly sexual. In the same article, assistant film professor Lisa Dombrowski stated, "Lara Croft in her padded bra was ridiculous and in *Catwoman*, no woman would design an outfit like that for herself."[23] Dombrowski highlights a point that is crucial to developing a new black action heroine. Unlike her predecessors in blaxploitation movies, this new heroine should deemphasize fashionable attire that illuminates her sexuality and instead, wear clothing attire that suits the woman of the twenty-first century.[24]

"Tied up not quite": Lara Croft (Angelina Jolie) prepares for one of her many action adventures as a tomb raider (a person who collects ancient relics) in retrieving the key and talisman from a sect who seek to control the world.

The reviews of *Catwoman* were harsh. Mark Holcomb of *The Village Voice* wrote, "This plodding, by-the-numbers superhero flick has all the feline grace of a walleyed mastiff."[25] David Rooney of *Variety* wrote, "[*Catwoman*] plays like a Lifetime movie on estrogen overdose, barely held together by a script that should have been tossed out with the kitty litter."[26] Critic Peter Travers of *Rolling Stone* stated, "The stench of the litter pan is all over this big-screen $90 million disaster-in-waiting" and Robert K. Elder of the *Chicago Tribune* called it "the *Showgirls* of superhero movies."[27] The general consensus among critics was that *Catwoman* did little to make Halle Berry a viable action heroine. With a budget of 90 million, critics and audiences expected more than what Berry could deliver. Berry, as good an actress as she is, was probably not right for the role, and the studio (after spending a significant amount of money to produce the movie) did little to market it. Instead of attempting to distance *Catwoman* from the character in the *Batman* series, it may have been wiser to market the film as an extension of *Batman* simply for comic book fans. There does not appear to be a rationale for choosing to distinguish Patience as a new heroine who is not in any way related to the Catwoman that audiences could identify from *Batman*. Since the failure of the movie, Berry's work has been limited to television movies except for another movie, *Gothika* (2003), that also failed to generate interest from audiences.

Initially, when I began reworking the chapters of this book and saw the attention surrounding Halle Berry's Jinx in *Die Another Day*, I believed she could bring the action heroine back to her racial origins. With that in mind, the last chapter was going to be devoted strictly to the black action heroine's metamorphosis which would aptly fit Berry's career. She began her career as an actress on a television sitcom titled *Living Dolls* (1989) that did not last a full year. After the show's demise, Berry took many roles on her path to becoming the first African American woman to win a Best Actress Oscar and possibly the first black actress since Grier and Dobson to draw the attention of audiences, critics and perhaps scholars to the action heroine. But audiences do not appear interested in the character judging from the last few films that focused on her. Also, studios continue to produce sub-par films centered on the action heroine, leaving one to consider whether or not audiences will once again eagerly embrace the character or if there is even room for an action heroine, let alone a revamped black action heroine, in today's films. As poorly made as *Aliens vs. Predator* is, Sanaa Lathan's character is different and she in fact could revitalize the action heroine genre and, more importantly, renew interest among those who remember the grittiness of Pam Grier's heroines in a contemporary black action heroine that appeals to everyone. Not only is audience interest in the genre waning, but film critics also appear to long for an empowered heroine. In a sub-article on action heroines, Susan Wloszczyna lists several possible solutions for creating a strong female protagonist in action-driven films beginning with the need for writers, producers and directors to take the character seriously. In reference to the comedic banter between Drew Barrymore, Lucy Liu and Cameron Diaz in the *Charlie's Angels* movies, Wloszczyna writes, "Don't be silly ... just because an action hero is a girl doesn't mean every day has to be a slumber party."[28] What critics saw as overtly sexual in Pam Grier's films, I see as reshaping African American femininity onscreen. Placing all of her heroines, particularly Coffy and Foxy Brown, within the social and political context of the 1970s, it was a time when African American women embraced their femininity in a way that they deemed appropriate. This meant adopting hairstyles and wearing clothing that emphasized the African heritage and used "black is beautiful" as a way to liberate themselves from dominant ideology's cultural norms of beauty. In trading traditional headwear associated with the lack of black femininity in film for a natural hairstyle such as the afro, all across the country black women began to hold a more visible discourse about the gender dynamics between black men and black women. Moreover, they also began to critique the feminist movement and how the focus of the patriarchal structure which impeded progress for all women created what Deborah King has referred to as a "multiple jeopardy"[29] for black women. This is the backdrop in which a new heroine emerged — the action heroine. It was never the intention of AIP to create a character that would have such lasting appeal within the action heroine genre. Moreover, the studio could never have anticipated that an African American actress would become such a popular culture icon that female rapper Foxy Brown adapted her moniker from Pam Grier's film character. Certainly, the studio had no idea when they were making Grier's movies that she would become *the* symbol of blaxploitation. Whether or not she likes the *face* of blaxploitation, and even though she has made many films since *Coffy*, Grier remains *the* most familiar and has a huge fan base directly tied to her involvement with blaxploitation. Despite film critics' and scholars' lack of fascination with either her characters or the genre itself, many in the black community responded favorably to her heroines. No clearer example of this exists than in Chapter 3 where Grier recounts overhearing a conversation between a woman and her boyfriend after seeing one of her films. The blaxploitation action heroines always operated on their own terms and that is different from the exotic other who used her sexuality to entice men. When Grier's heroines used their

"Angel power": It's all in a day's work for Charlie's Angels Dylan (Drew Barrymore, left), Natalie (Cameron Diaz), and Alex (Lucy Liu) as they dish out equal doses of cool detective work, combat skill and lethal feminine charm to survive their riskiest assignment ever.

"An angelic idea": Amid the rubble of the Charles Townsend Agency, Natalie (Cameron Diaz, left), Alex (Lucy Liu), and Dylan (Drew Barrymore) devise a plan to rescue their abducted lieutenant in command, the bumbling Bosley (Bill Murray, not shown).

sexuality it was an example of the ends justifying the means. In essence, when the character was exacting revenge against those who harmed her family, she used her sexuality as a weapon. There is a difference between the use of sexuality by blaxploitation heroines and how Dorothy Dandridge's Carmen used her feminine charms in *Carmen Jones*. I am unwilling to say that both Grier and Dobson were latter-day Jezebels as other film critics have suggested.

While it is clear that even blaxploitation heroines were fashioned in such a way to appeal to male fantasies, Grier's outfits were for the most part everyday clothing unless she was working undercover. Dobson's outfits were a bit flashier and fancier, but given the premise of Cleopatra Jones (a CIA operative who uses modeling as her disguise), the outfits seemed appropriate for the character. Lastly, Wloszczyna writes, "Don't forget the story."[30] Take a tip from TV where strong women thrive.[31] As Jessica Alba (the Invisible Woman in *Fantastic Four*) stated, "Men run the business, and when you see Elektra or Catwoman, it is clear they don't understand it's more than a hot girl kicking [butt]."[32] Often it behooves an actress to exert quality control herself. Sigourney Weaver did that in co-producing the last two *Alien* sequels. It is clear that the metamorphosis of a new black action heroine must be universal in the sense of defending the world, and not simply her community and family, if she is to have an opportunity to appeal to a wide spectrum of moviegoers and enjoy success. Of today's African American actresses, Vivica A. Fox has this appeal. Her character on the television series *1-800-MISSING* is highly action-oriented: She portrays an FBI agent who uses her wits and physical strength to apprehend suspects and solve cases. Although she is surrounded by a strong group of cohorts, the series is clearly focused on Fox's character. As the executive producer of the series, Fox has a voice in how her character is portrayed and also how the storylines develop. In Quentin Tarantino's *Kill Bill: Volume 1* (2005), she portrayed Vivian Green, a hired assassin who battles Uma Thurman's character. Green loses the battle, but Fox demonstrated that she could be the new black action heroine if given the opportunity in film, especially since the Lifetime Channel recently cancelled the series. Her character is an excellent model for a new black action heroine because as portrayed by Fox, the character is smart, sassy and even in high heel boots manages to run down and overtake villains when the need arises. Additionally, as executive producer of the show, she had greater flexibility and this route might be a viable way of creating a new black action heroine — with an African American woman as the producer and director. Such a move does not necessarily mean a better black action heroine; however, the perspective of a woman who is African American and involved in creating a character like this could result in a universal appeal, while maintaining her roots as an African American woman. Fox's character certainly falls into this category. In many ways, Fox's character Nicole Scott is a combination of all the blaxploitation action heroines. First, she is reminiscent of Grier's Coffy and Foxy Brown in her determination, as fashionable as Cleopatra Jones without the makeup and some of the outfits, but still possesses the ability to produce scenes that entail a lot of action and as sassy as Teresa Graves' Christie Love. Before Fox joined the show, Gloria Reuben, another African American actress, portrayed a more subdued agent. But, *1-800-MISSING* lacked the spark that ignited when Fox took over the role. She has demonstrated both on television and in *Kill Bill: Volume 1* that she too could be the next black action heroine.

For the moment, the interest in action heroine films in general has dissipated. To regain audiences, Larson offers several steps that may help the next action heroine:

1. Do fight demons. Don't fight only inner demons.
2. Do play well with others. Don't shun human society.
3. Do exhibit self-control. Don't exhibit mental disorders.
4. Do wear trendy clothes. Don't wear fetish clothes.
5. Do embrace girl power. Don't cling to man hatred.
6. Do help hapless men. Don't try to kill your boyfriend.
7. Do toss off witty remarks. Don't look perpetually sullen.[33]

Ultimately, writes Larson, the woman-searching-for-herself trope might work in other genres, but it's a bad fit for superheroes. For female fans, the superheroine saga is a fantasy about being in control. Successful heroines defy everyday restraints: They cheat gravity, physically overpower men, and deflect bullets with silver bracelets. The last thing women want to see is Supergirl whining about her boss, suffering through a mid-life career crisis, and being served divorce papers by Superman.[34]

The black action heroine faces a unique set of problems. As an African American woman, she shoulders the burden of appealing to all without ignoring the fact that she is a black woman. Such a feat is difficult, but there are actresses who could perform the task very well. However, this requires a willingness on the part of the film industry to create such a character. Secondly, selling the character to the audience could prove to be challenging. The way to do that is again by creating a black action heroine that is universal and in a storyline that is believable. Equally important, the black action heroine should not necessarily have the same traits as she did in blaxploitation, but instead be a strong protagonist who takes control of a crisis and handles it adeptly. Here, I am thinking of Jodie Foster who has portrayed several strong heroines (not necessarily in action-driven storylines). But, also when examining Grier's heroines from *Coffy*, a heroine who does whatever is necessary to settle old debts with her nemesis to a woman working as a fashion photographer who just happens to stumble onto a criminal plot in *Friday Foster*, the transformation of the black action heroine emerges. Unfortunately, this transformation was incomplete as Grier's later heroines were even more underdeveloped than Coffy and Foxy Brown. Also, studios were not thinking outside the confines of blaxploitation when casting Pam Grier and moving into mainstream roles was challenging because studio executives could not see her in other types of roles. With the right script and a defection from the blaxploitation films, Grier had the most potential to move into a mainstream role as an action heroine with universal appeal. Unfortunately, that could not happen in spite of the progress African American actresses had made in the 1970s.

Yet, even now, it would prove a difficult sell to create the types of heroines that actresses such as Foster portray. For as much progress that African American actresses have made in the film industry, racism is still very inherent and Halle Berry, Vivica A. Fox, Angela Bassett and countless others cannot break the invisible barrier that still exists. Ironically, black actors have had an "easier" road to travel in terms of portraying different types of characters and Denzel Washington's career epitomizes this. Washington portrays a variety of characters, and audiences appear to accept him in dramatic or action-oriented roles with little trouble. To build a better "(s)hero," a good script, director and actress are necessary. To build a new black action heroine requires the willingness of the studios to create such a character, but also the support should come from the African American community, particularly those in the film industry who yield power. There are few African Americans who have achieved that stature in Hollywood, but there are some such as Washington and Will Smith who can get projects started by lending their name. As talented and respected as Halle Berry is, she does not have the film industry clout of Washington and Smith or even Wesley Snipes who executive produced the sequels to his successful *Blade* (1998). Whether Berry stirs excitement with her remake of *Foxy Brown* remains to be seen, but in order for the metamorphosis of the black action heroine to be completed, it is clear that a developed character and a plausible storyline that generates audience interest must appear. Any of the aforementioned African American actresses are fully capable of achieving this metamorphosis, but unlike their predecessors Pam Grier, Tamara Dobson, Teresa Graves and Jeannie Bell, a new black action heroine *must* transcend racial barriers if she is to become as successful as Sigourney Weaver's Ellen Ripley. The task will be difficult, given the racism that still pervades the film industry, but one worth undertaking particularly in light of the contributions of African American actors. To borrow a famous popular culture phrase and a line that Cleopatra Jones might say, black actresses have "come a long way, baby" and perhaps, as the action heroine genre looks to revive interests among audiences, film critics and scholars, this could provide the perfect opportunity for the film industry to create a new black action heroine.

Epilogue

The book would have been enhanced with the inclusion of interviews from actors and actresses, producers and directors who are still willing to speak about this particular moment in cinematic history. I understand why many actors and actresses in particular were eager to distance themselves from these movies, and I also believe if there had not been such a backlash against blaxploitation and criticism of those involved, then many actors and actresses would freely discuss their experiences today. Any future study should focus on the connection between the genre and hip hop, which arguably has its roots in blaxploitation. Although both movements are clearly different, many hip hop artists have been influenced by the genre.

I began this book with a preface describing a few incidents in my childhood, and I would like to end it by reflecting on those incidents twenty plus years later. I believe that whatever has been said about the actresses of blaxploitation, they represented empowerment and beauty that did not conform to dominant ideology's notions of African American femininity. Articles and books on the action heroine are now a mainstay in film scholarship; yet some scholars fail to acknowledge the contributions of the blaxploitation actress to this iconic character in American popular culture. At the age of 12, I saw Pam Grier's *Coffy* for the first time and remember thinking there was something different about this character. By the 1980s, the action heroine had become a staple in film and television. As time passed, and particularly when I began my dissertation (on which this book is based), I revisited these movies and the genre and understood perfectly, as well as appreciated, what I could not fully articulate at 12. It sparked my interest enough to go back and look at my own family album to see a mother who received many compliments on her beauty, wore an Afro as high as Angela Davis' and carried herself in the same manner as Tamara Dobson's Cleopatra Jones without the glamour of being a CIA agent and fashion model, but with all of the glamour of being a wife and a mother.

The blaxploitation genre is clearly not without its share of problematic images and issues. This has never been in dispute. However, what they did for a young girl like me who realized 15 years after the fact (and what they may have done for many other African American women and young teenage girls) was confirm that black women were wresting control of their womanhood and femininity from others and no longer allowing others to define what they should look like or how they should act. This was an act of agency that, given the time, remains remarkable today. As demonstrated by the experiences of the actresses, it was not without a price, either, but one that was necessary. Progress has been very slow in the film industry for African American actresses, but the contributions of the 1970s blaxploitation actress to the action heroine have not gone unnoticed and hopefully, scholars and fans alike will restart a dialogue on the genre and examine the power that it brought to the film industry for a brief period.

Selected Filmography

Black Sister's Revenge (1976) Aka *Emma Mae*. Pro International. Running Time 100 minutes. *Executive producers* William Silberkleit, Peter J. Oppenheimer; *producer* Jamaa Fanaka; *associate producer* Arnie Magidow; *director-screenplay* Fanaka; *art director* Adel Mazen; *costumes* Stephanie A. Bell, Beverly Ventriss, Marva Farmer; *makeup* Dwaine Fobbs; *music* H.B. Barnum; *second unit director–stunt coordinator* Alex Brown; *assistant director* Henry Sanders; *sound* Don Sanders; *sound editor* Linda Dove; *camera* Stephen Posey; *editor* Robert Fitzgerald.

    Cast: Jerri Hayes, Eddie Allen, Charles D. Brooks III, Eddie Allen, Robert Slaughter, Malik Carter, Teri Taylor, Leopoldo Mandeville, Grammy Burdett, Laetitia Burdett, Eddy Dyer, Synthia James, Jewell Williams, Hank Smith, Michelle Davison, Ruth Delahoussaye, Garst Reese, Tyrone S.B. Thompson, Alex Brown, Charles Elder, John Laud, Dexter King, Stephanie A. Bell, Cherryl Mofitt, Sherri Drake.

    Plot: A young woman (Hayes) from the South moves in with her Los Angeles relatives. Enduring ridicule upon her arrival, she is eventually accepted by locals and robs a bank to free her drug-dealing boyfriend from jail.

Cleopatra Jones (1973). Warner Brothers. Running Time 89 minutes. *Producer* William Tennant; *co-producer* Max Julien; *director* Jack Starrett; *story* Julien, *screenplay* Julien, Sheldon Keller; *art director* Peter Wooley; *set decorator* Cheryl Kearney; *music–music director* J. J. Johnson; *additional music* Carl Brandt, Brad Shapiro, Joe Simon; *title theme* Simon; *assistant director* Julien, *stunt coordinator* Ernest Robinson; *hapkido karate master* Bong Soo Han; *sound* Bud Alper; *camera* David Walsh; *editor* Allan Jacobs.

Cast: Tamara Dobson, Shelley Winters, Bernie Casey, Antonio Fargas, Brenda Sykes, Bill McKinney, Dan Frazer, Stafford Morgan, Mike Warren, Albert Popwell, Caro Kenyatta, Esther Rolle, Paul Koslo, Joseph A. Tornatore, Hedley Mattingly, George Reynolds, Theodore Wilson, Christopher Joy, Keith Hamilton, Angela Gibbs, John Garwood, John Alderman.

Plot: A CIA super agent (Dobson) who works undercover as a fashion model returns to California to destroy Mommy (Winters), the villainess who runs a $30 million drug operation on the West Coast. After the police raid her boyfriend's (Casey) community center and drugs are falsely planted on one of its members, Cleopatra vows to destroy Mommy's heroin operation. The final scene is somewhat disappointing as the two women fight in an abandoned junkyard with Cleopatra dispensing of Mommy once and for all. Interestingly enough, Winters was not listed in the opening or closing credits of the movie.

Cleopatra Jones and the Casino of Gold (1975). Running Time 94 minutes. *Producer* William Tennant; *director* Chuck Bail; *based on characters created by* Max Julien; *screenplay* Tennant; *art director* Johnson Tsao; *music* Dominic Frontiere; *assistant directors* Bobby Canavarro, William Chaung Kin; *stunt coordinator* Eddy Donno; *Chinese fighting instructors* Tang Chia, Yuen Shian Yan; *sound* Cyril Swern; *sound effects* Billie Owens, Arthur Pullen, Bill Rivol; *special effects* Nobby Clark, Milt Rice; *camera* Alan Hume; *editor* Willy Kemplen.

Cast: Tamara Dobson, Stella Stevens, Tanny, Norman Fell, Albert Popwell, Caro Kenyatta, Chan Sen, Christopher Hunt, Lin Chen Chi, Liu Loke Hua, Eddy Donno, Bobby Canavarro, Mui Kwok Sing, John Cheng, Tony Lee, Rich King, Gigo Tevzadze, Lok Sing, Paul Che, Victor Kahn.

Plot: Cleopatra goes to Hong Kong to rescue two brothers (Albert Popwell and Caro Kenyatta), also CIA operatives, who were captured by Dragon Lady (Stella Stevens). Refusing to work with local police, she enlists the aid (unwillingly at first) of a woman private detective (Tanny) and her motorcycle outfit. Unbeknownst to Cleopatra, they have been warned by her superior (Norman Fell) to keep an eye on her and to help if she gets into trouble.

Together, the two women track Dragon Lady to her casino, rescue the brothers and destroy Dragon Lady. With such a zesty predecessor that explored all levels of her one-dimensional, superheroine character so efficiently, there is not much that a sequel can do to follow upon *Cleopatra Jones*.[1] By the time the sequel was made, blaxploitation had diminished and Dobson's flamboyant attire along with a weak plot could do little to improve on the original. Additionally, by 1975, blaxploitation was no longer profitable, making the sequel a guaranteed box-office disaster.

Coffy (1973). American International. Running Time 91 minutes. *Executive producer* Salvatore Billiteri; *producer* Robert A. Papazian; *director-screenplay* Jack Hill; *art director* Perry Ferguson; *set decorator* Charles Pierce; *wardrobe supervisor* James George; *makeup* Ray Brooks; *music–music director* Roy Ayers; *songs* Ayers and Carl Clay, Ayers and Roselle Weaver; *music arrangers* Ayers, Harry Whitaker; *music editor* Ving Hershon; *stunt coordinator* Bob Minor; *sound* Don Johnson; *sound effects* Gene Corso; *special effects* Jack DeBron; *camera* Paul Lohmann; *editor* Charles McClelland.

Cast: Pam Grier, Booker Bradshaw, Robert DoQui, Allan Arbus, William Elliott, Sid Haig, Barry Cahill, Morris Buchanan, Lee de Broux, Bob Minor, John Perak, Ruben Moreno, Carol Lawson, Linda Haynes, Lisa Farringer, Mivako Cumbuka, Ray Young, Wally Strauss, Gail Davis, Lyman Ward, Bobby Johnson, Nat Jones, Bibi Louis, Walter Blake.

Plot: A nurse (Grier) seeks revenge on the criminals who left her eleven-year-old sister in a vegetative state from a drug overdose. Coffy does not realize that her politician boyfriend (DoQui) has been working for Vittroni's organization. After her police officer friend (Bradshaw) is severely injured for threatening to expose the corruption by his colleagues, Coffy vows retribution. To reach Vittroni, she dons many disguises. She first infiltrates King George's prostitution ring, before finally reaching the guy who is responsible for her sister and friend's condition. She is shocked to learn that her boyfriend has been a part of this corruption and is almost willing to forgive him despite his betrayal of her until she returns to his house and finds him in bed with another woman. She kills him and walks out the door facing an uncertain future. Coffy has achieved her revenge with the last act of killing her unfaithful boyfriend.

Ebony, Ivory and Jade (CBS-TV, 8/3/79). Running Time 78 minutes. *Executive producer* Ernie Frankel; *producer* Jimmy Sangster; *associate producer* Art Seid; *director* John Llewellyn Moxey; *story* Ann Beckett, D.B. Cooper; *teleplay* Sangster, Annie Scott, Cooper; *art director* Rodger Maus; *music* Earle Hagen; *camera* Arch R. Dalzell; *editor* Seid.

Cast: Bert Convoy, Debbie Allen, Martha Smith, Donald Moffat, Nina Foch, Clifford David, Lucille Benson, Ji-Tu Cumbuka, Claude Akins, David Brenner, Frankie Valli, Ted Shackelford, Bill Lane, Ray Guth, Cletus Young and Quinn Redeker.

Plot: Mick Jade is a tennis pro turned entertainer turned government agent. He uses two singers, Ebony (Debbie Allen) and Ivory (Martha Smith), as his cover, posing as their manager. The setting is the Middle East, where the girls perform their dance-song act at a local club and Jade is involved with scientist Dr. Adela Teba (Nina Foch), who has developed a red oozing explosive that detonates in 80° temperatures. When the formula and the two performers disappear, Jade comes to the rescue. Later in Las Vegas, the trio prevent the Aladdin Casino and Theatre from being blown up.

Foxy Brown (1974). American International. Running Time 94 minutes. *Presenter* Samuel. Z. Arkoff; *producer* Buzz Feitshans; *director-screenplay* Jack Hill; *art director* Kirk Axtel; *wardrobe supervisor* James George; *set decorator* Charles Pierce; *makeup* John Norin; *music* Willie Hutch; *assistant director* Frank Beetson; *stunt coordinator* Bob Minor; *sound* John Dignan; *special effects* Roy Downey; *camera* Brick Marquand; *editor* Chuck McClelland.

Cast: Pam Grier, Peter Brown, Terry Carter, Antonio Fargas, Kathryn Loder, Harry Holcombe, Sid Haig, Juanita Brown, Sally Ann Stroud, Bob Minor, Tony Giorgio, Fred Lerner, Judy Cassmore, Jon Cedar, Kimberly Hyde, Esther Sutherland, Mary Foran, Roydon E. Clark, Don Gazzamici, Gary Wright, Fred Murphy, Edward Cross, Larry Kinley, Jr., Jack Bernardi, H. B. Haggerty, Boyd "Red" Morgan.

Plot: Often labeled by some critics as a sequel to *Coffy*, *Foxy Brown* is not really a sequel. Grier portrays the same character with a new name, but no real connection to Coffy other then her action heroine status. In this movie, Foxy Brown (Grier) dons disguises while seeking vengeance on the crooks who murdered her boyfriend and brother. After Ms. Kathryn (Kathryn Loder), the leader of a drug and prostitution ring, discovers Foxy's true identity, she orders her boyfriend Steve (Peter Brown) to take Foxy to a farm. The farm is actually a drug manufacturing operation run by two of Ms. Kathryn's henchmen, who inject Foxy with heroin then rape her in one of the most disturbing scenes of a blaxploitation movie with an African American actress as the lead character. Foxy escapes, burning down the farm with both men in it. She returns to the neighborhood and makes an impassioned plea to the local organized crime watch to assist her in her plans to end Ms. Kathryn's drug reign. The final scene is one of the most memorable ever as Foxy presents Ms. Kathryn with her boyfriend's severed parts in a jar.

Friday Foster (1975). American International. Running Time 90 minutes. *Producer-director* Arthur Marks; *based on the comic strip and on the story* *by* Marks; *screenplay* Orville Hampton; *costumes* Izzy Berne; *makeup* Louis Lane, Bob Westmoreland; *music* Luchi De Jesus; *song* Bodie Chandler; *assistant director* Gene De Ruelle; *stunt coordinator* Richard Geary; *sound* George Malley; *sound effects* John Post; *camera* Harry May; *editor* Stanley Frazen.

Cast: Pam Grier, Yaphet Kotto, Eartha Kitt, Godfrey Cambridge, Jim Backus, Scatman Crothers, Thalmus Rasaulala, Ted Lange, Tierre Turner, Paul Benjamin, Jason Bernard, Julius W. Harris, Rosalind Miles, Tony Brubaker, Carl Weathers, William Gill, John Anthony Bailey, Stan Stratton, James Cousar, Almeria Quinn, Alice Jubert, Candy All, Samuel Daris, Bebe Drake Hooks, Harold Jones, Charles Stroud, Mel Carter.

Plot: A fashion photographer stumbles onto an intriguing plot where the objective is to kill the first black billionaire. Along the way, several colorful characters (from Kitt to Cambridge) join Foster. They meet premature deaths because of their knowledge about the conspiracy to murder Blake.

Get Christie Love! (1974). Produced by Universal TV and Wolper Productions. Running Time 60 minutes. 22 episodes. *Executive* Lawrence Turman; *producer* Peter Nelson; *associate producer* Eddie Saeta; *director* William A. Graham; *story* Dorothy Unhak (novel); *teleplay* George Kirgo; *production supervisor* Conrad Holzgang; *original music* Jack Elliot, Allyn Ferguson; *stunt coordinator* Paul Baxley; *special effects* Gene Griggs; *sound* John Asman, James Mason; *cinematography* Meredith Nicholson.

Cast: Teresa Graves, Harry Guardino, Louise Sorel, Paul Stevens, Ron Rifkin, Lynne Holmes, Lee Paul, Titos Vandis, Tracey Roberts, William Hansen, Andy Romano, Davis Roberts, Bill Henderson, Debbie Dozier, Darlene Conley.

Plot: A police detective (Graves) goes undercover to break up a drug ring in Los Angeles. Christie does not get along with her superior (Guardino) who seems uncomfortable with a woman, particularly one who is outspoken and sassy as the taglines for the telemovie describe her. Nonetheless, despite their clashes, by the end of the movie, her boss grudgingly begins to warm to Christie's charm particularly because she solves and disbands the drug ring. Along the way, Christie gets into a few scrapes with the drug kingpin's (Stevens) girlfriend Helena Vargas (Sorel). After a few misunderstandings, the two (especially Vargas) grudgingly begin to admire Christie and they form a bond of sorts as Vargas lies dying from a gunshot wound. The television movie of the week appeared on ABC and was the first detective show that lasted a full season with a woman detective at the center. Graves earned a Golden Globe nomination for best actress in a television series for her portrayal and although *Get Christie Love!* only lasted 22 episodes, it laid the foundation for many shows starring women as detectives or working as private detectives.

Savage Sisters (1974). American International. Made in the USA and the Philippines. *Executive producers* John Ashley, Eddie Romero; *director* Eddie Romero, *screenplay* Harry Corner and H. Franco Moon, *original music* Les Baxter; *cinematography* Justo Paulino; *editor* Lori. J. Kranze and Isgani Pastor.

Cast: Gloria Hendry, Rosanna Ortiz, Cheri Caffaro, Sid Haig, Vic Diaz, John Ashley, Eddie Garcia, John Plater, Johnny Long, Alfonso Carvajal, Rita Gomez, Robert Rivera, Romy Rivera, Bruno Punzalan, Subas Herrero, Jonnee Gamboa, Dindo Ferndano, Angelo Ventura, Max Rojo, Leopoldo Salcedo.

Plot: Made in the same year as Grier's *Foxy Brown*, this was a cheap imitator starring Gloria Hendry, who was the first black actress to appear as a James Bond love interest in *Live and Let Die* (1973); she also co-starred in *Black Belt Jones* with Jim Kelly (1974). Here she stars as one of three women (with Ortiz and Caffaro) who become involved in tracking down a million dollars that a local general (Salcedo) plans on smuggling out of a country. The revolutionaries form an uneasy alliance with a con artist named Malavael (Haig) who double-crosses them. Before Jo Turner (Caffaro) and Mai Ling (Ortiz) can join their boyfriends, they land in jail under the watchful eye of Lynn Jackson (Hendry). Convinced by another con artist to help him escape and lead him to the million dollars, Hendry soon forms a bond with Caffaro and Ortiz in their quest to reunite with the revolutionaries and find the million dollars. Grier began her acting career in women-in-prison films and this movie is really no different from the others in its genre with the exception that Hendry had some success in mainstream movies before appearing in exploitation flicks.

Sheba Baby (1975). American International and Mid-America. Running Time 90 minutes. *Executive producer* Mike Henry; *producer* David Sheldon; *director* William Girdler; *story* Sheldon, Girdler; *screenplay* Girdler; *production designer* J. Patrick Kelly III; *music director–arranger* Higgins; *music consultant* Larry Maxwell; *stunt coordinator* Richard Washington; *special effects* Gene Griggs; *sound* John Asman, James Mason; *sound effects* Tony Di Marco-Nesco; *camera* William Asman; *editors* Henry Asman, Jack Davies.

Cast: Pam Grier, Austin Stoker, D'Urville Martin, Rudy Challenger,

Dick Merrifield, Charles Broaddus, Maurice Downes, Ernest Cooley, Edward Reece, Jr., William Foster, Jr., Mike Clifford, Rose Ann Deel, Durston, Robert Drane, Melvin Jones, Herman Thompson, Bill Wilson, Mary Minor, Henriette Brands, Joyce Jones, Bobby Davis, Walter Evans, Charles North, Bill Embry, Dennis Williams, Mike Abrams, Phil Kelley, Lloyd Poore, Mary Perries, Jackie Patterson, Richard Taylor, Joan Ray, Toni Gorman, Tara Lang, Jeanie Care.

Plot: Sheba Shayne (Grier) is a private detective living in Chicago. When her father (D'Urville Martin) refuses to give in to the local mob organization's demand to buy his insurance agency and is subsequently murdered, she returns to Louisville seeking justice. Grier portrayed the same character in all of her action films for American International Pictures. Made in 1975, *Sheba Baby* signaled the end of Grier's relationship with the studio as the movie performed very poorly at the box-office. It was not as revolutionary or interesting as *Coffy* and *Foxy Brown*, and it was clear that Grier and AIP were heading in different directions; thus it was not surprising that the studio dropped her not long after the release of this movie.

T.N.T. Jackson (1974). New World Pictures. Running Time 72 minutes Made in the USA and the Philippines. *Executive producer* Roger Corman; *producer* Cirio H. Santiago; *director* Cirio H. Santiago; *screenplay* Ken Metcalfe, Dick Miller; *cinematography* Felipe Sacdalan (Philip Sacdalan); *sound* William Arce (William Arkush); *editors* Barbara Pokras, Gervacio Santos.

Cast: Jeannie Bell, Pat Anderson, Stan Shaw, Ken Metcalfe, Percy Gordon, Max Alvarado, Chiquito, Joonee Gamboa, Leo Martinez, Imeldo Ilanan, Chris Cruz.

Plot: Diana "T.N.T." Jackson (Bell) travels to Hong Kong to find her brother's killers. She teams up with a local tavern owner and makes her way into the inner circle of the local crime ring before discovering that one of the men in the organization killed her brother. The final scene is anticlimactic as she fights one-on-one with her brother's killer using martial arts. At first she despises her reluctant cohort (Pat Anderson) but comes to grudgingly admire her. "T.N.T." Jackson is clearly a cheap imitator of Grier and Dobson's heroines; however Bell's character is in some ways more interesting in that martial arts is her primary means of protecting herself and outwitting the villains. She does not rely on weaponry or as many gimmicks as the other heroines in blaxploitation movies. Although not as well-known as Grier and Dobson; Bell's heroine belongs alongside the other heroines if for no other reason than the merging of two genres: action and martial arts in another genre.

Velvet Smooth (1976). Howard Mahler. Running Time 80 minutes. *producers* Marion Schild, Michael Fink, Joel Schmid; *associate producer* Janice Fink; *director* Michael Fink; *screenplay* Leonard Michaels, Jan Weber; *music* Media Counterpoint; *martial arts choreography* Owen Watson; *assistant director* Hal Hutkoff; *camera* Jay Dubin; *editors* Schild, Schmid.

Cast: Johnnie Hill, Emerson Boozer, Elise Roman, Owen Watson, Emerson Boozer, Rene Van Clief, Elsie Roman, Moses Illuya, Frank Ruiz, James Durran, Thomas Ageio, Wildrew Roldan, Sidney Filson, Sam Schwartz, Gary Catus, Tanka Ramos, Teddy Wilson, Chino Diaz, James Martin, Butch Oglesby, Jack Levy, Greer Smith.

Plot: Velvet Smooth (Hill) is a private detective with a support staff of women. She is hired by King Lathrop, the leader of the local gang, to find out who is behind the rash of outside action that is crowding his turf. By the time this movie was released, the interest in blaxploitation had peaked and declined, thus the movie was one of the last to emerge.

Notes

Preface

1. I have chosen to limit the discussion to my personal experiences that do not serve as a marker for all African-American women.
2. These terms are defined in Chapter 1.
3. Although she has had other significant roles, Sigourney Weaver's career in Hollywood has been defined by this character.
4. Many actors such as Fred Williamson, Jim Brown and the late Ron O'Neal appeared in this film as a homage to their roles in blaxploitation movies.
5. Jim Brown appeared as her husband in this picture. Ironically, they never co-starred in a movie together during blaxploitation's pinnacle of popularity.
6. Gregg Braxton, "She's Back and Badder Than Ever," *Los Angeles Times*, August 27, 1995.

Introduction

1. Richard A. Maynard, ed., *The Black Man on Film: Racial Stereotyping* (Rochelle Park, NJ: Hayden Book Company, 1974), VII.
2. Marilyn Kern-Foxworth, *Aunt Jemima, Uncle Ben, and Rastus: Blacks in Advertising, Yesterday, Today, and Tomorrow* (Westport, Connecticut: Greenwood, 1994), 79.
3. I am using the term Tragic Mulatto and Exotic Other interchangeably. While Tragic Mulatto is technically the correct term, Tragic Mulatto often has been used to describe a male and female who is of Mulatto origins.
4. Marilyn Kern-Foxworth, *Aunt Jemima, Uncle Ben, and Rastus: Blacks in Advertising, Yesterday, Today, and Tomorrow* (Westport, Connecticut: Greenwood, 1994), 88.
5. Cedric Robinson, "Blaxploitation and the misrepresentation of liberation," *Race & Class*, vol. 40, no. 1, 1998.
6. I borrow this term from Molly Haskell's "Here Come the Killer Dames," *New York Times*, May 19, 1975.
7. Throughout this book, I try to use the term "film" in a different context from "movies." I recognize that film is perceived as more artistic by reviewers, scholars and critics. It is not my intent to suggest that blaxploitation movies should be viewed as films; however, I do not believe they should be completely dismissed on the basis of aesthetics. In *At a Theater or Drive-In Near You: The History, Culture and Politics of the American Exploitation Film*, Randall Clark offers several criteria on which exploitation films, including blaxploitation movies, should be judged. My own personal assessment of the movies discussed here is based partly on recognizing that film critics are correct in their argument about the lack of cultural aesthetics in blaxploitation movies, but I am unwilling to dismiss the entire genre based on this criteria alone.
8. It is important to emphasize the contributions and creation of the action heroine

in Hong Kong cinema long before the character became part of popular cinema in the United States. Also, scholars have suggested that Diana Rigg's Emma Peel in the 1960s British television series *The Avengers*, with her male counterpart John Steed (portrayed by Patrick Macnee), was also an action heroine. While I agree that Rigg's character certainly fits the definition of action heroine, what is different in blaxploitation movies is the main plot is centered on the action heroine herself and not her male counterpart.

9. Junius Griffin, president of the local chapter of the National Association for the Advancement of Colored People, is credited with coining this term. In his dictionary on film terms, scholar Frank Beaver defines it as "a commercial-minded film of the seventies for black audiences." Although I have misgivings about using blaxploitation because it downplays the contributions of African-American actresses in bringing a new personae to the screen, I have chosen to use the word keeping in mind the social, political and economic context in which the genre emerged. In his dissertation *The 1970s As Hollywood's Golden Economic Age: A Critical Interpretative Analysis of the Blaxploitation Cinematic Movement* (University of Illinois-Urbana Champaign, 2000, p. 2), Eric Charles Pierson writes, "[A]ny definition must avoid the reductionism of simply stating that blaxploitation was a series of films marketed to the African-American audience in the early 1970s." Black action is an appropriate term for the movies discussed in this book; however, blaxploitation is more familiar to audiences, critics and scholars.

10. Charles Michener, "Black Movies" in *Black Films and Film-Makers: A Comprehensive Anthology from Stereotype to Superhero* (New York: Dodd, Mead, 1975), 243.

11. *Ibid.*

12. *Ibid.*

13. *Ibid.*

14. Edward Mapp, "Black Women in Films: A Mixed Bag of Tricks" in *Black Films and Film-Makers: A Comprehensive Anthology From Stereotype to Superhero*, ed. Lindsay Patterson (New York: Dodd, Mead, 1975), 197.

15. *Ibid.*

16. Charles Michener, "Black Movies" in *Black Films and Film-Makers: A Comprehensive Anthology from Stereotype to Superhero* (New York: Dodd, Mead, 1975), 246.

17. Chapter 1 offers a more detailed analysis of the types of limited roles African-American actresses portrayed prior to the 1960s.

18. Kathy Russell, Midge Wilson, and Ronald Hall, *The Color Complex: The Politics of Skin Color and Hair in the African American Community* (New York: Harcourt Brace Jovanovich, 1992), 143.

19. *Ibid.*, 70.

20. *Ibid.*, 71.

21. In the biography *Hattie*, author Carleton Jackson discusses the sting McDaniel felt from White's criticism.

22. Louis Robinson, "Pam Grier: More Than Just a Sex Symbol," *Ebony Magazine*, June 1976.

23. I am defining dominant way as the dominant ideology — that is to say the ideology that suggests African-American women must look a certain way in order to portray a part. This ideology is rooted in the historic placement and perspective of black women dating back to slavery. There are many books on the subject and one oft-cited work, *When and Where I Enter: The Impact of Black Women on Race and Sex in America* (New York: Morrow, 1984) by Paula Giddings, offers an insightful analysis of black women's history in American culture.

24. Randall Clark, *At a Theater or Drive-In Near You: The History, Culture and Politics of the American Exploitation Film* (New York and London: Garland, 1995), 150.

25. Mark A. Reid, *Redefining Black Film* (Berkeley and Los Angeles: University of California, 1993), 7.

26. *Ibid.*, 9.

27. *Ibid.*

28. *Ibid.*

29. *Ibid.*, 12.

30. *Ibid.*

31. *Ibid.*, 11.

32. *Ibid.*

33. *Ibid.*, 14.

34. *Ibid.*

35. *Ibid.*

36. Although she was not on par with Grier, Dobson and Graves as an actress, Bell is included because she played a woman seeking revenge on those who killed her brother in *TNT Jackson* (1974), one of the first blaxploitation movies to merge martial arts as a crucial component of the storyline, particularly with an African-American heroine.

Dobson's Cleopatra Jones alternates between martial arts and using guns.

37. Randall Clark, *At a Theater or Drive-In Near You: The History, Culture and Politics of the American Exploitation Film* (New York and London: Garland, 1995), 158.

38. Gerald Martinez, Diana Martinez, and Andres Chavez, eds., *What it Is, What it Was!: TheBlack Film Explosion of the 70s in Words and Picture* (New York: Hyperion Miramax Books, 1998), 54.

39. Philip Green, *Cracks in the Pedestal: Ideology and Gender in Hollywood* (Amherst: University of Massachusetts Press, 1998), 239.

40. *Ibid.*, 240.

Chapter 1

1. Richard A. Maynard, ed., *The Black Man on Film: Racial Stereotyping* (Rochelle Park, NJ: Hayden Book Company, 1974), 3.

2. James R. Nesteby, *Black Images in American Films, 1896–1954: The Interplay Between Civil Rights and Film Culture* (Washington, D.C: University of America Press, 1982), 2.

3. bell hooks, "The Oppositional Gaze" in *Black Looks: Race and Representation* (Boston: South End Press, 1992), 119.

4. *Ibid.*, 122.

5. *Ibid.*

6. Patricia Hill Collins, *Black Feminist Thought: Knowledge, Consciousness and the Politics of Empowerment*, 2d ed (New York and London: Routledge, 2000), 70.

7. K. Sue Jewell, *From Mammy to Miss America and Beyond: Cultural Images and the Shaping of U.S. Social Policy* (New York and London: Routledge, 1993), 36.

8. Patricia Hill Collins, *Black Feminist Thought: Knowledge, Consciousness and the Politics of Empowerment*, 2d ed (New York: Routledge, 2000), 70.

9. Mary E. Mebane, Review of *Cleopatra Jones, New York Times*, September 23, 1973.

10. Robert Stam, *Film Theory: An Introduction* (Malden, Massachusetts: Blackwell, 2000), 185.

11. Douglas Kellner, "Cultural Studies, Multiculturalism and Media Culture" in *Gender, Race and Class in Media: A Text Reader*, eds. Gail Dines and Jean M. Humez (Thousand Oaks, California: Sage Publications, 1995).

12. Throughout the book, exotic other, tragic mulatto and jezebel are used interchangeably.

13. Jessie Parkhurst, "The Role of the Black Mammy in the Plantation Household," *Journal of Negro History* 23, 1938, 351.

14. *Ibid.*

15. Cheryl Thurber, "The Development of the Mammy Image and Mythology," in *Southern Women: Histories and Identities*, eds. Virginia Bernhard, Betty Brandon, Elizabeth Fox-Genevese, and Theda Perdue (Columbia: University of Missouri Press, 1993), 89.

16. The clothing really depended on the film for the tragic mulatto. In the original *Imitation of Life* (1934), Fredi Washington's Peola wore dresses or skirts. When Lena Horne portrayed a seductress in *Cabin in the Sky* (1944), the tragic mulatto was more of a seductress. Although I use the term tragic mulatto and jezebel interchangeably, an argument can be made that the character is really two depending on how she is portrayed in a film.

17. K. Sue Jewell, *From Mammy to Miss America and Beyond: Cultural Images and the Shaping of U.S. Social Policy* (New York and London: Routledge, 1993), 39.

18. Kathy Russell, Midge Wilson, and Ronald Hall, *The Color Complex: The Politics of Skin Color and Hair in the African American Community* (New York: Harcourt Brace Jovanovich, 1992), 144.

19. Edward Mapp, "Black Women in Films: A Mixed Bag of Tricks," in *Black Films and Film-Makers: A Comprehensive Anthology From Stereotype to Superhero*, ed. Lindsay Patterson (New York: Dodd, Mead and Company, 1975), 196.

20. David Pilgrim, "Jezebel Stereotype," Ferris State University, July 2002, 1. Article retrieved March 2003.

21. *Ibid.*

22. George Alexander, "Credits Due: The Rise of Black Women in Hollywood," *American Legacy Woman*, 2002, 12.

23. *Ibid.*

24. *Ibid.*

25. Donald Bogle, *Toms, Coons, Mulattoes, Mammies and Bucks: An Interpretative History of Blacks in Film*, 3rd ed (New York: Continuum, 1994), 36.

26. Victoria Sturtevant, "'But things is changin' nowadays an' Mammy's gettin' bored': Hattie McDaniel and the Culture of Dissemblance," *Velvet Light Trap*, Fall 1999.

27. Ibid.

28. Edward Mapp, "Black Women in Films: A Mixed Bag of Tricks" in *Black Films and Film-Makers: A Comprehensive Anthology From Stereotype to Superhero*, ed. Lindsay Patterson (New York: Dodd, Mead, 1975), 197.

29. Victoria Sturtevant, "'But things is changin' nowadays an' Mammy's gettin' bored': Hattie McDaniel and the Culture of Dissemblance," *Velvet Light Trap*, Fall 1999.

30. Edward Mapp in "Black Women in Films: A Mixed Bag of Tricks" in *Black Films and Film-Makers: A Comprehensive Anthology From Stereotype to Superhero*, ed. Lindsay Patterson (New York: Dodd, Mead, 1975), 197.

31. Ibid.
32. Ibid.
33. Ibid.
34. Ibid.

35. Lena Horne, "Lena," in *Black Films and Film-Makers: A Comprehensive Anthology From Stereotype to Superhero*, ed. Lindsay Patterson (New York: Dodd, Mead, 1975), 142.

36. Ibid.

37. George Alexander, "Credits Due: The Rise of Black Women in Hollywood," *American Legacy Woman*, 2002, 14.

38. Jason Meyers, "How to Fight Like a Girl: The Roles of Women in Action Movies." Accessed March 2003, *www.home.earthlink.net/stik/girl/action*.

39. Ibid.
40. Ibid.

41. Yvonne Tasker, *Spectacular Bodies: Gender, Genre and the Action Cinema* (New York and London: Routledge, 1993), 1.

42. Personal interview with Bishetta Mishett, professor of communications at Howard University, April 29, 2005.

43. Ibid.
44. Ibid.

45. Susan Wloszczyna, "Holding out for a Heroine," *USA Today*, June 24, 2005.

46. Ibid.
47. Ibid.
48. Ibid.
49. Ibid.

50. Jason Meyers, "How to Fight Like a Girl: The Roles of Women in Action Movies," Accessed March 2003, *www.home.earthlink.net/stik/girl/action*.

51. Ibid.

52. It is worth noting that Stallone was not the only action hero in the 1980s as Schwarzenegger and Bruce Willis also starred in many action movies.

53. Jason Meyers, "How to Fight Like a Girl: The Roles of Women in Action Movies," Accessed March 2003, *www.home.earthlink.net/stik/girl/action*.

54. Donald Bogle, *Toms, Coons, Mulattoes, Mammies and Bucks: An Interpretative History of Blacks in American Film*, 3rd ed (New York: Continuum, 1994), 251.

Chapter 2

1. Ed Guerrero, *Framing Blackness: The African American Image in Film* (Philadelphia: Temple University Press, 1993), 82.

2. James P. Murray, "The Subject is Money" in *Black Films and Film-Makers: A Comprehensive Anthology From Stereotype to Superhero*, ed. Lindsay Patterson (New York: Dodd, Mead, 1975), 248.

3. Ibid.

4. Ed Guerrero, *Framing Blackness: The African American Image in Film* (Philadelphia: Temple University Press, 1993), 85.

5. James P. Murray, "The Subject is Money" in *Black Films and Film-Makers: A Comprehensive Anthology From Stereotype to Superhero*, ed. Lindsay Patterson (New York: Dodd, Mead, 1975), 248.

6. Ibid.

7. Michael Ryan and Douglas Kellner, *Camera Politica: The Politics and Ideology of Contemporary Hollywood Film* (Bloomington: Indiana University Press, 1988), 17.

8. Ed Guerrero, *Framing Blackness: The African American Image in Film* (Philadelphia: Temple University Press, 1993), 69.

9. Daniel Leab, *From Sambo to Superspade: The Black Experience in Motion Pictures* (Boston: Houghton Mifflin, 1975), 234.

10. Ibid.

11. Ed Guerrero, *Framing Blackness: The African American Image in Film*. (Philadelphia: Temple University Press, 1993), 70.

12. Mark A. Reid, "The Black Action Film: The End of the Patiently Enduring Black Hero," *Film History*, volume 2, 1988, 23.

13. Ibid.
14. Ibid.

15. Ed Guerrero, *Framing Blackness: The African American Image in Film* (Philadelphia: Temple University Press, 1993), 82.

16. *Ibid.*
17. *Ibid.*
18. Mark A. Reid, "The Black Action Film: The End of the Patiently Enduring Black Hero," *Film History*, volume 2, 1988, 24.
19. *Ibid.*
20. Daniel Leab, *From Sambo to Superspade: The Black Experience in Motion Pictures* (Boston: Houghton Mifflin, 1975), 85.
21. *Ibid.*
22. *Ibid.*
23. Ed Guerrero, *Framing Blackness: The African American Image in Film* (Philadelphia: Temple University Press, 1993), 74.
24. *Ibid.*
25. Mark A. Reid, "The Black Action Film: The End of the Patiently Enduring Black Hero," *Film History*, volume 2, 1988, 24.
26. *Ibid.*
27. *Ibid.*
28. *Ibid.*
29. *Ibid.*
30. *Ibid.*
31. *Ibid.*
32. Cedric Robinson, "Blaxploitation and the misrepresentation of liberation," *Race and Class*, vol. 40, no. 1, 1998, 2.
33. *Ibid.*
34. *Ibid.*
35. Mark A. Reid, "The Black Action Film: The End of the Patiently Enduring Black Hero," *Film History*, volume 2, 1988, 24.
36. Robert Fogelson, *Violence as Protest: A Study of Riots and Ghettos* (New York: Doubleday, 1971), 81.
37. Ed Guerrero, *Framing Blackness: The African American Image in Film* (Philadelphia: Temple University Press, 1993), 84.
38. *Ibid.*
39. Eric Charles Pierson, *The 1970s as Hollywood's Golden Economic Age: A Critical Interpretative Analysis of the Blaxploitation Cinematic Movement* (Ph. D. dissertation, University of Illinois-Urbana Champaign, 2000), 88.
40. *Ibid.*
41. Samuel Arkoff, with Richard Turbo, *Flying Through Hollywood by the Seat of My Pants: From the Man Who Brought You I was a Teenage Werewolf and Muscle Beach Party* (New York: A Birch Lane Press Book, 1992), 43.
42. Cedric Robinson, "Blaxploitation and the misrepresentation of liberation," *Race and Class*, vol, 40, no. 1, 1998, 7.
43. *Ibid.*
44. Samuel Arkoff, with Richard Turbo, *Flying Through Hollywood by the Seat of My Pants: From the Man Who Brought You I was a Teenage Werewolf and Muscle Beach Party* (New York: A Birch Lane Press Book, 1992), 43.
45. *Ibid.*
46. Pauline Kael, *Going Steady: Film Writings 1968–1969* (New York and London: Marion Boyars, 1994), 183.
47. Harvard Sitkoff, *The Struggle for Black Equality 1954–1992*, rev. ed. (New York: Harper Collins, 1993), 23.
48. *Ibid.*
49. Ed Guerrero, *Framing Blackness: The African American Image in Film* (Philadelphia: Temple University Press, 1993), 70.
50. *Ibid.*
51. Donald Bogle, *Toms, Coons, Mulattoes, Mammies and Bucks: An Interpretative History of Blacks in American Films* (New York: The Viking Press, 1973), 251.
52. Cedric Robinson, "Blaxploitation and the Misrepresentation of Liberation," *Race and Class*, vol. 40, no. 1, 1998, 10.
53. Donald Bogle, *Toms, Coons, Mulattoes, Mammies and Bucks: An Interpretative History of Blacks in American Films* (New York: The Viking Press, 1973), 251.
54. Oliver Slaughter, *A Study of Black Reactions to Blaxploitation Movies*, Master's thesis, Illinois Institute of Technology, December 1973.

Chapter 3

1. Thomas Johnson and David Fantle, "Coffy Time: An Interview with Pam Grier" *Outré* 9, 1997, 63–64.
2. Gerald Martinez, Diana Martinez, and Andres Chavez, eds., *What it Is, What it Was!: The Black Film Explosion of the 70s in Words and Picture* (New York: Hyperion Miramax Books, 1998), 73.
3. Ed Guerrero, *Framing Blackness: The African American Image in Film* (Philadelphia: Temple University Press, 1993), 100.
4. *Ibid.*
5. Marc Jacobson, "Sex Goddess of the Seventies," *New York Magazine*, May 19, 1975, 43.
6. Carrie Rickey, "Little Sheba's Comeback," *Voice*, March 4–10, 1981, 42.

7. Patrick Salvo, "Pam Grier: The Movie Super-Sex Goddess Who's Fed up with Sex and Violence," *Interview*, February 1976, 56.
8. Alan Ebert, "Pam Grier: Coming Into Focus," *Essence Magazine*, January 1979, 108.
9. One of the taglines from *Coffy*.
10. Marc Jacobson, "Sex Goddess of the Seventies," *New York Magazine*, May 19, 1975, 43.
11. Jamaica Kincaid, "Pam Grier: The Mocha Mogul of Hollywood," *Ms. Magazine*, August 1975, 50.
12. *Ibid*.
13. *Ibid*.
14. *Ibid*.
15. Louis Robinson, "Pam Grier: More Than Just a Sex Symbol," *Ebony Magazine*, June 1976, 33.
16. *Ibid*.
17. Dennis Hunt, *Los Angeles Times*, March 12, 1981, 7.
18. *Ibid*.
19. Alan Ebert, "Pam Grier: Coming Into Focus," *Essence Magazine*, January 1979, 107.
20. *Ibid*.
21. Gerald Martinez, Diana Martinez, and Andres Chavez, eds., *What It Is, What It Was!: The Black Explosion of the 70s in Words and Pictures* (New York: Hyperion Miramax Books, 1998), 50.
22. *Ibid*.
23. Alan Ebert, "Pam Grier: Coming Into Focus," *Essence Magazine*, January 1979, 10.
24. *Ibid*.
25. Hazel Carby, "It just be's dat way sometime: The sexual politics of women's blues," *Radical America*, 20, 1987, 9.
26. Gerald Martinez, Diana Martinez, and Andres Chavez, eds., *What It Is, What It Was!: The Black Explosion of the 70s in Words and Pictures* (New York: Hyperion Miramax Books, 1998), 146–147.
27. Alan Ebert, "Pam Grier: Coming Into Focus," *Essence Magazine*, January 1979, 10.
28. Cedric Robinson, "Blaxploitation and the misrepresentation of liberation," *Race and Class*, vol. 40, no. 1, 1998.
29. Arthur Knight, "Sex Stars," *Playboy's Sex in Cinema* (Chicago: Playboy Press, 1974) 142.
30. Tagline from *Foxy Brown*.
31. Gerald Martinez, Diana Martinez, and Andres Chavez, eds., *What It Is, What It Was!: The Black Explosion of the 70s in Words and Pictures* (New York: Hyperion Miramax Books, 1998), 138.
32. *Ibid*.
33. "Sheba Baby," *Variety*, April 23, 1975, 18.
34. Patrick Salvo, "Pam Grier: The Movie Super-Sex Goddess Who's Fed up with Sex and Violence," *Interview*, February 1976, 5.
35. *Foxy Brown* (1974).
36. Patrick Salvo, "Pam Grier: The Movie Super-Sex Goddess Who's Fed up with Sex and Violence," *Interview*, February 1976, 5.
37. *Sheba Baby* (1975).
38. Patrick Salvo, "Pam Grier: The Movie Super-Sex Goddess Who's Fed up with Sex and Violence," *Interview*, February 1976, 5.
39. *Ibid*.
40. Donald Bogle, *Toms, Coons, Mulattoes, Mammies and Bucks: An Interpretative History of Blacks in American Film* revised edition (New York: Continum, 1994).
41. Jill Gerston, "Pam Grier Finally Escapes the 1970s," *New York Times*, December 21, 1997, 17.
42. Alan Ebert, "Pam Grier: Coming Into Focus," *Essence*, January 1979, 10.
43. *Ibid*.
44. *Ibid*.
45. Thomas Johnson and David Fantle, "Coffy Time: An Interview with Pam Grier," *Outré* 9, 1997, 63–64.
46. *Ibid*.
47. *Ibid*.
48. James Robert Parish and George H. Hill, *Black Action Films: Plots, Critiques, Casts and Credits for 235 Theatrical and Made-for-Television Releases* (Jefferson, North Carolina: McFarland, 1989), 100.
49. *Ibid*.
50. George Alexander, "Credits Due: The Rise of Black Women in Hollywood," *American Legacy Woman*, 2002, 14.
51. *Ibid*.
52. *Ibid*.
53. Thomas Johnson and David Fantle, "Coffy Time: An Interview with Pam Grier," *Outré* 9, 1997, 63–64.
54. Gerald Martinez, Diana Martinez, and Andres Chavez, eds., *What It Is, What It Was!: The Black Explosion of the 70s in Words and Pictures* (New York: Hyperion Miramax Books, 1998), 53.
55. Personal interview, January 27, 2005.

56. Chris Holmund, "Wham! Bam! Pam! Pam Grier as Hot Action Babe and Cool Action Mama," *Quarterly Review of Film and Video*, vol. 22, no. 9, 102.
57. *Ibid.*
58. I use the word stigma here in a very loose context. I specifically use "stigma" to suggest that African-American actresses who starred in blaxploitation movies were labeled as blaxploitation actresses with the reasoning that they could only carry a film in this sub-genre. Producers refused to see black actresses such as Pam Grier and Tamara Dobson in roles beyond the action heroine and, frankly, being labeled as a bad-ass superwoman as part of the characters they portrayed did not help their chances of progressing to roles of more substance.
59. Chris Holmund, "Wham! Bam! Pam! Pam Grier as Hot Action Babe and Cool Action Mama," *Quarterly Review of Film and Video*, vol. 22, no. 9, 102.
60. *Ibid.*
61. Philip Green, *Cracks in the Pedestal: Ideology and Gender in Hollywood* (Amherst and Boston: University of Massachusetts Press, 1998).
62. Thomas Johnson and David Fantle, "Coffy Time: An Interview with Pam Grier" *Outré* 9, 1997, 63–64.

Chapter 4

1. Eric Charles Pierson, *The 1970s as Hollywood's Golden Economic Age: A Critical Interpretative Analysis of the Blaxploitation Cinematic Movement* (Ph. D. dissertation, University of Illinois-Urbana Champaign, 2000), 128.
2. Jack Haverstraw, "The Making of a Movie Star," *Sepia*, May 1975, 50.
3. *Ibid.*
4. *Ibid.*
5. *Ibid.*, 48.
6. Lucy Horton, *Ebony*, 1973, 146.
7. *Ibid.*
8. Jack Haverstraw, "The Making of a Movie Star," *Sepia*, May 1975, 47.
9. *Ibid.*
10. "Tamara Dobson: The Gorgeous Skyscraper," *Cosmopolitan*, October 1974, 46.
11. *Ibid.*
12. *Ibid.*
13. Jack Haverstraw, "The Making of a Movie Star," *Sepia*, 1975, 50.
14. *Ibid.*, 49.
15. Mary E. Mebane, Review of *Cleopatra Jones, New York Times*, September 23, 1973.
16. Yvonne Tasker, *Spectacular Bodies: Gender, Genre and the Action Cinema* (New York and London: Routledge, 1993), 23.
17. Chris Norton, "Cleopatra Jones 007: Blaxploitation, James Bond, and Reciprocal Co-Optation." Available online at *http://www.imagesjournal.com/issue04/features/blaxploitation.htm*. Retrieved on March 15, 2004.
18. *Ibid.*
19. *Ibid.*, 5.
20. *Ibid.*
21. *Ibid.*
22. Personal interview with Frances Gateward, professor of communications at the University of Illinois, April 29, 2005.
23. *Ibid.*
24. *Ibid.*
25. Mary Mebane, *New York Times*, September 1973.
26. Donald Bogle, *Toms, Coons, Mammies, Mulattoes and Bucks: An Interpretive History* (Rev Edition, New York: Continuum), 251.
27. *Ibid.*
28. "Cleopatra Jones: Tamara Dobson plays two-fisted crime buster in new black action flick?," *Ebony*, July 1973, 49.
29. *Ibid.*
30. Maurice Peterson, "Focus on Tamara Dobson," *Essence*, October 1977(?), 48.
31. *Ibid.*
32. "Cleopatra Jones: Tamara Dobson plays two-fisted crime buster in new black action flick," *Ebony*, July 1973, 49.
33. *Cleopatra Jones* (1973).
34. Kevin Thomas, "Cleopatra Battles the Dragon Lady," *Los Angeles Times*, August 27, 1975.
35. Jack Haverstraw, "The Making of a Movie Star," *Sepia*, May 1975.
36. *Ibid.*
37. Elley, Derek. "Cleopatra Jones and the Casino of Gold. *Film and Filming*, May 1976.
38. Todd McCarthy, "Cleopatra Jones and the Casino of Gold," *Hollywood Reporter*, June 18, 1975.
39. *Ibid.*
40. *Ibid.*

41. James Robert Parish and George H. Hill, *Black Action Films: Plots, Critiques, Casts and Credits, for235 Theatrical and Made-For-Television Releases* (Jefferson, North Carolina: McFarland, 1989), 98.
42. Jennifer DeVere Brody, "The Returns of Cleopatra Jones" in *The Seventies: The Age of Glitter in Popular Culture*, ed. Shelton Waldrep (New York and London: Routledge, 2000), 240.
43. *Ibid.*
44. *Ibid.*
45. *Ibid.*, 233.
46. Molly Haskell, "Here Come the Killer Dames," *New York Times*, May 19, 1975.
47. Personal interview with Francis Gateward, professor of communications at the University of Illinois-Urbana Champaign, April 29, 2005.

Chapter 5

1. Philip Green, *Cracks in the Pedestal: Ideology and Gender in Hollywood* (Amherst and Boston: University of Massachusetts Press, 1998), 219.
2. Universal Studios/Television News, 1974.
3. *Ibid.*
4. Richard Warren Lewis, "Then Time Out for Bible Study," *Television Guide*, November 30, 1974, 22.
5. *Ibid.*
6. "Will the Real Teresa Graves Stand Up?" *Ebony*, December 1974, 67.
7. Universal Studios/Television News, 1974.
8. "Will The Real Teresa Graves Stand Up"? *Ebony*, December 1974, 68.
9. "A Matter of Faith," *Television Guide*, November 16, 2002, 45.
10. *Ibid.*
11. "Will the Real Teresa Graves Stand Up?," *Ebony*, December 1974, 67.
12. *Ibid.*
13. *Ibid.*
14. Richard Warren Lewis, "Then Time Out for Bible Study," *Television Guide*, November 30, 1974, 23.
15. "Will The Real Teresa Graves Stand Up?," *Ebony*, December 1974, 68.
16. Richard Warren Lewis, "Then Time Out for Bible Study," *Television Guide*, November 30, 1974, 23.
17. *Ibid.*
18. *Ibid.*
19. *Get Christie Love!* (1974).
20. Get Christy Love article. TV Party.com.
21. *Ibid.*
22. "Will The Real Teresa Graves Stand Up?" *Ebony*, December 1974, 70.
23. After leaving AIP, Roger Corman started New World Pictures.
24. She appeared in *The Big Doll House*, *The Arena* and *Black Mama/White Mama* before 1973.
25. Tom Laughlin's *Billy Jack* trilogy is an excellent example.
26. John H. Dorr, "TNT Jackson," *Hollywood Reporter*, February 4, 1975.
27. Mack. "TNT Jackson," *Daily Variety*, February 13, 1975.
28. *Ibid.*
29. The martial arts stunts are more sophisticated than *Cleopatra Jones* and a bit fantastical, enough to attract audiences of both genres to the movie especially when nudity and violence are added in.
30. Diahann Carroll, "From Julia to Cosby to Oprah: Tuning in to 60 years of TV," *Ebony*, November 2005, 101.
31. *Ibid.*
32. *Ibid.*, 102.
33. *Ibid.*
34. *Ibid.*
35. http://www.jmannix.net/gail1.htm. Web site dedicated to the series *Mannix*, starring Mike Connors and Gail Fisher. Accessed on June 30, 2005.
36. *Ibid.*
37. K. Sue Jewell, *From Mammy to Miss America and Beyond: Cultural Images & Shaping of U.S. Social Policy* (New York and London: Routledge, 1993), 48.
38. *Ibid.*
39. Edward Mapp, "Black Women in Film a Mixed Bag of Tricks" in *Black Films and Black Filmmakers: A Comprehensive Anthology From Stereotype to Superhero*, ed. Lindsay Patterson (New York: Dodd, Mead, 1975), 198.
40. *Ibid.*
41. *Ibid.*
42. *Ibid.*
43. Donald Bogle, *Toms, Coons, Mulattoes, Mammies and Bucks: An Interpretative History*

of Blacks in American Film, 3d ed (New York: Continuum, 1994), 251.
44. *Ibid*.
45. Gerald Martinez, Diana Martinez, and Andres Chavez, eds., *What It Is, What It Was!: The Black Explosion of the 70s in Words and Pictures* (New York: Hyperion Miramax Books, 1998), 139.
46. Mark A. Reid, *Redefining Black Film* (Berkeley and Los Angeles: University of California Press, 1993), 87.
47. *Ibid*.
48. *Ibid*.
49. *Ibid.*, 88.

Chapter 6

1. Randall Clark, *At a Theatre or Drive-In Near You: The History, Culture and Politics of the American Exploitation Film* (New York and London: Garland, 1995), 150.
2. *Ibid*.
3. Mark A. Reid, "The Black Action Film: The End of the Patiently Enduring Black Hero," *Film History*, volume 2, 1988, 26.
4. *Ibid*.
5. *Ibid*.
6. Ed Guerrero, *Framing Blackness: The African American Image in Film* (Philadelphia: Temple University Press, 1993), 87.
7. *Ibid*.
8. Lerone Bennett, Jr., "The Emancipation Orgasm: Sweetback in Wonderland," *Ebony*, September 1971, 112.
9. The end of Van Peebles film states "dedicated to all the brothers and sisters who have had enough of the man."
10. Daniel Leab, *From Sambo to Superspade: The Black Experience in Motion Pictures* (Boston: Houghton Mifflin, 1975), 249.
11. *Ibid*.
12. *Ibid*.
13. James Murray, *To Find an Image: Black Films from Uncle Tom to Super Fly* (Indianapolis and New York: Bobbs-Merrill, 1973), 68.
14. *Ibid.*, 69.
15. Daniel Leab, *From Sambo to Superspade: The Black Experience in Motion Pictures* (Boston: Houghton Mifflin, 1975), 249.
16. *Ibid*.
17. Mark A. Reid, *Redefining Black Film* (Berkeley and Los Angeles: University of California Press, 1993), 84.
18. *Ibid*.
19. *Ibid*.
20. *Ibid*.
21. *Ibid*.
22. *Ibid*.
23. Ed Guerrero, *Framing Blackness: The African American Image in Film* (Philadelphia: Temple University Press, 1993), 97.
24. Daniel Leab, *From Sambo to Superspade: The Black Experience in Motion Pictures* (Boston: Houghton Mifflin, 1975), 259.
25. Personal interview conducted with Professor Eric Charles Pierson.
26. *Ibid.*, 99.
27. *Ibid.*, 164.
28. Ed Guerrero, *Framing Blackness: The African American Image in Film* (Philadelphia: Temple University Press, 1993), 95.
29. Charles Michener, "Black Movies," in *Black Films and Film-Makers: A Comprehensive Anthology From Stereotype to Superhero*, ed. Lindsay Patterson (New York: Dodd, Mead, 1975), 239.
30. *Ibid*.
31. Francis Ward, *"Super Fly": A Political and Cultural Condemnation by the Kuumba Workshop* (Chicago: Institute of Positive Education, 1972), 1–2.
32. *Ibid*.
33. Oliver Slaughter, *A Study of Black Reactions to Blaxploitation Movies*, Master's thesis, Illinois Institute of Technology, December 1973, 6.
34. Alvin F. Poussaint, "Cheap Thrills that Degrade Blacks," *Psychology Today* 7, 1974, 27.
35. Ed Guerrero, *Framing Blackness: The African American Image in Film* (Philadelphia: Temple University Press, 1993), 97.
36. *Ibid*.
37. *Ibid*.
38. Oliver Slaughter, *A Study of Black Reactions to Blaxploitation Movies*, Master's thesis, Illinois Institute of Technology, December 1973.
39. *Ibid*.
40. *Ibid*.
41. Eric Charles Pierson, *The 1970s as Hollywood's Golden Economic Age: A Critical Interpretative Analysis of the Blaxploitation Cinematic Movement* (Ph. D. dissertation, University of Illinois-Urbana Champaign, 2000), 99.

42. *Ibid.*
43. *Ibid.*
44. *Ibid.*, 126.
45. *Ibid.*, 103.
46. George Alexander, "The Credits Due: The Rise of Black Women in Hollywood," *American Legacy Woman*, 2002, 14.
47. *Ibid.*
48. Daniel Leab, *From Sambo to Superspade: The Black Experience in Motion Pictures* (Boston: Houghton Mifflin, 1975), 258.
49. *Ibid.*, 259.
50. Jamaica Kincaid, "Pam Grier: The Mocha Mogul of Hollywood," *Ms. Magazine*, 1975, 53.
51. *Ibid.*
52. Samuel Arkoff, with Richard Turbo, *Flying Through Hollywood by the Seat of My Pants: From the Man Who Brought You I was a Teenage Werewolf and Muscle Beach Party* (New York: A Birch Lane Press Book, 1992), 207.
53. Eric Charles Pierson, *The 1970s as Hollywood's Golden Economic Age: A Critical Interpretative Analysis of the Blaxploitation Cinematic Movement* (Ph. D. dissertation, University of Illinois-Urbana Champaign, 2000), 102.
54. *Ibid.*
55. "Pam Grier Expands Her Film Career," 1975, 58.
56. Eric Charles Pierson, *The 1970s as Hollywood's Golden Economic Age: A Critical Interpretative Analysis of the Blaxploitation Cinematic Movement* (Ph. D. dissertation, University of Illinois-Urbana Champaign, 2000), 106.
57. *Ibid.*, 107
58. *Ibid.*, 130.
59. *Ibid.*
60. Andres Martinez, Diana Martinez, and Andres Chavez, eds., *What It Is, What It Was!: The Black Film Explosion of the 70s in Words and Pictures* (New York: Hyperion Miramax Books, 1998), 92.
61. Randall Clark, *At a Theater or Drive-In Near You: The History, Culture, and Politics of the American Exploitation Film* (New York and London: Garland, 1995), 158.
62. Andres Martinez, Diana Martinez and Andres Chavez, eds., *What It Is, What It Was!: The Black Film Explosion of the 70s in Words and Pictures* (New York: Hyperion Miramax Books, 1998), 112.
63. *Ibid.*
64. James Robert Parish and George A. Hill, *Black Action Films: Plots, Critiques, Casts and Credits for 235 Theatrical and Made-for-Television Releases* (Jefferson, North Carolina: McFarland, 1989), xii.
65. *Ibid.*
66. *Ibid.*
67. *Ibid.*
68. Eric Charles Pierson, *The 1970s as Hollywood's Golden Economic Age: A Critical Interpretative Analysis of the Blaxploitation Cinematic Movement* (Ph. D. dissertation, University of Illinois-Urbana Champaign, 2000), 106.
69. *Ibid.*, 34.
70. *Ibid.*
71. *Ibid.*
72. *Ibid.*
73. Charles Kroengold, "Identity, Value, and the Work of Genre," in *The Seventies: The Age of Glitter in Popular Culture*, ed. Shelton Waldrep (New York and London: Routledge, 2000), 110.
74. To borrow Charles Kronengold's term, movies made by Burt Reynolds that featured his character outwitting law enforcement while transporting moonshine and Charles Bronson's vigilante movies might also be considered "white exploitation." Although Kronengold does not define what he means by white exploitation, using the same definition exchanging black for white might be useful as a working definition of what he means.
75. Charles Kronengold, "Identity, Value, and the Work of Genre" in *The Seventies: The Age of Glitter in Popular Culture*, ed. Shelton Waldrep (New York and London: Routledge, 2000), 110.

Chapter 7

1. Jason Meyer, "How to Fight Like a Girl: The Roles of Women in Action Movies." Accessed March 2003, *www.home.earthlink.net/stik/girl/action*.
2. *Ibid.*
3. Jeffrey A. Brown, "Gender and the Action Heroine: Hardbodies and the *Point of No Return*," *Cinema Journal* vol. 35, no. 3, Spring 1996, 52–71.

4. *Ibid.*
5. *Ibid.*, 57.
6. *Ibid.*
7. Yvonne Tasker, *Spectacular Bodies: Gender, Genre and the Action Cinema* (New York and London: Routledge, 1993), 16–17.
8. *Ibid.*
9. *Ibid.*
10. *Ibid.*
11. *Ibid.*
12. Jason Meyer, "How to Fight Like a Girl: The Roles of Women in Action Movies." Accessed March 2003, *www.home.earthlink.net/stik/girl/action.*
13. *Ibid.*, 1.
14. *Ibid.*, 2.
15. *Ibid.*
16. Donald Bogle, *Toms, Coons, Mulattoes, Mammies and Bucks: An Interpretative History of Blacks in Film*, 3d ed (New York: Continuum, 1994), 251.
17. *Ibid.*
18. Yvonne Tasker, *Spectacular Bodies: Gender, Genre and the Action Cinema* (New York and London: Routledge, 1993), 21.
19. *Ibid.*
20. Jason Meyer, "How to Fight Like a Girl: The Roles of Women in Action Movies." Accessed March 2003, *www.home.earthlink.net/stik/girl/action.*
21. *Ibid.*
22. Donald Bogle, *Toms, Coons, Mulattoes, Mammies and Bucks: An Interpretative History of Blacks in Film*, 3d ed (New York: Continuum, 1994), 252.
23. Jason Meyer, "How to Fight Like a Girl: The Roles of Women in Action Movies." Accessed March 2003, *www.home.earthlink.net/stik/girl/action.*
24. *Ibid.*
25. *Ibid.*
26. Yvonne Tasker, *Spectacular Bodies: Gender, Genre and the Action Cinema* (New York and London: Routledge, 1993), 149.
27. *Ibid.*, 149.
28. Jeffrey A. Brown, "Gender and the Action Heroine: Hardbodies and the *Point of No Return*," *Cinema Journal*, vol. 35, no. 3, Spring 1996, 62.
29. Jason Meyer, "How to Fight Like a Girl: The Roles of Women in Action Movies." Accessed March 2003, *www.home.earthlink.net/stik/girl/action.*
30. *Ibid.*
31. *Ibid.*
32. Yvonne Tasker, *Spectacular Bodies: Gender, Genre and the Action Cinema* (New York and London: Routledge, 1993), 151.
33. *Ibid.*
34. Jeffrey A. Brown, "Gender and the Action Heroine: Hardbodies and the *Point of No Return*," *Cinema Journal*, vol. 35, no. 3, Spring 1996, 54.
35. *Ibid.*, 66.
36. *Ibid.*, 68.
37. Yvonne Tasker, *Spectacular Bodies: Gender, Genre and the Action Cinema* (New York and London: Routledge, 1993), 132.
38. Jason Meyer, "How to Fight Like a Girl: The Roles of Women in Action Movies." Accessed March 2003, *www.home.earthlink.net/stik/girl/action.*
39. *Ibid.*
40. Yvonne Tasker, *Spectacular Bodies: Gender, Genre and the Action Cinema* (New York and London: Routledge, 1993), 138.
41. Jason Meyer, "How to Fight Like a Girl: The Roles of Women in Action Movies." Accessed March 2003, *www.home.earthlink.net/stik/girl/action.*
42. *Ibid.*
43. Jeffrey A. Brown, "Gender and the Action Heroine: Hardbodies and the *Point of No Return*." *Cinema Journal*, vol. 35, no. 3, Spring 1996, 52.
44. *Ibid.*, 60.
45. *Ibid.*
46. Yvonne Tasker, *Spectacular Bodies: Gender, Genre and the Action Cinema* (New York and London: Routledge, 1993), 149–150.
47. *Ibid.*
48. *Ibid.*
49. *Ibid.*
50. Jason Meyer, "How to Fight Like a Girl: The Roles of Women in Action Movies." Accessed March 2003, *www.home.earthlink.net/stik/girl/action.*
51. *Ibid.*
52. Jeffrey A. Brown, "Gender and the Action Heroine: Hardbodies and the *Point of No Return*," *Cinema Journal*, vol. 35, no. 3, Spring 1996, 56.
53. *Ibid.*, 56.
54. *Ibid.*, 63.
55. *Ibid.*, 64.
56. *Ibid.*
57. *Ibid.*, 65.

58. Owen Glieberman, review of *Point of No Return*, *Entertainment Weekly*, April 2, 1993, 31
59. Jeffrey A. Brown, "Gender and the Action Heroine: Hardbodies and the *Point of No Return*," *Cinema Journal*, vol. 35, no. 3, Spring 1996, 56.
60. *Ibid.*, 68.
61. *Ibid.*
62. *Ibid.*
63. Jason Meyer, "How to Fight Like a Girl: The Roles of Women in Action Movies." Accessed March 2003, *www.home.earthlink.net/stik/girl/action*.
64. *Ibid.*
65. *Ibid.*
66. Yvonne Tasker, *Spectacular Bodies: Gender, Genre and the Action Cinema* (New York and London: Routledge, 1993), 135.
67. *Ibid.*
68. *Ibid.*
69. *Ibid.*
70. *Ibid.*
71. Stephanie Mencimer, "Violent Femmes," *Washington Monthly*, September 2001, 3.
72. *Ibid.*, 5
73. *Ibid.*
74. *Ibid.*
75. *Ibid.*
76. *Ibid.*
77. *Ibid.*
78. *Ibid.*
79. *Ibid.*
80. *Ibid.*

Chapter 8

1. *http://www.girlswithguns.org/index.htm*. Accessed June 3, 2005.
2. Gerald Martinez, Diana Martinez, and Andres Chavez, eds., *What it Is, What it Was!: The Black Film Explosion of the 70s in Words and Picture* (New York: Hyperion Miramax Books, 1998), 53.
3. *http://www.nmstudios.com*. Accessed November 2, 2005.
4. *http://www.nmstudios.com*. Accessed November 2, 2005.
5. Christina Larson, "Seven Mistakes Superheroines Make: Why the Latest Action-Babe Flicks Flopped," *Washington Monthly*, March 2005. Retrieved from *http://www.washingtonmonthly.com/features/2005/0503.larson2.html*.
6. *Ibid.*
7. *Ibid.*
8. *Ibid.*
9. *Ibid.*
10. *Ibid.*
11. *Ibid.*
12. Personal interview.
13. *Ibid.*
14. *Ibid.*
15. *Ibid.*
16. Christina Larson, "Seven Mistakes Superheroines Make: Why the Latest Action-Babe Flicks Flopped," *Washington Monthly*, March 2005. Retrieved from *http://www.washingtonmonthly.com/features/2005/0503.larson2.html*.
17. *Ibid.*
18. *http://www.girlswithguns.org/index.htm*. Accessed June 3, 2005.
19. Stefanie Powers, *The Girl from U.N.C.L.E.*, also deserves mention for her series about a woman who works for the federal government and tries to stop enemy plots. It was a spin-off from the successful *The Man from U.N.C.L.E.* series starring Robert Vaughn.
20. Susan Wloszczyna, "Holding Out for a Heroine," *USA Today*, June 24, 2005.
21. *Ibid.*
22. *Ibid.*
23. *Ibid.*
24. *Ibid.*
25. *http://www.girlswithguns.org/index.htm*. Accessed June 3, 2005.
26. *Ibid.*
27. *Ibid.*
28. Susan Wloszczyna, "Holding Out for a Heroine," *USA Today*, June 24, 2005.
29. "Multiple jeopardy" is based on the fact that African American women must contend with race, gender and class issues.
30. Susan Wloszczyna, "Holding Out for a Heroine," *USA Today*, June 24, 2005.
31. *Ibid.*
32. *Ibid.*
33. Christina Larson, "Seven Mistakes Superheroines Make: Why the Latest Action-Babe Flicks Flopped," *Washington Monthly*, March 2005. Retrieved from *http://www.washingtonmonthly.com/features/2005/0503.larson2.html*.
34. *Ibid.*

Selected Bibliography

Alexander, George. "Credits Due: The Rise of Black Women in Hollywood." *American Legacy Woman*, 2002.
Arkoff, Samuel Z., with Richard Turbo. *Flying Through Hollywood by the Seat of My Pants: From the Man Who Brought* You I Was a Teenage Werewolf *and* Muscle Beach Party. New York: A Birch Lane Press Book, 1992.
Bennett, Lerone, Jr. "The Emancipation Orgasm: Sweetback in Wonderland." *Ebony*, September 1971.
Bobo, Jacqueline. *Black Women as Cultural Readers*. New York: Columbia University Press, 1995.
Bogle, Donald. *Toms, Coons, Mulattoes, Mammies and Bucks: An Interpretative History of Blacks in American Film*. First and 3d eds. New York: Continuum, 1973 and 1994.
Braxton, Gregg. "She's Back and Badder Than Ever." *Los Angeles Times*, August 27, 1995.
Brody, Jennifer DeVere. "The Returns of Cleopatra Jones." In *The Seventies: The Age of Glitter in Popular Culture*, ed. Shelton Waldrep. New York and London: Routledge, 2000.
Brown, Jeffrey A. "Gender and the Action Heroine: Hardbodies and the *Point of No Return*." *Cinema Journal*, vol. 35, no. 3, Spring 1996, 52–71.
Carby, Hazel. "It just be's dat way sometime: The sexual politics of women's blues." *Radical America*, 20, 1987.
Carroll, Diahann. "From Julia to Cosby to Oprah: Tuning in to 60 Years of TV." *Ebony*, November 2005.
Clark, Randall. *At a Theater or Drive-In Near You: The History, Culture and Politics of the American Exploitation Film*. New York and London: Garland, 1995.
"Cleopatra Jones: Tamara Dobson plays two-fisted crime buster in new black action flick." *Ebony*, July 1973.
Collins, Patricia Hill. *Black Feminist Thought: Knowledge, Consciousness and the Politics of Empowerment*. 2d ed. New York and London: Routledge, 2000.

Dines, Gail, and Jean Humez, eds. *Gender, Race and Class in Media: A Text Reader.* Thousand Oaks, California: Sage Publications, 1995.
Dorr, John H. "TNT Jackson." *Hollywood Reporter,* February 4, 1975.
Ebert, Alan. "Pam Grier: Coming Into Focus." *Essence Magazine,* January 1979.
Fogelson, Robert. *Violence as Protest: A Study of Riots and Ghettos.* New York: Doubleday, 1971.
Foxworth-Kern, Marilyn. *Aunt Jemima, Uncle Ben, and Rastus: Blacks in Advertising, Yesterday, Today, and Tomorrow.* Westport, Connecticut: Greenwood, 1994.
Gerston, Jill. "Pam Grier Finally Escapes the 1970s." *New York Times,* December 21, 1997.
Giddings, Paula. *When and Where I Enter: The Impact of Black Women on Race and Sex in America.* New York: Morrow, 1984.
Gleiberman, Owen. Review of *Point of No Return.* Entertainment Weekly,
Green, Philip. *Cracks in the Pedestal: Ideology and Gender in Hollywood.* Amherst and Boston: University of Massachusetts Press, 1998.
Guerrero, Ed. *Framing Blackness: The African American Image in Film.* Philadelphia: Temple University Press, 1993.
Haskell, Molly. "Here Come the Killer Dames." *New York Times,* May 19, 1975.
Haverstraw, Jack. "The Making of a Movie Star." *Sepia,* May 1975.
Holmund, Chris. "Wham! Bam! Pam! Pam Grier as Hot Action Babe and Cool Action Mama." *Quarterly Review of Film and Video,* vol. 22, no. 9, 2005.
hooks, bell. *Black Looks: Race and Representation.* Boston: South End Press, 1992.
Hunt, Dennis. *Los Angeles Times,* March 12, 1981.
Jacobson, Marc. "Sex Goddess of the Seventies." *New York Magazine,* May 19, 1975.
Jewell, K. Sue. *From Mammy to Miss America and Beyond: Cultural Images and the Shaping of U.S. Social Policy.* New York and London: Routledge, 1993.
Johnson, Thomas, and David Fantle. "Coffy Time: An Interview with Pam Grier." *Outré* 9, 1997.
Kael, Pauline. *Going Steady: Film Writings 1968–1969.* New York and London: Marion Boyars, 1994.
Kellner, Douglas. "Cultural Studies, Multiculturalism and Media Culture." In *Gender, Race and Class in Media: A Text Reader,* eds. Gail Dinea and Jean M. Humez. Thousand Oaks, California: Sage Publications, 1995.
Kincaid, Jamaica. "Pam Grier: The Mocha Mogul of Hollywood." *Ms. Magazine,* August 1975.
Kronengold, Charles. "Identity, Value, and the Work of Genre." In *The Seventies: The Age of Glitter in Popular Culture,* ed. Shelton Waldrep. New York and London: Routledge, 2000.
Larson, Christina. "Seven Mistakes Superheroines Make." *Washington Monthly,* March 2005. Retrieved November 2, 2005, from *http://www.washingtonmonthly.com/features/2005/0503.larson2.html.*
Leab, Daniel. *From Sambo to Superspade: The Black Experience in Motion Pictures.* Boston: Houghton Mifflin, 1975.
Lewis, Richard Warren. "Then Time Out for Bible Study." *Television Guide,* November 30, 1974.
Mapp, Edward. "Black Women in Films: A Mixed Bag of Tricks." In *Black Films and*

Film-Makers: A Comprehensive Anthology From Stereotype to Superhero, ed. Lindsay Patterson. New York: Dodd, Mead, 1975.

_____. *Blacks in American Films*. Metuchen, New Jersey: Scarecrow, 1972.

Martinez, Gerald, Diana Martinez, and Andres Chavez, eds. *What It Is, What It Was!: The Black Film Explosion of the 70s in Words and Pictures*. New York: Hyperion Miramax Books, 1998.

"A Matter of Faith." *Television Guide*, November 16, 2002.

Maynard, Richard A., ed. *The Black Man on Film: Racial Stereotyping*. Rochelle Park, NJ: Hayden Book Company, 1974.

McCarthy, Todd. "Cleopatra Jones and the Casino of Gold." *Hollywood Reporter*, June 18, 1975.

Mebane, Mary E. *New York Times*, September 23, 1973.

Mencimer, Stephanie. "Violent Femmes: On the big screen today, action babes are on top. Here's why men love it." *Washington Monthly*, September 2001. Retrieved November 2, 2005, from *http.www.washingtonmonthly.com/features/2001/0109. mencimer.html*.

Meyers, Jason. "How to Fight Like a Girl: The Roles of Women in Action Movies." Accessed March 2003 from www. home.earthlink.net/ stik/girl/action.

Michener, Charles. "Black Movies." In *Black Films and Film-makers: A Comprehensive Anthology from Stereotype to Superhero*, ed. Lindsay Patterson. New York: Dodd, Mead, 1975.

Murray, James P. *To Find an Image: Black Films From Uncle Tom to Super Fly*. Indianapolis and New York: Bobbs-Merrill, 1973.

_____. "The Subject is Money." In *Black Films and Film-makers: A Comprehensive Anthology from Stereotype to Superhero*, ed. Lindsay Patterson. New York: Dodd, Mead, 1975.

Nesteby, James R. *Black Images in American Films, 1896–1954: The Interplay Between Civil Rights and Film Culture*. Washington, D.C: University of America Press, 1982.

Norton, Chris. "Cleopatra Jones 007: Blaxploitation, James Bond, and Reciprocal Co-Optation." PUB INFO???

Parish, James Robert, and George H. Hill. *Black Action Films: Plots, Critiques, Casts and Credits for 235 Theatrical and Made-for-Television Releases*. Jefferson, North Carolina: McFarland, 1989.

Parkhurst, Jessie. "The Role of the Black Mammy in the Plantation Household." *Journal of Negro History* 23,1938.

Patterson, Lindsay, ed. *Black Films and Film-Makers: A Comprehensive Anthology from Stereotype to Superhero*. New York: Dodd, Mead, 1975.

Peterson, Maurice. "Focus on Tamara Dobson." *Essence*, October 1977(?).

Pierson, Eric Charles. *The 1970s as Hollywood's Golden Economic Age: A Critical Interpretative Analysis of the Blaxploitation Cinematic Movement*. Ph. D. dissertation, University of Illinois–Urbana Champaign, 2000.

Pilgrim, David. "Jezebel Stereotype." Ferris State University, July 2002. Retrieved March 2003.

Poussaint, Alvin F. "Cheap Thrills that Degrade Blacks." *Psychology Today* 7, 1974.

Reid, Mark A. "The Black Action Film: The End of the Patiently Enduring Black Hero." *Film History*, vol. 2, 1988.

_____. *Black Lenses, Black Voices: African American Film Now*. Lanham, Maryland: Rowman and Littlefield, 2005.

_____. *Redefining Black Film*. Berkeley and Los Angeles: University of California Press, 1993.

Rickey, Carrie. "Little Sheba's Comeback." *Voice*, March 4–10, 1981.

Robinson, Cedric. "Blaxploitation and the Misrepresentation of Liberation." *Race & Class*, vol. 40, no.1, 1998.

Robinson, Louis. "Pam Grier: More Than Just a Sex Symbol." *Ebony Magazine*, June 1976.

Rubin, N. Interview with Pam Grier. *Onion Magazine*. Accessed April 20, 2003, from *http://www.theonionavclub.com/avclubFebruary2002*.

Russell, Kathy, Midge Wilson, and Ronald Hall. *The Color Complex: The Politics of Skin Color and Hair in the African American Community*. New York: Harcourt Brace Jovanovich, 1992.

Ryan, Michael, and Douglas Kellner. *Camera Politica: The Politics and Ideology of Contemporary Hollywood Film*. Bloomington: Indiana University Press, 1988.

Sims, Yvonne Denise. "From Headscarves to Afros: Redefining African-American Femininity in 1970s Selected Black Action Films." In *Ethnic Media: Taking Control*, vol. 2, eds. Guy Meiss and Alice Tait. Dubuque: Kendall/Hunt, 2005.

_____. "From Mammies to Action Heroines: Female Empowerment in Black Popular Cinema." Dissertation, Bowling Green State University, 2000.

Sitkoff, Harvard. *The Struggle for Black Equality 1954–1992*. Rev. ed. New York: Harper Collins, 1993.

Slaughter, Oliver. *A Study of Black Reactions to Blaxploitation Movies*. Master's Thesis. Illinois Institute of Technology, December 1973.

Stam, Robert. *Film Theory: An Introduction*. Malden, Massachusetts: Blackwell, 2000.

Sturtevant, Victoria. "'But things is changin' nowadays an' Mammy's gettin' bored': Hattie McDaniel and the Culture of Dissemblance." *Velvet Light Trap*, Fall 1999.

Tasker, Yvonne. *Spectacular Bodies: Gender, Genre and the Action Cinema*. New York and London: Routledge, 1993.

Thomas, Kevin. "Cleopatra Battles the Dragon Lady." *Los Angeles Times*, August 27, 1975.

Thurber, Cheryl. "The Development of the Mammy Image and Mythology." In *Southern Women: Histories and Identities*, eds. Virginia Bernhard, Betty Brandon, Elizabeth Fox-Genevese and Theda Perdue. Columbia: University of Missouri Press, 1993.

Waldrep, Shelton, ed. *The Seventies: The Age of Glitter in Popular Culture*. New York and London: Routledge, 2000.

Ward, Francis. *"Super Fly": A Political and Cultural Condemnation by the Kuumba Workshop*. Chicago: Institute of Positive Education, 1973.

"Will the Real Teresa Graves Please Stand Up?" *Ebony*, December 1974.

Wloszczyna, Susan. "Holding Out for a Heroine." *USA Today*, June 24, 2005.

Index

Action hero 18, 43–44, 46–47, 90, 150, 176, 184, 204
Action heroine 4–6, 9, 16–22, 25–28, 31, 42–50, 68, 72, 90–92, 96, 100, 104, 106–8, 112, 114, 120–21, 123, 142, 147–48, 150–51, 154–58, 161–62, 164–73, 175–77, 179–81, 183–84, 187–89, 191–92, 196, 201–2, 207, 210–12
Action movies 20, 43, 47, 67, 70, 91, 136, 142–43, 146, 148, 150–151, 167, 204, 210–12
African American: beauty 15 79, 83, 128; femininity 4, 6, 10, 13, 18, 26, 28, 32, 41, 42, 44, 94, 100–1, 124, 126, 142, 191; sexuality 25, 79–81, 89, 96, 121, 129, 151, 154, 164, 167, 181, 184, 186; womanhood 4, 40–41, 74, 169
Afro 11, 42, 56, 68, 80–83, 184, 192
Aliens 9, 21, 147, 150, 154–58, 165, 167, 183
American International Pictures (AIP) 13, 18–19, 21, 45, 48–49, 55, 62–66, 68–69, 72, 77–78, 82, 86–87, 90, 166, 128, 129, 133, 136–140, 142, 143, 145, 171, 184, 199, 208
American popular culture 25, 191
Amos 'n' Andy 41, 52, 64, 102, 197
Arkoff, Samuel Z. 45, 62–66, 69, 90, 129, 139–40, 196, 205, 210
Audience reception 27
Aunt Jemima 7–8, 14–16, 25, 30–33, 35, 40–44, 60, 68, 70, 83, 110, 125, 127, 201
The Avengers 202

Baby boomers 52, 54
Baker, Josephine 11, 33, 80, 169–70
Baldwin, James 57–58
Barrymore, Drew 50, 184–86
Bassett, Angela 179, 189
Beavers, Louise 11, 34–36, 38, 40, 42, 79, 87, 124, 169–70
Bell, Jeannie 4–6, 8, 10, 16, 18, 20, 22, 26–30, 42, 48–50, 68, 70, 120–24, 127–29, 1380–39, 142, 146–47, 149, 151, 154, 170, 179, 189, 193, 199, 202
Bennett, Lerone, Jr. 73, 131, 209
Berry, Halle 22, 64, 173–75, 177–78, 183, 189
Beulah 20, 79
The Bionic Woman 1, 79
Birth of a Nation 33, 131
Black: action heroine 21–22 44–46, 90, 147–48, 169, 172, 175, 177, 179–81, 183, 187–89; femininity 3, 5, 7–8, 11–12, 16, 29, 31, 34, 40, 42, 80–83, 125, 184 *see also* African American femininity; feminist thought 30; film 10, 14–16, 37, 39, 58–60, 69, 72–73, 81, 87, 89–93, 98, 100, 109, 126–33, 135–44, 170–73, 181; nationalism 54, 67, 81
Black Feminist Thought 29
Black is beautiful 15
Black Panther Party 61, 67, 81, 131
Blackman, Honor 20, 180
Blaxploitation 3–6, 8–10, 13, 15–23, 26–30, 33, 42–49, 53–55, 58–60, 65, 67–72, 74–78, 82, 86–87, 89–94, 99–102,

217

108–11, 113, 116–17, 120–25, 127–49, 151, 154, 157, 162, 166–68, 170–76, 181, 184, 186–88, 191–192, 194–96, 199–202, 205, 207, 209–10
Blue Steel 47
Bogle, Donald 12, 34, 42, 68, 74, 87, 98–99, 151, 154, 170, 203–8, 211
Bond, James 22, 30, 49, 93, 96–99, 106, 122, 124, 126, 156, 197–98, 207
Bonnie and Clyde 47–48, 55, 180
Brando, Marlon 63
Brown, Jeffrey A. 148–49, 156–57, 160–63
Brown, Jim 4, 18, 58, 60, 66, 70, 140, 201
Bucks 60, 68, 72, 203–8, 211

Cambridge, Jeffrey 130, 197
Carby, Hazel 80, 206
Caricatures 5, 7, 18, 25, 42, 58, 69, 102, 125
Carroll, Diahann 16, 39, 42, 68, 79, 117, 124–25, 141, 170, 208
Casey, Bernie 96, 194
Cash, Rosalind 10, 197
Catwoman 22, 49, 173, 175, 181, 183, 186
Charlie's Angels 1, 50, 111, 173, 184, 185
Christy 1, 115, 208
Civil Rights Movement 8, 15, 60–61, 65, 70, 72, 110, 171
Clark, Randall 16, 201–3, 209–10
Claudine 140–41
Cleopatra Jones 6, 19–20, 22, 48–50, 93–94, 96–102, 104–9, 111, 113, 118, 120, 122, 124, 132, 137–38, 140, 179, 186–87, 189, 192–94, 203, 207–8
Cleopatra Jones and the Casino of Gold 19, 94, 104, 137–38, 194
Coffy 4, 6, 13, 16–17, 19, 22, 47–48, 50, 68, 72, 75–77, 79, 81, 83–84, 87, 89–91, 93–94, 101–2, 111–14, 118, 120–24, 128, 140, 145, 180, 184, 187–88, 191, 195–96, 199, 206
Coalition Against Blaxploitation 135
Coalition of Blaxploitation 72, 139
Collins, Patricia Hill 29–30, 203, 205
The Color Purple 30
Columbia 45, 55, 63, 180
Connor, Sarah 48, 158, 160–61, 164–165; *see also* Hamilton, Linda
Coons 203 8, 211
Corman, Roger 64, 72, 90, 199, 208
Cotton Comes to Harlem 130
Crain, Jeanne 62
Cultural myths 5, 25, 29, 40, 41, 72, 75
Curtis, Jamie Lee 62, 136
Cutthroat Island 47

Dandridge, Dorothy 11–12, 33–34, 37–40, 42, 66, 169–70
Davis, Angela 9, 11, 19, 72, 80–82, 85, 195
Davis, Geena 21, 47–48, 50, 165–67
Davis, Ossie 130
Dean, James 51, 63
Decoy 20
Diaz, Cameron 50, 184–86, 198, 200
Die Another Day 49, 183
Dobson, Tamara 4–6, 8, 10, 13, 16, 18–20, 22, 26–30, 42–43, 46–50, 68–70, 90, 93–96, 98, 100–1, 104–6, 108–12, 116, 118, 120–21, 123–25, 127–29, 137–138, 140, 142, 145–47, 149, 151, 154, 167, 170, 179, 183, 186, 189, 194, 199, 202, 207
DVDs 4, 8, 91

Eastside/Westside 42
Eastwood, Clint 44, 130
Ebony 73, 94, 100–1, 113–14, 121, 131, 195–96, 202, 206–9
Elektra 172–73, 186
Elise, Kimberly 179, 200
Everywoman 119
Exotic Other 5–6, 8–9, 11, 14–16, 22, 31–33, 40–42, 44, 60, 83, 98, 101, 110, 142, 201, 203
Exploitation 16–17, 44, 47–48, 50, 63, 72, 76, 90–91, 94, 100, 122, 129, 133–34, 140, 143, 146, 171, 198, 201–3, 209–10

Fathom 181
Fonda, Bridget 55, 148, 162
Foster, William 14–15, 57, 59, 199
Fox, Vivica A. 22, 177, 179–80, 187, 189
Foxy Brown 4–6, 13, 17, 22, 47, 48, 68, 71, 77, 79, 81–85, 87, 89, 91, 92, 102, 108, 112–114, 118, 120–123, 128, 129, 140, 145, 168, 173, 174, 180, 184, 187–189, 196, 198, 199, 206
Friday Foster 17, 19, 77, 83–87, 91, 102, 108, 124, 142, 188, 196
Fuzz 93

Gale, Cathy 20
Garland, Beverly 20
Garner, Jennifer 172
Gateward, Frances 98, 110, 174–75, 207–208
Gaze 28, 29, 31, 128, 162
George, Nelson 6
Get Christie Love! 20, 27, 50, 79, 113, 114, 119, 123, 127, 136, 142, 197, 198, 208
The Girl from U.N.C.L.E. 180
Gone with the Wind 11, 18, 26, 34–36
Graves, Teresa 4–6, 8, 10, 16, 18–20, 22,

26–27, 29–30, 42, 49–50, 70, 79, 111–17, 119–21, 127, 129, 138, 142, 147, 149, 154, 170, 179, 189, 197, 202, 208
Green, Philip 20, 91, 111, 203, 207, 208
Grier, Pam 3–6, 8, 10, 13, 16–22, 26–30, 42–43, 45–50, 68–81, 83–84, 86–95, 99–100, 104, 108–12, 114, 116–21, 123–25, 127–29, 136–40, 142–43, 145–47, 149, 151, 154, 167, 170–72, 179–80, 183–84, 186, 188–89, 195–99, 202, 206, 207, 210
Griffin, Junius 71–72, 75, 135, 202
Griffith, D. W. 33, 53, 131
Guerrero, Ed 52, 204, 205, 209
Guess Who's Coming to Dinner 57, 62

Hall, Ronald 33, 131, 202, 203
Hamilton, Linda 21, 48–50, 82, 158–62, 167, 194
Hendry, Gloria 144, 198
Hepburn, Katharine 57, 63
Hill, Jack 83, 90, 128, 195, 196
hooks, bell 28–29, 197, 203
Horne, Lena 11–12, 33–34, 37–40, 42, 65–66, 169–70, 203, 204
Hurst, Fannie 35

In the Heat of the Night 60

Jackie Brown 3, 6, 21, 71, 91, 143
Jacqueline Bobo 29
Jewell, K. Sue 29–30, 32, 126, 193, 203, 208
Jezebel 30, 32–34, 38–39, 43, 68, 83, 99, 127, 203
Jolie, Angelina 89, 182
Julia 20, 42, 79, 117, 118, 124, 125, 208
Julien, Max 93, 101, 193–94

Kellner, Douglas 30, 53, 203, 204
Kern-Foxworth, Marilyn 7, 201
King, Martin Luther 54, 60
King, Tara 20; *see also* Thorson, Linda
Kramer, Stanley 62
Kuumba Workshop 134, 209

Larson, Christina 172–73, 176, 187–188, 212
Lathan, Sanaa 180
Leab, Daniel 53, 57, 204, 205, 209, 210
Liu, Lucy 50, 184–86, 194
A Long Kiss Goodnight 165
Loving v. State of Virginia 57
Low budget films 114, 116

Macho goddess 99
The Mack 93

Mainstream action heroes 44
Malcolm X 54, 61
Mammy 5–13, 15–16, 18, 22, 25–26, 30–37, 39–42, 44, 60, 68, 76, 80, 83, 90, 98–99, 101, 110, 124–27, 141–42, 203, 208
Mannix 42, 117, 124–25, 208
Mapp, Edward 10, 33, 202, 203, 204, 208
Martial Arts 17, 20, 84, 93, 106, 109, 121–123, 140, 145, 199, 200, 202, 203, 208
McCarthy, Joseph (McCarthyism) 65–66, 105, 108, 207
McDaniel, Hattie 11–12, 32, 34–38, 40, 42, 74–76, 79, 124, 169–70, 202, 203, 204
McKinney, Nina Mae 11, 33, 37, 39, 83, 170, 194
McQueen, Butterfly 33
Mebane, Mary 96, 98–100, 203, 207
Melinda 9
Mencimer, Stephanie 165–66, 212
Merritt, Theresa 126–27
Meyer, Jason 43, 47, 148, 150, 154–58, 160–64, 210, 211, 212
Micheaux, Oscar 14–15, 59
Mishett, Bishetta 45, 90, 204
Modesty Blaise 181
Morley, Rob 181
Mulvey, Laura 162

NAACP 12, 38, 53, 57, 73, 75, 135, 139
Neal, Larry, 59
Nesteby, James 25, 203
Newton, Huey 131
Nichols, Nichelle 16, 42, 68, 117, 125, 170
Nicholson, Jim 45, 62–66, 140, 197

Oppositional gaze 28–29, 31
Original Gangstas 143
Outlaws 21, 47–48, 147, 180

Parkhurst, Jesse 31, 203
Parks, Gordon 58, 133, 137
Patrick Moynihan Report 141
Peel, Emma 20, 202; *see also* Rigg, Diana
People United to Save Humanity (PUSH) 72, 135
Pierson, Eric C. 145, 202, 205, 207, 209, 210
Pinky 62
Point of No Return 162
Poitier, Sidney 10, 18, 56–58, 60, 62, 66–67, 70, 101, 133, 145, 171
Police Woman 1, 47, 111
Poussaint, Alvin 73, 209

220 INDEX

Queen of the B's 71, 76; *see also* Grier, Pam

A Raisin in the Sun 56
Rambo 43–44, 161–62
Rebel Without a Cause 63
Red Scare 65
Reddick, Lawrence 25
Reefer Madness 52
Reid, Mark A. 14–15, 54, 128, 171, 202, 204, 205, 209
Reynolds, Burt 93, 134, 194, 210
Rigg, Diana 20, 180–81
Ripley, Ellen 6, 9, 16–17, 22, 26, 46–47, 129, 149–51, 153–58, 165, 167–68, 172–173, 176, 180, 189; *see also* Weaver, Sigourney
Ritt, Martin 9
Robertson, Hugh 9
Robeson, Paul 65–66
Robinson, Cedric 8–9, 68, 82, 193, 201, 202, 205, 206
Rolle, Esther 117, 126–27, 194
Roundtree, Richard 47, 69, 131, 133, 145
Russell, Kathy 33, 202, 203

St. Jacques, Raymond 130
Sands, Diana 56–57, 126
Sapphire 7–8, 14–16, 18, 23, 25, 30–33, 40–42, 44, 60, 68, 70, 83, 102, 110, 126, 127; *see also* Wade, Ernestine
Sarandon, Susan 21, 47, 48, 50, 166–67
Schwarzenegger, Arnold 44, 47, 146, 160–61, 165, 176, 204
Scott, Hazel 37–39, 90, 195
Sepia 93, 94, 105, 207
Shaft 19, 46, 48, 58, 66, 68–69, 72, 100, 113, 116–17, 131–33, 135–37, 143, 145, 171, 174
Sheba Baby 17, 19, 77, 84, 91, 124, 142, 198–99, 206
Skin color 1–2, 33, 36, 202, 203
Slaughter, Oliver 134–35, 205, 209
Smith, Jada, Pinkett– 179
Smith, Will 176, 189
Snipes, Wesley 146, 168, 176–77, 189
Snoop Dogg 6
Sounder 9–10, 137, 141
Stallone, Sylvester 44, 145–46, 160, 162, 176, 204
Stam, Robert 30, 203
Star Trek 42, 117–18
Stereotypes 8–11, 13, 23, 27, 34, 40, 41, 68–70, 83, 90, 99–100, 102, 105, 110, 117, 120, 123, 125–26, 131, 134, 136, 139, 141, 147, 151, 163–64, 169, 181

Stevens, Stella 107–8, 194, 197
Superhero 99, 183, 188, 202–204, 208, 209
Superheroine 172, 181, 188, 194, 212
Sweet Sweetback's Baadasssss Song 19, 67, 130, 132, 135

Tanny 194
Tarantino, Quentin 3, 21, 71, 143, 184, 187
Tasker 44, 96, 98, 150, 151, 156–158, 161, 164, 204, 207, 211, 212
The Terminator 48, 158
The Terminator 2 158
Textual analysis 30
Thelma and Louise 47, 164, 165, 167
Thorson, Linda 181
Thurber, Cheryl 203
T.N.T. Jackson 19–20, 28, 48, 50, 120–24, 128, 136, 142, 199
Tomb Raider 50, 173, 182
Toms 60, 203–8, 211
Tracy, Spencer 57
Tragic Mulatto 32, 33, 37, 38, 40, 42, 98, 99, 124, 125, 201, 203
20th Century–Fox 55, 124,
Tyson, Cicely 9–11, 42, 68, 76, 80, 113, 141, 143, 170

Van Peebles, Mario 66–68, 130–31, 209
VHS 4, 91
Victorian womanhood 32, 33
Vidor, King 37, 83

Wade, Ernestine 41
Warner Brothers 13, 21, 45, 48, 55, 63, 68, 93, 105, 128, 180, 193
Washington, Denzel 144, 146, 176, 177, 189
Washington, Fredi 33, 36, 83, 170, 203
Waters, Ethel 11, 39, 79
Weaver, Sigourney 9, 17, 21, 46, 49–50, 150, 153–54, 156–58, 165, 167, 171, 180, 187, 195
Welch, Raquel 181
White, Walter 12, 36
Williamson, Fred 4, 47, 61, 66–67, 69, 113, 140, 142–43, 145, 171, 201
Willis, Bruce 43, 47, 146, 162, 204
Wilson, Midge 33, 113, 194, 199, 200, 202, 203
Winfield, Paul 9
Winters, Shelley 93, 108, 194
Wloszczyna, Susan 181, 184, 186, 204, 212
Wright, Richard 59, 196

www.ingramcontent.com/pod-product-compliance
Ingram Content Group UK Ltd.
Pitfield, Milton Keynes, MK11 3LW, UK
UKHW041950140426
5217IPUK00014B/734